Fourteen

Fourteen

*Growing Up
Alone
in a Crowd*

Stephen Zanichkowsky

BASIC
BOOKS

A Member of the Perseus Books Group

Published by Basic Books,
A Member of the Perseus Books Group

Designed by Janice Tapia
Set in 10.5-point Electra LH Regular

Zanichkowsky, Stephen.
  Fourteen : growing up alone in a crowd / Stephen Zanichkowsky.
    p. cm.
  ISBN 0-465-09400-7 (hard : alk. paper)
    1. Zanichkowsky, Stephen. 2. Adult children of dysfunctional families—United States—Biography. 3. Problem families—United States—Case studies. I. Title.

  HQ536 .Z36 2002
  306.87—DC21

                                                     2002001518

02 03 04 05 / 10 9 8 7 6 5 4 3 2 1

Our parents:

Johanna	October 24, 1920
Martin	November 22, 1921

The four oldest:

Martha	February 26, 1943
Louise	April 1, 1944
Martin	March 22, 1945
James	August 29, 1946

The girls:

Anne	October 23, 1948
Catherine	June 16, 1950

The three boys:

Paul	August 7, 1951
Stephen	July 21, 1952
Anthony	September 13, 1953

The three girls:

Elizabeth	October 11, 1954
Grace	October 22, 1955
Rita	April 25, 1957

The babies:

Jane	September 18, 1960
Stephanie	October 25, 1961

Contents

Acknowledgments, ix

Prologue, xi

1
The Annunciation, 1

2
All My Children, 23

3
Crowds, 31

4
Hunger, 53

5
My Two Afflicted Children, 73

6
The Expanding Universe, 95

7
Satisfaction, 109

8
Our Father, 133

9
The Fear, 147

10
Liftoff, 161

11
West, 189

12
In the New World, 203

13
The Unconsoled, 213

14
Death of the Patriarch, 227

15
Saint Joan, 237

Epilogue
1998, 255

Acknowledgments

I wish to thank New York Press for first publishing my work; Ellen Kozak for teaching me to take myself seriously; my editor, Liz, and my agent, Lisa, for taking a chance; Jennie Greene and Selby Frame, for their editorial suggestions; my hosts, Ellen and Miguel, for their enormous hospitality; Charis Conn; the *Atlantic Monthly*; and Paula Balzer. I wish to thank my brothers and sisters for their courage and generosity during the interviews; this book is dedicated to them. All my life I've been asked the same question: What was it *like* growing up with all those kids? This book is one of fourteen possible answers. There are stories in this book that people in this book will find uncomfortable reading. I've tried to write about my childhood with honesty and integrity, and hope for all of us that time really does heal all wounds.

Prologue

I, Johanna Zanichkowsky, do hereby make, publish and declare this to be my last will, and hereby revoke all other wills and codicils heretofore made by me. I am not unmindful of my children: Martha Burns; Louise Naples; Martin Zanichkowsky; James Zanichkowsky; Anne Zanichkowsky; Catherine Andruskevich; Paul Zanichkowsky; Stephen Zanichkowsky; Anthony Zanichkowsky; Elizabeth Zanichkowsky; Grace Borriello; Rita Zanichkowsky; Jane Zanichkowsky; and Stephanie Zanichkowsky, and I intentionally omit my said children from the provisions of my will. The omission of my said children from the dispositive provisions of this will is not due to any lack of affection for them.

What can I say? My mother wrote that. Or anyway she signed it, or at least she didn't change the wording when she had the chance in the last eleven months she spent outliving her husband. Mom died of a disintegrated aorta on February 20, 1992. When the fourteen of us kids got together in the funeral parlor in south central New Jersey, it was only the second time all the siblings had shared the same room in thirty years. The other time was eleven months earlier, in the same funeral parlor, when our father died. The time before that was in 1961. There were other times probably, but not very many, and not with a camera handy. There are only two pictures of our whole family together, one taken by our brother Marty, and one by an outsider, and those were taken the same year. There aren't any others because we never all lived together as a family; the first kids were already on their way out the door before the last ones were brought home from the delivery room. And we were so . . . disconnected—I can't think of a better word—after we left the nest and went our separate ways that it was considered a family reunion if only eight or ten of us showed up. Even when Dad died it was doubtful that all the kids would come to the funeral, and Mom made special phone calls to those kids, like me, who she thought might steer clear. It didn't occur to me at the time what this meant, that my mother had felt it necessary to ask her children to please come to their father's funeral. Perhaps, once he was physically gone, in a little corner of her mind she began to understand that the man she knew as her husband was an entirely different person from the man we knew as our father. Did she allow herself to imagine what he'd meant to the rest of us? What would it be like for a wife of fifty years to wake up and not only find that her husband was gone, but discover almost at once (but not instantly: it would take her a few seconds to remember the missing person was also the father of her children) that her man had been two people, the first a stranger to her and the other a stranger to her children?

Nobody had to make calls when Mom died. We phoned each other about the time and place, about motels and car arrangements, but no one had to solicit promises of attendance. We'd all be there, and not just because their estate would need to be settled; it had something to do with the way we kids had tried to rethink our mother in her last eleven months. She was not loved more than our father had been; that wouldn't be entirely accurate. A few of us (most notably Jimmy, Annie, and Steffie) actively despised her. To most of us, though, she was just less clear-cut than our father had been, an unfathomable mystery figure. There was more room to wonder what she might have been like in another setting, with a different husband, with a few less kids, with better health and perhaps the same opportunity for education her husband had enjoyed. Many of the kids had made some effort to try to understand her in those last eleven months. Some had even tried to befriend her, making the drive to the middle of nowhere to visit her in that depressing retirement village of Whiting, New Jersey, among the ancient white people and single-story houses set on perfect lawns. Our efforts didn't really pan out, because our mother was fairly unapproachable in the end; but who knows, maybe it was that sad inability to reach her in those last months that allowed us to feel closer to her after she died. Dad had died in two seconds; in all the decades before that instant, we'd never seen him shed a tear or break down in weakness. But Mom's fragility during those last months made us want to get to know her. Only her weakness allowed us to know she'd actually suffered a loss; her tears showed us we now had to understand what it meant that a woman's husband had died and the woman now had nothing more she wanted to live for.

She looked terrible, lying there in the coffin all pasty and stiff and I could say lifeless, because they're supposed to make it look like she's only sleeping. They'd done a terrible job on her. My father had at least looked like a dead guy, but here it looked as if they'd just picked a stiff out of the catalog and dolled her up to resemble Johanna. She looked like neither a sleeping person nor a dead one, just one more grotesque figurine being dispatched to the netherworld before the doors closed. I wandered in and out of the viewing room many times over the few days of the wake, but the thing in the coffin couldn't give me any sense of whether or not my mother was dead. I took her picture; I still have it on my refrigerator, but looking at it doesn't affect me. It's as if I'm waiting for it to tell me something about my mother that I should already know.

We fourteen sat on tan metal folding chairs, the kind they used to have in the grade school auditorium when we were kids. We formed a shallow semicircle, facing our oldest sister, Martha, who stood before us with a bunch of papers in her hand. Our cousin Tommy slouched against a corner at the back of the room, keeping his distance. Maybe he wanted the fourteen of us to feel unified in our loss, and felt that sitting among us would be an intrusion. Or maybe he wanted to see how we'd support each other, to make sure we could, now that our parents were gone. It felt odd to me, though, having Tommy there; why couldn't it just be the fourteen of us? I tried to recall if it'd ever been like that, all of us kids together without our parents around, but I don't think that ever happened.

Martha read to us from the will. Martha the first-born, the dutiful, the child who by far had caused our parents the least grief. Martha who became a nurse, married a union guy, had her three kids and brought them up good Catholics, stayed married, didn't drink, never strayed to another bed. Martha who as a nurse made countless trips to the central New Jersey wastelands to see our mother through her last days. Martha who my parents always knew would do whatever they asked.

I'd only seen wills being read on television, solemn readings in libraries and drawing rooms, trophy heads and family portraits on the walls, decanters of brandy and fine linen hankies for the disconsolate. Or more formal readings in the lawyer's office, a fat desk in the center, walls lined with books. By comparison, ours seemed a slapped-together affair, an emergency meeting in a shoddy room, all of us trapped like insects between the cheap carpeting and fluorescent lighting and motel-quality wallpaper. It never occurred to me they'd have the reading right there in the funeral home. It seemed indecent, with our mother resting in her coffin one room over, as if she were just lying down in there, too damned tired to come in and read the thing herself.

There was no lawyer. Mom and Dad had asked Martha many years earlier if she would agree to be the executrix of their estate, and as the sickeningly obedient eldest daughter (as she described herself, always with an illustrative gag and a laugh), she'd agreed without question. She'd never *not* done what they'd asked, and had no reason to stop with what would probably be their last request. We never knew she'd been offered the job and never knew she'd taken it. Afterwards, when we were pissed at her and the letters flew back and forth, she explained that she'd agreed to their request without ever knowing or even considering what their will might contain, and that if she'd known ahead of time what they were going to do, she would have refused to help them do it. She would have foisted the job upon Tommy, who was the alternate.

Those letters weren't about her doing the job; they were about the size of our parents' estate. We'd been shocked by what Mom and Dad had written, especially that they'd thought it necessary to name each of us by full first and last name (applying the surname Zanichkowsky to those daughters whose spouses they could not acknowledge), as if we might try to contest the fact that we were their kids. There was a quality of finality in that naming, as if we were now officially their children for the first time, as if they'd taken possession of us only with the naming, so that they'd have the legal authority to dismiss us in the next sentence. After the shock wore off, we needed something to focus our attention on, and the extent of our parents' estate seemed a logical subject.

What had we missed out on? How badly had they done it to us? But when we asked Martha to tell us the final evaluation, she wouldn't do it. It would only make things worse, she said; no good could come from our knowing; they'd asked her not to discuss it with the rest of us. And we thirteen became resentful. First of all, because we really did want to know. It's not good enough knowing your favorite team has lost; a loyal fan needs to know how much they lost by. Second, we resented her deciding whether or not we *needed* to know, whether it would be *good* for us to know. We were tired of authority, and Martha's behavior smacked of her being "in charge." She seemed to be holding herself above us, and we got pissy over it. Maybe, we said, you don't want us to know because you got a percentage for handling their affairs, and you don't want us to know how much it came to? Why, we asked, are you bothering to conceal a simple number, which in any event will become a matter of public record in six months?

In the end, all the letters really asked was why Martha chose to side with our parents, rather than with us.

I still have those letters, copies of the ones my siblings sent to Martha, and her replies to them. I solicited them when I started this book. I keep them in a file cabinet, next to my copy of the will. It all blew over eventually, but it was expensive. For a long time after that reading it wasn't fourteen of us at all, but thirteen and one. But of course, Martha had no way of knowing in advance just what she was going to be reading to us and we, under duress perhaps, saw fit to kill the messenger.

And there's the first mystery. Why had Mom and Dad chosen the messenger from among us kids? Their lawyer could have done it, or Father Goggin, the New Hampshire priest who knew most of us toward the end and had also witnessed their will. Father Kruzas from Annunciation could have done it, Father Kruzas who had baptized each of us into the Roman Catholic faith; who had re-celebrated our parents' wedding on their twenty-fifth anniversary; who had said both their funeral masses and had even baptized my father into the faith. Why hadn't they charged one of those trusted outsiders with this task? Hadn't they thought about what it was going to do to us to have to listen to our own sister read it to us? Did they even consider whether such a thing would bring their children closer together or drive them further apart?

I'm calling this the first mystery even though the actual first mystery will never be resolved: Was this their last will and testament? Our sister Catherine clearly remembered a conversation she had with Mom and Dad in 1986, right before they left New Hampshire for the retirement village in New Jersey. They'd called her at work and asked her to stop by, saying that there was something important to discuss. During that conversation, they told Catherine they had redone their wills in preparation for moving, and had named Martha as executrix, with Catherine as the alternate. That later will, however, has never been unearthed. The will at the reading named Martha as executrix, with Tommy as alternate; it was dated 1979, a few months after the youngest of us, Stephanie, turned eighteen.

The second mystery is what our mother had been thinking in those last eleven months she outlived her husband. Because the will that Martha read to us (and assuming there was no later version because why wouldn't they have destroyed the earlier one?) had existed for twelve years. It sprains my memory to recall all the holiday visits and birthday cards and weddings that had taken place during those twelve years, with my parents knowing all the while what they'd written. Not them: most of us felt that Dad hadn't liked us in the first place, that there'd be no need for him to spell out in the will whether he'd had any affection for us or not. But hadn't it bothered Mom, with us sitting around her Christmas table, while stashed in the safe one room away were the documents of our disinheritance? All right, a lawyer had written the actual language; never mind that it was the lawyer whose kids we baby-sat, whose lawn I used to mow. And all right, he was paid to write out in legal terms no more and no less than our parents' wishes and intentions, and to make it all airtight. Still, Mom had outlived Dad and lawyer both; everything she'd owned with her husband was now hers, to do with as she pleased. Yet in those last eleven months, when she could have softened what we felt as Dad's contempt for us, she'd done nothing to counter his wishes. Was this because she couldn't alter her husband's intentions, or because she shared them? Could she not subvert his intentions to reassure her children? Or did she feel no need to change anything, because they'd already changed the will to a kinder, gentler version in 1986?

Martha held up pretty well during the reading. Her face registered a kind of dull amazement, almost curiosity, but not genuine outrage. I figured she was reading the stuff for the first time, that she hadn't seen the will in advance; no one could have rehearsed those facial gestures. She didn't start crying until a bit later, when it came to naming the token gifts, the little trinket each of us would be granted from their estate. Martha had worked with Mom on the list, during Mom's last few days in the hospital. Mom said she wanted to leave each of us kids a little something, a personal item that wouldn't mean much in the appraisal of the estate. Family things she didn't want to see end up at auction. Probably, Martha was crying because of her memory of working on that list at Mom's bedside, trying in vain to help our mother be nice to us. Martha was crying because she, the perfectly obedient eldest daughter, had been snookered by her own mother.

We sat in our little arc of metal folding chairs while Martha shuffled around through her papers for the list. She seemed to be stalling for time, as if worried that reading the list to us would verify and make permanent the primary fact of the will: our repudiation. She began to read through her tears from the list. Jane got Mom's wedding rings, because she was the only daughter who'd never been married. Paul got Dad's Civil War musket; Martha herself got the sugar bowl, and Annie got Mom's charm bracelet. Elizabeth got the good silverware in its felt-lined mahogany box. It went on like that for the fourteen of us. I got the silver coins my mother started hoarding when they quit minting silver and started dispensing those cheap alloy coins. One of the silver dollars I'd seen before; it had cost me a beating with the stick. I'd stolen it from Mom thirty years earlier and tried to buy a Tootsie Roll with it; the guy running the mom-and-pop store down the corner knew enough about our family to call my parents and turn us both (me and the dollar) in. Now I had it back.

Even cousin Tommy got something, the fine ebony crucifix with the silver Christ. Grandfather had brought it with him from the Ukraine, and it had been present at every baptism and funeral since the day our parents were married. Tommy's widow has it now.

After the readings, we returned to the same motel we'd stayed at the year before; we drank in the same bar. You'd think that after they got done raising the fourteen of us they wouldn't have had much left over, but that was not the case. Mom and Dad had left $97,000 to each of three charities, none of which, surprisingly, was the Roman Catholic Church. They'd left $8,000 to each of twenty-one grandchildren, some of whom were with us in the bar. Those kids had no reason to feel sheepish, because they had no way of knowing beforehand either that they'd been written in or that we fourteen had been written out. Many of them we hadn't seen in years; where in the old days our entire family existed within the boundaries of Brooklyn and Queens, these kids had materialized from as far away as Wisconsin and California. After they departed the bar, we cheered ourselves by singing "Eight Grand" to the Beatles tune "Hey Jude." (A few months later, Rita sent me an envelope with $8,000 in Monopoly money, with a note explaining how, with further searching, they'd found my share hidden at Mom and Dad's house. I still have the Monopoly money; I keep it next to the silver dollars.) We drank and sang with somber abandon, and drifted off to our rooms. Jane, Martha, and Catherine stayed at the house. Jane slept in Mom's bed and said it was spooky.

The next day, they put our mother in the ground a few feet from where they'd put our father less than a year before. As with Dad, we didn't get to see her off. Insurance regulations; hilly terrain. Our parents had chosen to be buried in some obscure military burial ground in a town whose name will never slip my memory because it never even registered there in the first place. Is that why they decided to get buried in the middle of nowhere? Because they'd only feel that much worse about it if they got buried right down the street and still their family didn't come by to visit?

The day after Mom was buried, we cleaned out their house. It was their lawyer who encouraged us. The will had shocked him; he advised us to help ourselves to our parents' estate while his back was turned. He had no stomach for the auction. He would not be surprised, he said, if he came in next week and discovered that our parents had lived like paupers, in an empty shell of a house. We took books, bedding and blankets, the liquor, the bath towels, and the canned goods. We took pots and pans, the dull plastic bowls we'd eaten soup and cereal from ten thousand times.

Knives and forks. The freezer, the coffee tables, the lamps. The long wooden benches that had served as dining room seating for decades. (The safe, however, proved worthless: no gold, no stocks or bonds, no hoard of emergency cash, no valuable and ancient jewels; it was filled with dark chocolate.)

We were in a frenzy of taking. It was the hunger Hemingway described in *A Moveable Feast*, the hunger that cannot be satisfied with eating. We were taking symbols, as if to convince ourselves with trophies that things had been better than we'd like to admit or remember. Because we'd seen in print, their print, something we'd suspected all along but hadn't allowed ourselves to believe until now: Our parents hadn't loved us. Or if they had, the definition of love would have to be reconfigured, as would the definition of family.

We now understood that our family consisted entirely of two things: remembered stories, and what we could squeeze into the trunks of our cars. We began forming those first questions about what message, if any, our parents had meant to send in that last sentence. Sooner or later, we knew, we'd be able to laugh at it; laughter had been our salvation all along. (A year after the funeral, Martha called me on the telephone about something. I'd just stepped out of the shower. She asked me what I was up to. "I'm drying myself off with my inheritance," I told her.) But laughter, we knew, would take a while to save us this time.

I looked around our parents' living room. The faces of my siblings were quite amazing for their variety, in spite of the common denominator of grim and pitiable determination. You'd never know what some of them thought of their mother or her passing, from studying them. Yet there was no mistaking one common feature: In spite of any grief or dismay or even relief that remained from the events of the weekend, the kids' (as we've always called ourselves) satisfaction at the looting was marred by an evanescent and wary quality. Each face carried the expression a homeless guy might have after walking away from the deli with a side of ham stuffed under his coat: a determined contentment that doesn't quite mask the understanding that his life will be the same as it's always been in a few days, once the ham is gone.

Many things occurred to me in the next few hours. I noticed, as if for the first time, that seven of the fourteen of us, half of us, were living alone. Among the twelve kids who'd gotten married, there'd been thirteen divorces. Five had chosen not to have children of their own; two of us had never married, and those twelve who had married had collected twenty spouses. These numbers, which had been mere statistics the day before, suddenly took on the weight of *consequences*. As I watched my brothers and sisters (and yes, myself) scurrying through the maze of our parents' home, literally filling their pockets with spoils, I began to think about our past. I wondered just how much our family *weighed*.

And here lies the great mystery. What is a family? By which I mean, what was *our* family? Surely not those same grim and pitiable faces scurrying like rats from house to car and back again? Weren't we more than that? I felt compressed, assaulted by a series of questions as I observed my siblings: How had it come to pass that our parents had died alone while all fourteen of their children were still living? Why had they written us off? Where had all our broken marriages come from? What had the fourteen of us inflicted upon our parents? Why had it taken thirty years and two funerals to bring the fourteen of us into the same room? And mostly, why would the fourteen of us never (because I knew this already, and seven years later would turn out to be right) share a room again?

I became interested in the influence the crowd had had upon itself, on its individual members. I knew as I watched the house empty out that it was the end of something, but I wasn't sure what. Even though we were all adults, it felt to me as if the fourteen of us were at that moment being spun off from the parental gravity for the first time, into new and incalculable orbits.

What would become of us?

❖   ❖   ❖

Maybe five years after my mother's funeral, I was sitting in a New York bar with my sister Elizabeth, discussing—as is inevitable, when any of us kids get together—our family, the funerals, our divorces, the will, the other kids. Liz told me she was getting ready to leave her husband. I sat there for a second, imagining her being married, wondering how she'd managed to believe in herself and her future solidly enough to marry in the first place, to have three children. I realized one reason she could think about leaving her husband was that she could imagine someone better, that she was capable of *choosing*; Elizabeth knew, on a fundamentally operational plane, that she was lovable. And for that one second, I realized I'd spent my entire adult life unable to love or be loved on that level, unable to choose love for myself. The feelings could have overwhelmed me, but they were too fleeting; I'm too well guarded now to fall apart in one second anymore.

I lowered my head to the bar. Her husband had been the most admired of the spouses; even though her kids were difficult, Elizabeth's marriage had been seen as one of the most enviable, stable, rewarding. If their marriage couldn't last, every apparently stable thing was an illusion. We got to talking about the role a sound sense of self plays in a good and solid and lasting relationship. We started speculating about the sources of self-identity, wondering how much, if at all, the source lay in being singled out by one's parents at a certain age for specific positive attention, for individual recognition. Liz mentioned our mother's lack of interest in the kids as individuals, and this puzzled me. I suggested to my sister that, while I might not have been interesting to my mother while I was in diapers, it seemed odd she wouldn't have developed a curiosity about me as I began to develop an identity of my own, perhaps when I started toddling around and using language.

Liz said to me, "You weren't interesting to Mom as Stephen Zanichkowsky when she named you that, so why should you become more interesting to her as a toddler, when she's already tearing her hair out over her other toddlers?"

I felt a mixture of shock and relief and gratitude. It was as if she'd been observing my entire life from down the street, a privileged outsider making a documentary film. It came upon me suddenly, as if for the first time, that this woman sitting next to me, this female who as a girl of twelve had caused me innumerable wet dreams, this woman who now taught Faulkner at the University in Madison, whose wedding I had skipped and who was getting ready to leave her husband and start over, this person had had the same parents as I did. She knew who I was; she knew about my mother; she knew that as the eighth child I was always beyond (in fact had been born already beyond) my mother's interest and concern. In one sentence, she had newly identified herself to me. In addition, she had stated our mother's case perfectly: We fourteen had inundated our mother before she ever knew what hit her. I'd always suspected my mother hadn't loved me, but it'd taken twenty years for Elizabeth's handful of words to enlighten me as to why, to explain the full meaning of a single phrase: Our mother had been overwhelmed.

Sitting in that bar, it occurred to me that while we kids saw our parents as the distant and troubling "them," our parents had probably experienced us in the same way. What had the fourteen of us done to our parents? What had been their dream on that wedding night back in 1942, and how had we demolished it? What had our father done to our mother in exacting the fourteen of us from her?

Now I understood something about my parents I hadn't thought about before: We fourteen, collectively, had happened to them.

Suddenly, I became thankful for that will, for that weekend of frenzied plundering. Our parents' estate turned out to be worth about $600,000; one-fourteenth of that, had it fallen into my lap, would have been sufficient to distract me for years. Such a windfall might have erased all the questions that had occurred to me while we looted their house. I might have left my parents' house thinking, "Well, imagine that, they loved us after all." I might have settled for the false solace of a consolation prize. Instead, I traded in the silver coins (but not the silver dollars) for a few hundred dollars in cash. I got a tape recorder and spent three years questioning my siblings about what had transpired while I'd lived among them for an entire childhood, unable to pay attention.

1

The Annunciation

Our family originated in Brooklyn, but by the time I came along in 1952 we had moved to Queens, and all I remember of Brooklyn is the one square block surrounding Annunciation, the parish that served as the center to the Lithuanian community in Williamsburg. That block always came to me in reverse. We'd drive in from Queens, two full cars even in my earliest recollections. We three youngest boys shared the back seat in the wagon, which faced out the rear window. That was no picnic. Once you got done making faces at the guy driving behind you and found out he wasn't amused, you had to just sit there all the way to Brooklyn while he stared you down. Sometimes I worried maybe he'd call Dad and tell him I was being snotty. It's confusing for a kid, riding backwards and having all the landmarks spring out at you from the corners of your eyes; you couldn't even read the exit signs on the Brooklyn Queens Expressway. But eventually the Kosciusco Bridge would appear, we boys just called it the Erector Set Bridge, and I knew we were almost there.

Annunciation was quite stunning, even for a little kid like me. The entire interior was done with gold leaf and tile and darkly suggestive paints and looked like a page from an illuminated manuscript. The stained glass was so beautiful I once licked the different colors to see if they had any flavor; all I got for my curiosity was the bitter metallic taste of ancient church dirt. Planted out front, behind a black fence of wrought iron spears, was an intimidating black crucifix; mutant tulips radiated like spokes from the haloed intersection, upon which was mounted a tiny shelter, which in turn held another miniature crucifix. I remember the pavement around the church and school buildings. It was smooth as taffy from years of soft tires; bottle caps had been impressed in the surface and planed flush by a thousand leather soles. That blacktop was why they invented roller skates. If I discovered an embedded nickel or dime I'd become bitter, having no way to excavate it.

A crowd would accumulate outside Annunciation after services, old men and women who were probably younger then than I am right now. It was like a town meeting. The women seemed solidly built in their shiny metallic 1950s dresses and no-nonsense cigarettes and that hard, slutty red they used for lipstick and nail polish back then. Stockings still had seams, and nobody had fur except maybe the incidental fox collar. The men wore hats and wing tips and brown suits. They'd lean with an elbow between two spearheads on the iron fence, talking church business through blue clouds of Chesterfield smoke and wagging copies of the parish newspaper at one another. These were your serious Catholics, pros raised on Latin, assembling to pray on the side because Sunday wasn't enough. They had their own clubs: the Holy Name Society; the Sodality; the Perpetual Rosary ladies; the sinister-sounding and males-only Nocturnal Adoration Society, which met to pray the rosary in shifts throughout the weekend, when temptation ran high. When my father died, the NAS appeared mysteriously during his funeral in identical sports jackets, said a rosary in twenty minutes flat, and walked out; they never even introduced themselves. There were people at Annunciation who'd had crucifixes of woven palm hanging on the same nail in their bedrooms for thirty years, with miniature holy water fonts hanging on other nails by the front doors.

They stuck together. Annunciation was a community in the most literal sense, something I never understood even while standing right in the middle of it. The elders would scrape together scholarship money for promising local kids. I remember taking the test even though I was going to attend high school in New Hampshire; all you had to do to qualify was be baptized at Annunciation. (I didn't make it, and couldn't understand my father's disappointment: It was money we didn't have yet, so why was he upset at the loss?) The parish would sponsor Communion breakfasts and Easter dinners and Christmas parties. All the families would attend with their kids, and no matter how many kids appeared, Santa, having dispensed with the Chesterfield and donned the proper attire, would hoist each of us onto his lap, ask if we'd been a good kid, and bestow a gift. The women prepared roast beefs, sauerkraut with white lima beans, stuffed cabbage, kielbasa with horseradish, boiled potatoes, red cabbage, black bread that weighed a ton. This is probably why they looked so stout; I don't have any recollections of what one would call elegance, grace, statuesque beauty. Although, to be fair, I might not have recognized those qualities as a boy, and besides, these women, my mother included, were all in their forties by then and had had a bunch of kids.

We always called the mass by its hour. The Nine was in Latin, the Eleven in Lithuanian. The families had names like Skarulys, Shula, Sertyvytis (our mother), Klimas, Gula, Salesky. You could hear Polish and Russian on that corner, you might hear Hungarian.

Mom spoke Lithuanian as a child at home, and didn't learn English until she started school. We kids did not learn Lithuanian, however. One of my mother's few regrets, she told me near the end, was their decision to keep the language for discussions between themselves. Because there were so many of us at home, only a separate language could grant them privacy. I could sense as a kid that we were being excluded—something about their tone and the shifty looks. But what reason could there be for speaking like Martians? When I first heard the language, it wasn't its strange beauty that affected me; I just couldn't understand what they needed to talk about that didn't involve us kids. This was my first inkling of the coming division between us kids and our parents—their need for a separate language.

The priests were assigned families in those days, sort of like the shepherd looking after a particular flock. Our family priest was a pudgy, balding, avuncular, bespectacled Lithuanian named Father Bruno Kruzas. He said last rites for my mother's parents after they died of separate heart diseases the same October afternoon in 1946. He baptized all us kids except for Louise; he'd called in sick that day. Even long after we'd moved from Williamsburg, Mom and Dad would take each new kid and drive back to the old neighborhood, so Father Kruzas could initiate the child, as if there were some critical and lifelong advantage to be gained if your starting blocks were anchored at Annunciation. We all wore the same white lace baptismal dress, made by our mother's mother (my oldest sister, Martha, has it now). Father Kruzas presided over our parents' twenty-fifth wedding anniversary celebration, when they repeated their vows. When Mom and Dad died, it was Father Kruzas who buried them. Then he died. His reputation among us kids today isn't so hot; we've often debated how much influence he'd had in steering Mom and Dad towards the extreme Roman Catholic right. I was too young to know anything about such things, but Father Kruzas was the first authority figure to rub my head instead of knuckling it, and I had no problem with that. Marty and Louise insist he was gay, but I was the cutest little teenager you could want and he never tried anything with me.

And if the priest's job was to look after the flock, that's what Father Kruzas did. He was the one who found the psychiatrist when our brother Jimmy needed help. And he found an eye doctor who owed him a favor when Annie needed an operation to uncross her eyes. He helped Jimmy with an apartment in Brooklyn when no one else would rent him one. More than once, he came by to bless our house; sometimes he'd set up an altar and say mass in our living room. Even I, a little kid, knew there was something special about having a mass said right in your own home. The ritual took on a special significance. There was the old black crucifix, the one that would follow us around to the bitter end; there was Father Kruzas, right next to me instead of up at the altar at Annunciation. It was his voice that made the mass special: just reasonable human volume, almost a whisper, because he didn't need to fill the church.

I returned to Annunciation in 2000, to take pictures. I looked up to the organ loft and remembered Jimmy singing the Ave Maria up there when I was a kid. Nothing about the interior has changed except that the votive candles are now electrified: The smoke and wax of my childhood have been replaced by flickering metallic elements that ignite themselves at the drop of a coin. The Eleven is still preached in Lithuanian (the Nine is in Spanish now), and the congregation at that service remains the immaculate white of my memory. In the congregation, I saw my sister's godmother, Isabelle Armatys, who remembered me from the old days; she was still driving in from God knows where to attend the Eleven. There were many more women than men now, devout and white-haired old ladies with skin like candle wax, palms together with fingertips heavenward, just like we'd been taught. Whereas religious men make me nervous with their righteousness, these women seemed attractive in their piety. They'd endured the deaths of almost everybody they knew; they'd said an Avogadro's number of Hail Marys by now and were certainly going to heaven if there was such a place. There were probably one or two who'd known Dad's sister, the one who'd caught fire on Easter Sunday back in 1924, while playing Jack-Be-Nimble over the leaf fire. Although they might not know it, some of those old women probably knew me; with fourteen of us kids, we'd been a central feature at Annunciation and had tapped a lot of the local community to supply us with godparents.

Still, after thirty years' absence, I didn't *recognize* the place, which upset me. I had anticipated being transported to the sanctuary it had always represented to me, and was dismayed not to feel any sensations whatsoever. On the right-hand wall about halfway down the aisle was painted a small pastoral scene; only then did I begin to appreciate my surroundings. I remembered sitting near that painting as a kid, imagining it as a window, dreaming myself out of the pew and into the two-dimensional meadow.

I talked to the current pastor, Father Vito, who'd had the job of burying Father Kruzas, a few years after Kruzas had buried Mom and Dad. He actually knew of us, because he'd been the assistant at Annunciation in Kruzas's day. Father Vito told me nothing in the interior had been changed, that my memory must be faulty. In fact, he had just spent $100,000 repainting the interior exactly the way he'd found it when he first took over. At the redecorating, he said, he'd only moved a few statues around. He speaks six languages and considered becoming a historian before being called to the priesthood. After all these years, Father Vito thinks he should either reconstruct the altar, or rename the church. It depicts the Ascension of Mary into Heaven, he says, not the Annunciation.

The Annunciation grade school is right across the street from the church, but only the two or three oldest kids went to school there. The Communion breakfasts were held down in the basement cafeteria, the Christmas parties up in the auditorium on the top floor. The auditorium has the same massive red velvet stage curtains, cheap loudspeakers, and decorative floral paint job that it had when I was a kid. This really amazed me. Although I couldn't remember the church, I could understand why successive pastors would retain the original scheme. But the auditorium was just a hall, and it had taken such a beating I couldn't imagine why they wouldn't have repainted it in forty years. I recognized it immediately, neurologically. We'd battled a huge snowstorm to get to Cousin Tommy's wedding reception there when I was seven or eight. I remember scouting that school from basement to attic every time we went there, starting from when I was four or five. Nothing was locked back then, and my brothers and I would go up and down the stairs, in and out of dark hallways. For years after that, well into my teens, I'd have dreams about the place, the smell of dry wood and linoleum wax and cabbage, dreams in which the architecture became more and more disorienting, the passageways more mysterious and convoluted. It would take longer and longer to complete an exploratory circuit, to find my way out. Nowadays I wonder if those darkly paneled corridors had been trying to warn me about something.

Only on the days we drove over to Annunciation did I experience too much to eat, the kindness and smiles of strangers, becoming invisible to my parents, games of tag in the hallways without scoldings, unsupervised bowls of brightly colored ribbon candy, an unexpected Christmas present. It was there I learned the tragedy of Christ's Passion, first learned the Christmas songs of Bing Crosby and Nat Cole, discovered the intimidating beauty of the pipe organ. At Annunciation I first experienced the gild and brocade and incensed pageantry of Christianity, the intoxication of ritual. I knew the occasions and would count off the days in impatience.

And maybe that's my strongest sensation and memory of Brooklyn: the anticipation of feeling safe in the halls of Annunciation; looking forward to those few days a year when, lost in ritual and excess, I could be certain almost nothing would go wrong.

❖   ❖   ❖

Annunciation came to us from my mother's side of the family. In forty years of our attending church activities there, we never once strayed from that center, and I never knew until recently that the church of my father and his father, the Russian Orthodox church, was right down the street. Nor did I know how different two adjacent Christian churches could be, nor how much trouble those differences had caused in our family.

As far as I've been able to determine, our family's difficulties began with the differences between the Christian crosses. The familiar crucifix, the Roman Catholic cross of my youth, has just the one crossbar, about shoulder height, where the arms go. Some images of it depict a footrest, a disturbing feature: Its only purpose could be to prolong the torture by preventing the victim's body weight from tearing him off the cross. The Russian Orthodox cross is called the patriarchal cross, and not without reason. It is frequently depicted with a skull and crossbones at the base. In addition to having a more generous footrest than the Roman Catholic model, it has another horizontal member, shorter and slightly above the one for the arms. It's not really a crossbar, that upper horizontal, though it's much more substantial than the piece of parchment in the same location on the Roman Catholic cross of my youth. On the patriarchal cross, it's more like a name-plate. I'm just not sure whose name would go up there, the guy who does the crucifying, or the guy who gets nailed. If I had to guess, based upon the story of my father and his father, I'd say it's the guy who does the job. That would be the patriarch; his name prominently displayed above his work would be an admonition to take him seriously.

All four of my grandparents came to this country before the out-break of the First World War. They came from eastern Europe, from countries about to be sucked into the Soviet Union. My father's parents, who only met in Brooklyn, had sailed from the Ukraine and settled in a community of their compatriots in Williamsburg. My mother's parents came from Lithuania; they met and married in the Lithuanian community in Cleveland in 1906, then came to Brooklyn and settled in a similar community, right down the street from the Ukrainians.

All four, one supposes, had the idea of a better life in mind. This decision to leave your homeland often meant leaving your entire family behind, and my grandparents were no exceptions. That was the best way, the only way, to make a new start. It would not surprise me to learn they were encouraged to flee, encouraged by people too old to take to the sea, too set in their ways to be bothered much by the changing of the guard. But I have no way of knowing their motivations. Two of my grandparents were dead before I was born, and one before I could speak; the only grandparent I knew was my father's father, Yakim, and he died long before I thought to ask him questions. Had I thought about it, had I heard the stories about my father and his father while Yakim was still alive, I would have asked him about his relationship with my father.

Yakim first visited the United States from the Ukraine in 1909 but returned home shortly thereafter. He came here for keeps in 1916, to avoid becoming entangled in the Revolution back home. He married a Ukrainian named Katherine Mudryk the following year. They had two daughters, and my father, Martin, was their only son. Grandfather's church, the Russian Orthodox Cathedral of the Transfiguration, sits at the corner of North Twelfth and Driggs. It is a mystical place, filled to the ceiling with icons and capped with a huge onion dome. Signs of God's omnipotence and secrecy abound at the service. The altar is hidden behind a screen, the Host is consecrated without witness. Confessions take place in public; the priest covers the head of the penitent with a silk cloth, but he knows who the sinner is. The women have their own secret society: the Sisterhood of Myrrhbearing Women. The congregation does not participate; there is just a continuous call-and-response between the choir and the priests. Everything is chanted, even the Gospel, as if it would be impudent to petition God with normal human speech. The Russian Orthodox do not recognize the pope as God's representative here on earth, and their service is not about humans and their desire to approach God; it is about God, the ultimate Patriarch.

The Roman Catholic Church of the Annunciation sits a few blocks away, in the shadow of the BQE at North Fifth and Havermeyer. Annunciation is not nearly as opulent as Transfiguration. It is the church for the Lithuanian community, who are mostly Roman Catholics, and my mother's family were members. Here, the people sing hymns to God from the organ loft; here, the service takes place in full view of the congregation, who also sing. God is more approachable to Catholics, whose brand of Christianity seems less severe. There are private confessionals, for example, and the altar is in plain view. But the Roman Catholic service, stripped of its Latin decades ago, lacks color; it feels completely Americanized. The only magic left at Annunciation takes place in Lithuanian at the Eleven.

It wouldn't surprise me, if I could go back to the 1930s and observe the street scene, to discover that the Orthodox and Roman communities mingled because of their common eastern European cultural heritage, more than they remained apart because of differences in religious dogma. They ate the same foods, their languages were only millimeters apart, they shared adjacent homelands (Ukraine can be loosely translated as *borderlandia*, or "land near the border"), and they'd left those countries for similar reasons. Maybe there was more of a social scene at Annunciation than there was at the Russian church.

I know my father associated more with Annunciation kids. He played on their CYO basketball team, and whenever and however he decided to become a Catholic, he studied Roman Catholic doctrine there. It's certainly possible he decided to become a Catholic after associating with Catholics in his free time. He may have found their brand of Christianity more forgiving, or at least less oppressive, than Grandfather's.

But it's equally possible he made the decision to convert after meeting my mother. One way or another, he dropped out of the Orthodox Church in favor of the Roman, and there his troubles began.

It seems ironic, or maybe just plain sad, that Grandfather should have come all those thousands of miles, in part to escape the oppression and religious intolerance of the Soviet Union, only to end up visiting religious intolerance upon his only son, whom he eventually disowned. And it seems even more sad that this only son, my father, would then abandon us, his own children, over issues of religious intolerance. But that's what happened. Both Yakim and Martin were uncompromising, strong-willed, and brooding; it depresses me to imagine both men sticking so hard by their principles that they doomed themselves to lives of mutual alienation and hostility.

Grandfather had brought the Orthodox religion with him to America and raised his kids with it. But his son happened to fall in love with Johanna Sertyvytis, an Annunciation girl. She was quite a babe, tall and dark-haired, and it isn't out of the question that Dad would have been willing to follow her over to her parish. It was love at first sight for both of them. In a story my mother told many times, they'd both gone to the dance with other dates, and both had sworn them off that same evening. My mother went home that night and told her mother she'd met the man she was going to marry. Later on, she insisted Martin was a Catholic when they met, but others in the family say Dad became a Catholic only once he became enamored of Johanna.

There's always been serious disagreement among us kids about which of our father's decisions came first, church or wife, and it's no mystery why my father wouldn't want to enlighten us: It might pave the way for us to disagree with him. In the end, the order of my father's choices doesn't matter much, as they were both mistakes. Dad had trouble with his father over both decisions, both happened at approximately the same time, and either choice by itself would have been sufficient to rend father and son asunder.

Grandfather didn't see a marriage; his only son was not going to abandon the faith of his ancestors, nor marry a Catholic, nor disobey his father. It didn't matter to Grandfather that both sides were actual Christians, and it didn't matter to him that he himself had married a Catholic, because he was the patriarch: When he married, his wife began attending the Orthodox church on their wedding day. What bothered Yakim was that Johanna, the *woman*, would not abandon Annunciation, whereby she forced her beau, the man, to make poor choices.

My mother was a serious Catholic, so much so that I can't conceive of her considering a change of religious affiliation, even to marry Mr. Right. If one of the parties was going to switch horses to make a marriage, it wasn't going to be her. And the man would have to volunteer; if anything, my mother was always brutally fair. I can't imagine her demanding of someone else, someone she loved, an action she wouldn't consider for herself. So I'm guessing she was correct, that Dad had already become, or was working on becoming, a Catholic by the time they met. My mother would have had no reason to lie about that. Unless, of course, she *had* forced our father's conversion and then felt guilty later in life for all the trouble she'd caused.

Dad's sister Olga remembers Grandfather being fully outraged that Martin had chosen to forsake the Orthodox religion; in fact, Yakim booted him out of the house over it. My father then went to live with his friend Alex Skarulys, another Lithuanian Catholic. Whether he would have endured all that trouble in the hopes of marrying Johanna, I don't know, but he remained enthralled with her, she with him, and they were determined to marry. But Martin was still a minor, and living at home or not, he needed his father's permission to do so.

Grandfather continued to prohibit his son's marrying, but Martin was intent, and hauled his father into court to make him explain this refusal to a judge. Grandfather had no experience with American justice; where he came from, the father was the only judge. He was outraged that his son would dishonor the patriarchy by contesting his father's wishes. Probably, he was shamed, for in his homeland, this would be a public humiliation. But he didn't have a good answer for the judge, who sided with my father. When the judge asked if there was anyone over twenty-one in the room who might be willing to sign on as Martin's legal guardian, Johanna's sister-in-law, Sophie, agreed. Sophie then granted Martin permission to marry Johanna. Grandfather bolted the courtroom, disowned his son, and refused to attend the wedding, which took place on what would become known after the war as Memorial Day, 1942.

This rift lasted until Katherine, on her deathbed, made Yakim swear that he'd patch things up with their only son. And he did, although it took a long time. For many years, our mother remained invisible to him; Grandfather would send greeting cards to the house, but with no mention of his son's wife's name on the envelope.

That's about all I know about Grandfather's relationship with his son. Yakim was one of six children; he had three children that we knew of. He lived to be ninety, but his wife died while I was an infant, and I never knew her. He never learned to drive a car; he'd walk from the nearest bus stop, always carrying his two shopping bags filled with treats for us kids when he came to visit. He was outspoken; after my father had had seven kids, Grandfather pulled him aside and told him he should learn to keep his zipper up. His silver hair, slight stature, and exotic accent lent him an air of mystery. I did not go to his funeral, not because I didn't like him, but because I was angry with my father at the time and could not bring myself to offer him the comfort of my presence at his father's death. It is one of my regrets.

Grandfather was not a warm person. He was not actually cold, but you could tell he was one of those men who'd be impossible to get to know more than superficially. It turns out he'd suffered a great loss, one that may have caused him to harden up, especially toward his children.

Yakim originally had four children, not three. This I never knew until after my parents died. He'd had a daughter in 1918, soon after arriving in this country. Her name was Anne. In 1924, she was six years old and her little brother, my father, was two. That year, on Easter Sunday, a neighbor was burning raked leaves in the gutter, still a common practice when I was a child. The story passed down is that the fire had died out, and Anne and some neighborhood girls were jumping over the remains. Their dresses fanned the ashes into new flame, and Anne's dress caught fire. Her last words were an apology for ruining her dress.

Grandfather was thirty-one years old at the time of the fire. He tried to replace his lost daughter, going against tradition and naming another daughter, born in 1925, with the name of the dead child. This story makes me wonder if he'd closed down emotionally and psychologically from his children after that fire, to protect himself from further loss. At two years old, my father probably would have been too young to remember the loss of his older sister. But no child is too young to miss the withholding of parental love, and Grandfather's withholding of that love did something to my father.

My father's childhood consisted of strict rules, the literal interpretation of them, respect for authority, and a keen awareness of the high price of disobedience. From this childhood, he learned that the world operated by sheer force of will, that the stronger will prevails. Thirty years after his troubles with his own father, when we younger kids began to marry spouses Dad disapproved of, he behaved the same way Grandfather had. Mom and Dad refused to attend our weddings; they would not acknowledge our spouses or allow them to spend the night under their roof; their holiday greeting cards came to us with only one name on the envelope. If you were visiting them over the weekend, you had to attend mass on Sunday; your kids had to be baptized. My father was a man of hard work, determination, ambition, pride; he never asked anybody for anything. Those are productive values that lead to high achievement, that saw my parents through the war. Certainly, they helped Dad support fourteen children without our once skipping a meal. But those values are hard on the spirit. They solidify around the man like armor, and my father, like all men who hold such values too long, became unapproachable.

 I know even less about my mother's family. She had one brother and one sister, and the sister, Helen (Tommy's mother), was without a husband. Helen was fourteen years older than my mother. From my perspective, this put her in another category entirely, and I never understood that she was my mother's sister until I was twenty. Helen was always alone when she came to visit or when we saw her at Annunciation; her husband might have been an alcoholic, or he might have walked out on her, or both; such things weren't talked about in those days. The brother, Leon, ran a pharmacy and was something of a pool player.

I know almost nothing about my mother's childhood except that she was born in Brooklyn and that she didn't learn English until she started school. I remember she seemed pretty knowledgeable about prizefights. I don't know whether she listened to them because her father did, or because she happened to like fights. She told me how she accidentally missed the Schmeling-Louis fight in 1938. It was a one-rounder, all of which took place while she was in the bathroom taking a pre-fight leak. She was pissed that Schmeling had beat Louis in 1936 and was happy to see him go down, but since he went down in the one minute she'd been in the can, he was even more of a "no-good," which was the worst thing my mother ever called anybody.

Since I was the eighth child, our early days in Brooklyn were already ancient history by the time I learned to talk, so much so that even my mother's birthplace remained a mystery. For some reason, I thought she'd been born in the Russian section of Brighton Beach, maybe because she'd often talked about shopping there. Brighton Avenue runs under the elevated tracks going out to Coney Island, and was "the Strip" for the eastern Europeans. The shop signs were all in Cyrillic, and that's where she'd buy kielbasa and pomegranate juice, lokum, pigs' knuckles, head cheese, livers, and hearts.

I went down to Brighton one day and took a few rolls of film, thinking to show her pictures of her old neighborhood. I brought them with me to the retirement place in New Jersey, on the last visit I had with her after my father died. That's when she told me she'd been born in Williamsburg.

In wedding photographs, my mother is a looker: a tall, well-assembled, darkly vampish beauty, sharply dressed, hungering for a glamour her own mother from the old country would never have dreamed of. Johanna was not shy: Those pictures are of one who is seductive and knowing, a woman so comfortable with her own beauty and physical stature as to be aware of the possibility of them as tools. Dark hats, long dresses, red trim on lips and fingernails; they spent their honeymoon at the Waldorf-Astoria (ten dollars a night), dancing nightly to the big bands and taking breakfast in bed. She preferred Artie Shaw to Benny Goodman on clarinet, and could tell you why. She sang arias in Italian and German along with the Saturday afternoon operas on the radio.

Martin was handsome too, olive-skinned and soft-eyed, intelligent and dashing and clever. A sharp pencil mustache. You could tell by his eyes he'd be the president of the company some day. They looked great together; Johanna's own mother saw to that, sewing at home the stylish dresses her daughter would wear at night.

Two weeks after the honeymoon, my mother was in the hospital with spinal meningitis inflicted upon her by the sloppy work of a drunken dentist. Exactly nine months after the wedding, Martha was born, and within a few years, there were no choices left. Each time Johanna awoke, all the minutes and seconds of her life were accounted for, all the pennies. Most of the time she awoke between 1942 and 1961, she was pregnant. With the first four or five pregnancies, she added so much weight to her frame that her back was ruined, and her body was taxed to its limits long before she could have derived much pleasure from its use. In one of my earliest memories of her, she is sitting straight up on a kitchen chair; a length of clothesline runs through a pulley in the ceiling, with a harness around her head at one end and a huge brass cylinder at the other, uncoiling Mom's backbone with grim makeshift mechanics.

I imagine all the days on which she must have had the same thoughts, employed the same words, because so many of those days were the same, identical. I imagine how tired she must have become with the sameness, with knowing that everything was preordained for as far into the future as she dared to imagine.

By the math of it, my mother got pregnant on their honeymoon, and I wonder how my parents spent the first nine months of their marriage, waiting for Martha to arrive. I can't imagine my father talking with my mother about the pregnancy. He was in the navy by then, but spent a lot of time at the Brooklyn Navy Yard, so he saw quite a bit of his new wife. They must have spent some time listening to the radio, because both of them were fa-

miliar with the opera, swing bands, the comedy routines, the se-
rials, Dodgers games, the fights. And they were early buyers of
records: opera and Broadway musicals and pop vocalists. We
kids were familiar with Sinatra and Cole, Goodman and the
Dorseys.

I've never seen the Brooklyn projects our family lived in before I was born. Martha thinks they were subsidized military hous-
ing down by the Navy Yard. Louise remembers the place as a two-
bedroom apartment, with Mom and Dad and the baby in one
bedroom, and the kids in the other. Lou was five years old when
we moved to Queens and, since Annie was born in 1948, it means
Mom had five children in Brooklyn before moving on. She would
pin a few dollars and a shopping note inside Martha's pocket and
send her out to the store; from the second floor kitchen window
she'd watch her progress across the street. "She could stay home
with the kids while I did it," Martha muses. "Kids . . . I must have
been six years old."

I don't know exactly where Dad was during this time. He was
twenty-one when Martha Marie was born early in 1943, and he
was in the navy, but he wasn't in the war itself. Paul tells me he
was on a destroyer hunting for German subs along the eastern
seaboard when the destroyer engaged a whale. The whale was
sunk, the destroyer incurred some rudder damage, and my father
spent most of the war dry-docked with his ship in the Yard. On
board, he might have been a radar or radio operator, since that
was his field of expertise in school. I'm not certain about any of
this, however, because Dad never talked about his past, at least
not with me. I would bet he never saw combat though, because
when my turn came and I applied for conscientious objector status, there was no compassion from him at all, no hard wisdom
passed down from the father who'd tasted war to his son who was

on the way. Instead, he bullied me with the brave and desperate rhetoric of a guy who'd never been shot at but could still boast about defending his country. I'm not accusing him of cowardice: I'm as big a pussy as the next guy. But even my friends who came back from Vietnam with bullet holes in them listened to my anti-war ravings and never held my cowardice against me. Then again, antiwar sentiment was easier to come by in 1970 than it had been in 1943.

It's clear that our father wasn't at sea very much, because he saw a lot of his wife during the war. Louise Marie was born in the spring of 1944, Martin (Jr.) Michael was born in the spring of 1945, and James George in the summer of 1946. There are one or two crinkly-edged, black-and-white pictures of our father in a sailor suit, holding a baby or two. He looks like a strong, wiry, handsome, no-nonsense guy, which in fact he was. He was also an angry guy, very angry in fact, with that ability to flash into violence like a vapor exploding into flame. He was not a guy you'd want to have walk in on you while you were tapping his wife, even if you were much bigger than he was.

Not that our mother would have had the desire, or the strength, or even the time, for anybody else. What she looks like in pictures from that time is another story: just pre-haggard, hair pulled back in preparation for grief, shapeless drudge-wear, the bulk already beginning to accumulate. With those first kids, my mother had her hands full before she was twenty-five. When I talk to the four oldest about those days, their earliest recollections (keeping in mind that by the time they were old enough to *have* recollections, there were ten of us) are that our mother was shot.

Johanna was twenty-six years old and struggling with those first four babies (Jimmy was two months old) when her parents died on the same October afternoon in 1946, three hours apart, of separate heart diseases. This was in the Woodhaven section of Queens, where Louise lives today. While Mom's mother was out shopping, her husband had a heart attack; when she came home and saw them loading her husband into the ambulance, she keeled over with a stroke. He was sixty-three, she was fifty-six. It even made the local paper; we have a picture of them in their twin parallel coffins, heads surrounded by flowers in the Lithuanian tradition.

Mom often said the worst years of her life were during that late Brooklyn period, minding five (Annie had arrived) preschoolers and doing all the housework, her parents gone, and Dad right down the street at the Yard, unavailable for duty on the home front. She couldn't have known that she was getting her first look at what the next twenty-five years were going to look like.

2

All My Children

"*I* will greatly multiply your pain in childbearing; in pain shall you bring forth children, yet your desire shall be for your husband, and he shall rule over you." Only God could have outlined the course of my mother's life with such cold and detached accuracy, and with so few words. Our mother did not steer her life; it just happened to her, in Kant's words, as an uncontrolled sequence of events, one following another with inconceivable rapidity. The Catholic girlhood in Williamsburg, a daughter of tailors. She dreamed of escaping the tedium of her parents' needle trades, but there was no opportunity for college. So she fell in love and married the boy next door; that could still happen, back then. But then the kids started coming, with Kant's inconceivable rapidity.

This is something I can't even imagine. Who was this woman, what were her days like, the workload; what was the first thing she thought about when she opened her eyes in the morning? What thread or cable snapped on that October afternoon in 1946 and left her in free-fall? I imagine a mother who even with a house full of kids was probably more alone at twenty-six than she was ever going to be again until, at seventy, she awoke from her nap and began outliving her husband.

At the same time, I wonder how she couldn't have figured out that each time she slept with my father it was going to get worse. She could get pregnant just looking at his underwear. They say we make our own beds, but the hardest thing for me to do as I contemplate my mother's experience is come to some understanding as to exactly how much of her misery was her own fault. Yet . . . what is *fault?* She loved, honored, and obeyed both her husband and her God, by the strictest and most old-fashioned interpretation of those words, and where's the fault in that? Did she honor her suffering? Offer it up to God as penance for her sins? What sins? Had she, in moments of darkness or bravery, dreamed of birth control, of saying no to her husband in the bedroom? Or had she been too obedient to even consider those things?

She was alone because her husband was not helping her and would not allow anyone else to do so. He was deeply proud and stubborn, almost defiant, concerning his young family. He wouldn't accept any outside help, even long after such help would have been not only necessary, but humane. Maybe he was trying to prove to his father that he didn't need help, that he made his own decisions and solved his own problems. Because our father was hardworking, determined, and smart, there's no getting around it. Nothing was ever neglected at our house; he could build a television from scratch, mow his own lawn, fix his own car, solder his own pipes. The only thing he had to pay to have done was put soles on his shoes.

But he was ignorant of the brutality of motherhood, and insensitive to his wife's needs; maybe the only thing he neglected was the most important thing: his family. "I can remember that Dad's mother wanted to be helpful," Martha says, "and would come over and help. Dad was opposed to the idea that we needed any kind of help. I think Mom also had that stiff-necked attitude, that we can do for ourselves." But our mother couldn't afford that attitude for long. She'd gained all that weight with those first pregnancies; the story is that she gained forty pounds just with Martha, and never lost half of it. By the time she was thirty-five, which is even before my memories of her begin, she was sleeping on the floor because she couldn't find a mattress stiff enough to support her back. Dad eventually stuck a sheet of plywood between the box spring and mattress.

It seems impossible that Dad would not have seen that the housework and the pregnancies and the children were taking a toll on his wife, and I'm left wondering what he did with her, to-gether as a couple, when he wasn't working. I know they went to socials and dances at Annunciation. But I wonder what they talked about, if he expressed any concern for her feelings and her health, if he showed any interest in her daily routine. It wasn't un-heard of for grandparents to help out new mothers in those days, especially not with Mom's parents being dead so early on and the house filling up so quickly. Yet, from the stories I collected from the older kids, our father did nothing while Mom was swamped. "He forbid his own mother to do any work in his house," Louise, the second child, says, "saying he was perfectly capable of taking care of his own family. Nana was welcome to visit, but she was not to iron or do any laundry or do any work in the house."

Louise tells another story, one that illustrates Dad's lack of un-derstanding and compassion concerning his wife's most intimate and fundamental activity: motherhood. Once infant Martha was fed and put to bed, he would not allow Mom to attend to the baby if she started crying in the middle of the night. His feeling was that you had to train the infant, not spoil it; the baby was fed, her diaper was changed, she has nothing to cry about. But whatever informed this feeling, our father took it too far. "Dad physically held her back," Louise says, "and Mom tells of crying in bed while Dad is holding her down, not letting her go inside and take care of the baby. Mom told me this story. She told it to Rita also."

The strange and amazing and sad thing is, our mother had started out married life hoping for twelve sons. This I only found out from talking to Martha and Louise, long after Mom was gone. I was really surprised by that one. It was the first story I'd ever heard concerning my mother that made me think of her as ignorant. Even as a boy, although I never wondered what my mother thought about large families, I'd attached a type of backwardness to the idea because, I thought, only poor people practiced uncontrolled *breeding*. That word breeding disgusts me; it reminds me of those nature programs on television, where they show the clear-white larvae oozing by the millions from the insect mother's opening. I've often wondered if both our parents had really wanted a large family; I suspected that my father, being a convert and therefore a more virulent strain of Catholic, had forced his will upon Mom. I could never accept the fact, or even the possibility, that someone as worn-out as my mother was after, say, ten children would opt for six more pregnancies. If you asked her, though, she disavowed having had any say in the matter: "We wanted as many children as God saw fit to grant us." I'd heard these words from her many times and never once liked hearing them. Nobody, I thought, could be so resigned to, unaffected by, or detached from what worked out to be 144 months of being pregnant.

It was much easier for me to believe it was Dad's idea, mass-producing Catholics for the Church. The party line back then was that it was better to deprive your kids of material benefits than it was to deprive them of brothers and sisters. But if I think about it now, I can see my father trying to prove to Grandfather the intensity of his conversion, or rubbing that conversion in his face, with the number of us. It nauseates me to imagine my father simply demanding sex from my mother, but it could have been that way (it's unimaginable to me that it could have been the other way around). Or perhaps they just wound up on the wrong side of all the bad luck that can happen to you when you don't use birth control and you love each other. Still, I thought we were primarily his fault.

But I was wrong. As an adult mother of twelve (at the time) children, Mom was interviewed by a student writer for the Bishop McDonald's newspaper; this was where she had gone to high school, and where her eldest daughter, Martha, was now a student. The student was writing a story about the continuity of mother/daughter pairs at the school. In that interview, our mother said she'd had a desire for twelve sons from a very young age, as a teenager. She'd had the twelve kids by then; the only regret she'd own up to was that they weren't all boys. Mom told Louise this story, and Martha had seen it in print.

Still, it must have been pretty clear in the end, even to Mom, that whatever she'd been dreaming about (my guess is she'd been dreaming about the Apostles) could never be aligned with what she or anybody else could have sanely wanted. But you just couldn't tell, with her. Maybe she *had* wanted us all. Or maybe, since it was God who'd given us to her, she couldn't deny her naive and youthful wanting, at least not out loud; nor could she wish to give us back. It's easier for me to see the twelve sons not as an actual wish, but as a foolish and idealized teenage sentiment that, once factualized by our births, would be difficult to repudiate in a Catholic newspaper.

I don't know why I've never wanted to believe all us kids were none of her idea. Maybe because it would force me into assigning to her some responsibility for her own suffering. Because she did suffer, and I wanted my father to be accountable for it. She was the one who got pregnant on their honeymoon, who spent every day of her life at home. As a kid I believed, or at least felt, that women dwelled in some mysterious and sanctified state of grace, that they were somehow elevated above the generations of men who had written the laws and waged the wars and created the religions and churches. Women were *innocent* in the most fundamental way. And my father seemed so powerful to me; it was easy for me to imagine he'd caused everything, had caused my very surroundings to come into existence. Was it possible that even my mother's moods were his doing, that her actions and feelings were delineated by his influence? It wasn't difficult for me to hold my father responsible for transporting my mother away from a state of grace; I mean, why would my mother have brought any suffering upon herself?

My father was a man in motion, a hard worker and a high academic achiever. He got into Brooklyn Tech when it was still a tough school. He then spent seven years of nights at Cooper Union, full scholarship, taking a degree in electrical engineering. During the day, once he got out of the navy, he worked at an electronics firm on Long Island. He soon started his own outfit with a partner; he was already working for himself. And here is the source of my resentment: Dad was out of the house night and day, assembling a full academic and professional career before he was thirty, all the while explaining to his relatives that things at home were fine, his wife could handle the kids.

And maybe this would have been okay with me. All it might have taken was for my mother to have kept her health, for her parents not to have died on that bleak October afternoon, for her to have had three or four kids like everybody else, for there maybe to have been years instead of months between those pregnancies, for her to have had a shot at college. But my father, in his arrogance and his pride, seemed not to care about his wife's plight, her experience of the outside world; nor would he let the outside world know of that plight. Sure, you read about it all the time, how the wives in those days (and even these days) sacrifice themselves for their husbands' careers. But I'd never seen what those sacrifices cost. And maybe to him there was no plight, because that's what wives did back then, stayed home having babies. But most wives aren't pregnant sixteen times.

Marty wasn't taking care of his family; he was fathering it and working hard to finance it, but aside from marinating his kids in conservative Catholic thought, he wasn't investing any time or attention in them, and very little with his wife. He had ambition; he was going to the top; he probably would have worked the same hours whether he had fourteen kids or two. All the families we knew were set up with that clean division of labor between provider and caretaker. Only in our family's case, the division seemed more extreme, preordained; we kids had occurred with such immediacy and speed and finality that our mother never even had time to express any of the anger or resentment she might have felt about being besieged by motherhood and house-wifery. She'd had no time to devise words for the loss or surrender or stripping away of any preexisting, independent desires and ambitions she might have held. She began on May 30, 1942, to sign herself as Mrs. Martin Zanichkowsky not because this was the custom of the times, but because, whether she could see it coming or not, there was no Johanna anymore. Interestingly, once all of us were gone from the house, she began to refer to herself once again as Johanna. Unfortunately, there were thirty-odd years in there in which the housewifery and motherhood got on top of her completely. Like a black hole, her children became the gravity sink around which she collapsed.

She would endure one more insult before leaving Brooklyn, one more physical insult to her body, although the price wouldn't become apparent for many years. Mom was twenty-eight when her fifth child, Anne Marie, was born in October 1948. My mother was in reasonably sound health and Anne herself offered no physical impediments. It should not have been a difficult birth, but it was. The details are sketchy; this is yet one more story I knew nothing about until after our parents were dead.

At the exact moment of our mother's final contractions, there was no doctor present in the delivery room. There was only the nurse, untrained and unskilled in actual delivery, when the baby began to emerge from the birth canal. The nurse was unsure of everything except that she couldn't deliver the baby by herself. She pushed Annie backwards, up into the birth canal, and squeezed my mother's knees together to prevent the baby from popping out; she yelled for the doctor. That's all it took. The doctor arrived and delivered what appeared to be a physically healthy baby.

At the time, nobody knew. But the damage was done; Annie had suffered a lack of oxygen to the brain in those few backwards seconds. There was no diagnosis, no lawsuit, no remedy. Nobody ever heard or mentioned the nurse's name. The damage wouldn't become obvious until Annie reached third grade. There, she'd hit a learning barrier she'd never overcome. My mother never told me this story; I heard it from Martha and Louise, who had gotten it from Mom. "That's the kind of thing you have to watch out for," she told Louise, "when you go to have babies of your own."

3

Crowds

I was born in 1952, exactly nine months after Bobby Thomson hit that homer off Ralph Branca to rob the Dodgers of the pennant. In 1952, the United States demolished the island of Elugelab by fusing hydrogen into helium in a primitive H-bomb. *The Old Man and the Sea* was published and contraceptive pills were developed. *High Noon* was screened and Lever House was built in midtown New York. Britain detonated its first atomic bomb and Schweitzer won the Nobel Peace Prize.

But of course I knew nothing about those things. My earliest memory might be the sound of prayer. Not only church prayer, but the long sessions of prayer at home during Advent and Lent. By the time I became aware of my surroundings, there were a dozen of us kids, plus Mom and Dad; since our parents ate in another room, praying was the only activity we practiced as a group. I couldn't understand the words, but there were certain sounds and smells that brought a sense of quiet and reassurance. The droning voices, hypnotic and calming; they made me feel safe long before I understood this to be a need. And the sound of Latin—why was the melody of this language so calming? And candles: the smell of melting wax and its aftersmoke; the dim, yellow, flickering light and strange, uneasy shadows; the thin black ribbon of smoke escaping the flame, rising straight, then disintegrating in chaos.

I remember Rita being born, then my mother being sick, then Jane being born. I was in bed, in the room I shared with my four brothers, when someone called from the hospital. The news of Jane's birth didn't interest me, and I didn't share the joy and antici- pation of the other kids, collected in the hall. The girls played mommy with the carriage in which Jane would sleep, the carriage parked in the hallway because all the rooms were full. Why didn't I join them? Could I have already felt, as a kid, that there were enough of us with twelve, that it had been over three years since Rita had arrived, that I hadn't seen diapers and baby bottles or even the crib itself in so long that I'd allowed myself to feel there would be no more need of those things? No, it wasn't anything reasonable or rational. It was my unconscious reaction to the further expan- sion of the crowd, which I didn't know yet was my own family.

The chaos of many kids, the sense of emergency as the older kids rushed to prepare the rest of us for school. The yelling for clean school uniforms; somebody making up dozens of peanut butter and jelly sandwiches and stuffing them into brown paper bags; someone at the ironing board, pressing jumpers and blouses. My mother looking tired; you just knew she was going straight back to bed the minute the house had emptied out. I don't re- member anything about my father from this time; he either left before we prepared for school, or I just wasn't paying attention. He had yet to take his place at my center. But without knowing much about him, it seemed prudent to steer clear of him.

I became aware of my mother, remember her picking me out of the bassinet during a thunderstorm and holding me in her arms to quiet me. Sometimes, when I'd done some mischief, she'd call me to her bedroom. She'd be lying down, her day's energy already expended before noon; very quietly, she would say, "Kneel," and indicate a place for me at her bedside. It'd be quiet and peaceful in there, and I felt she cared about me in spite of my annoying her. One day, I was around five, I took some striped canvas we had lying around from some old beach chairs. I found a needle, figured out how to thread it, and stitched two pieces together. My mother found it and called me over and said, "Did you do this?" So . . . I had *done* something. Because of the ever-present sounds of yelling and hitting, I backed away. But she said something like, "That's very nice," and looked at it for quite a while. I wonder now if I'd caught her in a moment of reflection, or brought her to such a moment with my handiwork, about her own parents having been tailors. I remember a sense of contentment or warmth flowing between us; maybe it was relief.

Mostly, though, I remember the incessant motion and commotion. The chaos on weekends, when no one went to school. That's when the bigger chores around the house would get done, when Martha or Louise bathed the three of us boys in the tub, when Dad fixed things around the house. Mom singing along with the radio; was she a bit happier on weekends, with her man at home? Perhaps. But our father wasn't lending her a hand with us; he used his skills and his time maintaining our physical surroundings, but he didn't spend time with the kids. He never took four or five of us out for a pointless car ride just to give Mom some quiet. I wonder if he went into shock on weekends, when he had to spend two whole days with the rest of us. Did he recognize or understand, as they readied us for Sunday mass, that these endless preparations were something our mother dealt with seven days a week?

They fed us at a single long, dark table, mahogany or walnut, a refectory table we'd picked up from Annunciation. We sat on two long benches, heavy dark-stained pine, as if in the mead hall of a great castle. Our parents had chairs, but they ate in the kitchen; they joined us on holidays and for the Sunday meal. Every morning we ate cereal from dull plastic bowls, followed by a soft-boiled egg. Those eggs, boiled a dozen at a time in a huge saucepan, cracked into our little glass cups and stirred with a teaspoon; we called them clucked eggs, after the sound of the spoon against the glass. You couldn't get them down, but if you waited too long, trying to fish out the umbilical cord, the yellow would cool and begin to solidify, a hard gold crust forming at the cup's circumference. But they'd make you eat it eventually, no matter what, and there was little sense in stalling. Many of those eggs were dumped behind the radiators, tossed out an open window. Or eaten that same night for supper, congealed.

It was about this time I first remember Mom opening up her candy store. I think she did it to save herself the worry of all us kids running down to the corner store, together or separately, to spend our allowances. She'd go down to the wholesaler's and buy boxed sets of Bonomo's Turkish Taffy, Sugar Babies, Necco Wafers, Bit-O-Honey, and all the other brands, and every afternoon we kids would buy the stuff from her with nickels not ten minutes old. It was impossible to save your money, with kids on both sides of you munching away, and we all became candy addicts. I've often been asked if Mom made a profit from us, and I hate to think about it, because she might have; she had to be getting the stuff cheap, buying in bulk like that, but we paid her the going store rate. While I can't imagine her earning money off her young children, it's possible I just don't have enough imagination.

When I started first grade in 1958, there were four girls living in the attic, the five of us boys in the front bedroom, and three girls sharing a bed in the middle bedroom. We kids had been subdivided into groups by now: Martha, Louise, Marty, and Jimmy had become known as "the four oldest"; Annie and Catherine were "the girls"; Paul, myself, and Tony were "the three boys"; and Elizabeth, Grace, and Rita were "the three girls."

It would be two years before Jane came along; my mother was suffering her miscarriages at this time. Jane and Steffie would be known as "the babies."

It had turned loud and violent at home; our parents had lost control of their family and were beating the kids with the stick and the strap. Sometimes we knelt on rice for our trespasses. I'd heard the sounds of punishment while I was still drinking milk from a bottle. The sound of Jimmy, constantly under the stick. And somehow, at six years old, I knew my mother was overwhelmed, swept away on the tide of us.

Except for mealtimes, I have few memories of the house as a whole. Our bedroom was my world, and it was there I felt the pressure of other people, that there were too many of them. That's where all my rights to privacy and ownership were surrendered, the room being too small for anybody living in it to not know everything about it, on a molecular level. I can see it now as a chamber of macabre distractions, as dreamt by cartoonist Gahan Wilson. In one corner, a boy picking his nose and wiping it on the wall for years, until a large, discolored area materialized on the paint adjacent to his pillow. Jimmy outfarting Marty—to amuse us, or to best his older brother in at least one area? The smell of tightly packed bodies and wet beds. I no longer remember what fears caused me to wet mine. Paul says his began with a fear of prowling demons, which gradually became a fear of Dad yelling at him for breaking some unspoken regulation against walking around at night. We shared the middle two beds, sandwiched be-tween Marty and Jimmy, four beds parallel with maybe a foot in between. Jimmy was laid up with a broken leg for a while, hit by a car. His seemingly interminable presence there bothered me; what little snatches of privacy I might find under my own sheets were now evaporated. One day he bet me I couldn't guess the combination to his lock; the prize was a pack of Violets, square purple lozenges coveted for their strange flavor. I guessed the sequence in a dozen tries (the only miracle that's ever happened to me) and he tried to deny it, but I opened the lock for myself afterwards. I never told him, because having the numbers was worth a lot more than having the candy; it wasn't that he had anything worth locking up, it was that I had one of his secrets.

We boys had nothing to play with but the room itself. We'd climb up the dresser, mount the bedroom door by standing on the knobs, and push off from the wall; the object was to fly our way in for an air assault on one of the beds, while avoiding a crash landing. We'd argue over whose turn it was to heat tomorrow's underwear on the radiator, or search Marty's stuff for candy or loose coins.

We rocked in bed like a pack of caged monkeys, a symphony of creaking metal frames. We each had our own style. Tony lay flat on his back, rocking his head violently from left to right, as if possessed by dybbuks; Marty and Jimmy rocked on their sides, semi-fetal position, in what might be described as uniform harmonic motion. Paul and I knelt on our mattresses, hands on the metal frames at the foot of the bed; we'd spring down on our haunches with enough energy to launch us back into the next cycle, clattering the headboards against the wall. Mom and Dad would scream at us to quit rocking, but we were a bunch of neurotic kids already; what else could we do with all our energy once they sent us to bed? (Old habits die hard; Louise didn't quit rocking until the day before she married, and Marty and I still rock today when sleep eludes us.)

There wasn't one sock or quarter or candy bar or book of matches in that room that escaped the notice of all who lived there, almost to the point where if you stole an item from someone and hid it, they'd still know where it was. All possible hiding places were known and exploited: inside your shoe, on the ledge of the bed frame that held up the mattress, inside the valance box of the venetian blinds, a dime stashed down the rubber well containing the zipper of your rain boots. Nothing was mine, not even a hiding place.

I was never a brave kid. I learned to live life tentatively at an early age and never took risks. Once in a while I'd sneak up the attic stairs to where the four girls slept, but I never got very far; my two oldest sisters kept strange, pointy-headed dolls on their neatly made beds, which spooked me into minding my own business. I couldn't enter the back yard if the neighbor's cat was sleeping on the path; I'd go back inside and play with toys. I would never challenge anyone, even a girl, for a park swing. By the time I started school, I was already intimidated by authority and tried to stay inconspicuous. On my second day, I wandered into the wrong classroom. Not knowing what to make of it, I began to cry. It never even occurred to me to ask the Sister where I was supposed to be. That would mean calling attention to myself, something I'd learned at home to avoid at all costs. That was the cardinal rule: Don't call attention to yourself. It wasn't something anybody warned you about; you just figured it out from observation as you went along.

And that's something in itself, how attention became a negative thing. I remember talking to Rita about this recently. As far down as she was at number twelve, she'd still learned to value invisibility. "I used to do things in the dark," she says, "so as not to be seen. Because a lot of times at home, being seen was a threat. You could automatically be slapped or yelled at for what you were doing, or be ridiculed by Dad. I had this pathetic need for privacy. . . . I still have an unlisted phone number."

Dad drove a silver Pontiac sedan, and Mom had the Woody, one of those oak-paneled station wagons. We three boys always rode with her in the back of the wagon when we went to Annunciation or the beach. I don't remember a lot of trips to other places, except once in a while to one of the few aunts who didn't mind having all "Marty and Joan's kids" over. There were too many of us for general visiting, and taking us all to the movies or a museum was out of the question. Everything took two cars, and always cars; it would have been a nightmare to haul us around on public transportation. We took trips to Jones Beach, which was the cheapest and nearest entertainment. There was an enormous sense of relief at the shoreline, because we were outside, with fewer rules and less supervision. We had inflatable sea horse rings and sand-castle tools. The waves always impressed me, their fluidity and sound, and I fell in love with the ocean before I could spell the word. There was a lot to be said for the sight of my parents sitting in their beach chairs, doing absolutely nothing. Dad swam, but I don't recall Mom going in anywhere past her ankles. Some of the older kids never learned to swim, either. Louise says Mom used to wash their hair in the kitchen sink and rinse it by dunking the kid with more than sufficient enthusiasm. As a consequence, they became terrified of the water, and even today it's not easy for Lou's husband to get her on a sailboat.

❖   ❖   ❖

I knew school would come eventually. My mother brought me along when she registered Paul for first grade at Saint Theresa's. This was the biggest building I'd ever been inside. It was the first time I'd seen a nun. Paul got a first-grader starter kit, and Sister gave me a holy card so I wouldn't go home empty-handed. Shortly thereafter, Paul left the house every morning with the others and returned in the afternoon. Now I could see it: School separated the big kids from the little kids, and it meant one less kid at home during the day. It also proved the existence of life outside the house.

Once Paul became a big kid, I was next. But although I spent a year as the oldest kid left at home, I only remember a few things from that time. Tony shattering the glass pushing up on the storm window by his bed, cutting the hell out of both his arms; the time I caught Jimmy searching Mom and Dad's bedroom; Tony falling from the slide at the park, splitting his head open; Jimmy disappearing from our bedroom when they sent him to the institution.

School itself didn't mean as much to me as being a school-kid rather than one of the kids at home. But there was no preschool or kindergarten for us, and the jump from the unorganized chaos at home to the formal studying in first grade was a transition I didn't make very well. I was just getting used to living in the dreamland inside my head when the agenda was thrust upon me: reading, arithmetic, spelling, religion, art, and music. There were sections on the report cards for cleanliness, social habits, conduct, and self-control. I got lousy grades, partially because my penmanship was so poor that Sister couldn't read my homework. In reality, the change was just too shocking; the classroom was so different from my house, I simply didn't know what to do with myself. I became obsessed with the physicalities of school: the smell of pencil grinds at the sharpener, the pledge of allegiance, roll call, the public address system, and mostly, my desk. I had the same desk every day, and it never occurred to me that anybody else ever used it. That desk was my first private space. All I remember otherwise are the movies they showed on Wednesday afternoons. My mother would fold up two pennies in a bit of paper and staple the ends closed; that was my fare. They showed monster movies like *The Crawling Eye*, and I became addicted to cheesy black-and-whites.

It came as something of a surprise, once I started first grade, to learn that some of my classmates were the youngest child in their family and that other families had only four or five kids in them. I couldn't define it; it just seemed strange that their families were already complete and mine was still growing. It wasn't about our numbers, not as I recall; the awareness of numbers only came later. This was about our family still being in progress. And there was nothing to compare us to. There weren't any families like ours on our block, nor on television. Although I didn't understand it yet, my relationship with the outside world was beginning to form around the concept of my family. What I carried to friends at school was the gang of us, rather than just myself as an individual. I wondered, when I met a new kid, if he knew about my brothers and sisters. He wasn't meeting me personally, back there in second grade, he was meeting my whole family; as he looked at *me*, I imagined him silently wondering about *us*. And maybe that's where some of my bafflement came from: I soon realized that some outsiders saw my family as a subject of astonishment or, later, derision. My earliest sensation about my family was the feeling of being part of a crowd, feeling tied to its motion, being seen by others as part of a group. My siblings, who I never learned to take one at a time, whose names I could never pronounce except in chronological order, who I never knew were part of my picture frame; my family, like lightning bugs in a jar.

I began to escape. Not physically, of course, because physical escape was impossible; there was never an empty room to escape to. I began living inside my head, spacing out while talking to people. My brothers were first. I learned to talk to them while paying attention to them for seconds at a time, then fractions of seconds, alternating their fractions with fractions kept for myself, filling their fractions with the visible manifestations of paying attention to them in such a way as to give the illusion of my undivided attention, while in fact, I was in a world of my own. My sisters were all over the place, and the only way around that was to screen them out. I never even took them seriously until puberty, when the sight of their strange chests began to energize a part of me that until that time hadn't even required a name.

Walking the five blocks to school brought my first experience of physical distance, my first experience outside the home. Gradually, I expanded into new territory. In my free time I roller-skated into terra incognita (metal clip-ons, with skate key), and learned that my family, while defining my galaxy, did not constitute the entire known universe. I remember the first time I skated four or five blocks in an unknown direction, stopped, looked around. I realized that nobody there knew who I was, and that nobody who knew me knew *where* I was. This hadn't happened in school; my siblings had been there before me, and the nuns knew all about me, anticipated me, before I got there. But if I skated in another direction, I could be in the middle of nowhere. It was my first lesson in self-and-other, in self-and-nothing, in learning how to be alone. How strange to think my first experience of solitude took place on a city street.

But what was happening at home that caused me to seek comfort and salvation in solitude? Why couldn't I learn to share my troubles with those around me, those most likely to understand them, my brothers? Could I already have felt, at six or seven, that nobody would understand me? Or was it shame, that inflammation of the ego that inhibited me from revealing myself to others, and so closed me off to the possibility of understanding myself?

The experience of shame came to me once I started school, when I began to meet people from the "outside" who asked questions about us. Maybe it wasn't shame at first, maybe it was just embarrassment at being the center of attention for the first time, and not even for anything about me particularly, but because of the size of our family.

I was the eighth child born into a household on its way to becoming twice that size, so there was already plenty going on before I arrived. I was born into a system with an established order, with people cemented into positions long before I got there. As I got older, the biggest kids gradually filled me in with things I needed to know, as if I were a new hand at the factory and needed to learn which drawers certain tools were kept in. They showed me where the shoe polish was kept, how to fry an egg (because on Sundays we could have our egg fried or scrambled if we didn't want clucked), where to put my laundry in the basement. I learned about Mom's miscarriages, because all the rest of us resembled a line of ducks, and outsiders sometimes asked about the three-year gap between Rita and Jane. The bigger kids told me about our religion, our relatives, our nationality. They told us when bath night was and how often to change my underwear. (No one, however, had an answer as to why all the girls had the same middle name: Marie.)

Armed with these bits of information, I could, to a limited extent, fend for myself when new friends asked me about my family. This usually happened in the first week of school. My older siblings had all been through it. "It won't register on them right off," they'd say. "They'll see a handful of Z's scattered throughout the school, you can't miss the name, but they won't make much of it.

They'll notice it in church on Sunday. Then they'll ask you, that following Monday." And so it was. We would troop in as a mob, as close to the front as Dad could get us; we'd fill half of two pews. This would be at the Nine at Saint Theresa's, the mass for whole families. Just our appearance at the Nine made me cringe, although I didn't understand exactly why. As I write this I can't help wondering what my parents thought, or *felt*, individually and as a couple, as we filed in like that. Did they ever wonder what others thought about the number of us?

That following Monday, my classmates would ask about my family. Since all the other students were white and Catholic and wore the same uniform, there was only one subject left for them to ask about that might promise excitement: our numbers. Why were there so many of us? What did we eat? How could we afford it? Stupid things, or at least innocent. Like how did we decide which channel to watch at night? Did we eat in shifts? How many bathrooms in the house?

For the most part, I answered truthfully. Although I'd already learned to lie to my parents to avoid physical punishment, I hadn't yet learned the value of lying to outsiders. So I told them that we ate canned vegetables and slept so many to a room, that we got bathed three at a time (once a week, by an older sibling) and that there wasn't much television because we got sent to bed pretty early because otherwise (this knowledge only came later) our parents wouldn't get any peace and quiet and would become even more overwhelmed. I still remember feeling that I could not avoid answering their questions; I had been trained to answer immediately. Yet I felt bad when I answered. It was my first experience of pain other than the stick.

Since I never asked those kinds of things of the other students (we'd learned at home not to ask questions), their questions and my answers made me feel there was something unusual about our family. At the same time, instinct told me to hold my tongue about certain topics. Because there were things at home I never shared with my classmates, did not know could be explained, things that hurt me before I knew how to put that sensation into words. The image of all of us lined up on those wooden benches, for example; why did that make me sad? Food ladled prison-style directly from pots and pans onto the plates, no serving dishes on the table and everything made of some nameless and unbreakable material. And kids getting yelled at or beaten right before or after supper. I know this was mostly Dad's job and that, since he worked during the day, the evening was the only time for discipline. But it lent to the supper table an element of morbid court entertainment (again the mead hall), not to mention fear. Did the other kids from school get yelled at every day? Did other parents hit their kids?

And the fact that our parents always ate in the other room. Did other parents eat in a separate room from their kids? And all the food we dumped down the toilet and behind the radiators because each of us kids had something we couldn't stomach, and we'd get sick of seeing the same things appear: not just clucked eggs, but canned wax beans, cream cheese, chick peas, boiled hot dogs, turnips. I remember days I went to school without my peanut butter and jelly sandwich, because the image of the mass production of those sandwiches hurt me. But why? Perhaps the sameness of our sandwiches was a reminder that, to outsiders, we kids were all the same, interchangeable. I needed to demonstrate to my schoolmates that I wasn't attached to, defined by, limited to what was available under our roof. I could be independent of the others: "Oh, I don't feel like eating lunch today." Sometimes, on the walk to school, I would discard my sandwich (but not the brown paper bag; that had to be used for a week, or else) and endure hunger, as if punishing that morning's sandwich maker for the painful images at home. I'd end up in the cloakroom, searching for food in the coats of my classmates. Yet I would feel neither hunger nor guilt for stealing snacks from my friends, only a sense of being lost, of feeling pathetic. I became a sugar addict, and even today I will eat candy for lunch if nobody's looking; I hardly even feel guilty about it anymore.

And how could I explain that our mother locked us in our rooms when she needed to get away for a few hours? Or, as was to follow, that I couldn't call a friend on the phone because the phone was locked as well, with a little brass cylinder keyed to the first finger hole, so we couldn't dial out? That if you wet the bed while you were locked in, it meant a beating with the stick? I was too young to know that even Martha, the teenager left in charge of the rest of us when Mom and Dad went out, was locked in, that my pleading to be let out for the bathroom was useless because there was no one unlocked enough to set me free. "I lived in the front bedroom before the five boys moved in there," she says. "I remember sitting up and being terrorized, watching out the window and having to go to the bathroom so bad I couldn't stand it, because we'd get a beating if we wet the bed. I remember being very frightened, feeling very responsible, trying to plan strategies in case there was a fire."

Mostly, I could not explain the fact of the crowd. I was already embarrassed, as if even at my young age I knew there was something wrong with there being so many of us. Sexually uninformed, I still detected off-color insinuations directed at my parents, especially from the boys. Even an innocent question like "Why did they have so many kids?" caused me a nameless discomfort, a soft inner heat I wouldn't learn until much later was called shame. It wasn't the shame of intercourse itself, because how can a kid too young to know even the mechanics of sex feel disgust at the thought of his parents' fucking? But there was some other category of abuse: Our parents were overdoing . . . *something*. Whatever occult or mysterious or secretly pleasurable practice it was that made my mother grow babies *inside* her, our parents did it much more often than my friends' parents. And simply because my friends questioned it, I assumed there must be something wrong with it.

But I didn't understand exactly what *was* wrong, and I never asked the older kids how I should answer my classmates. I don't know why; maybe part of me understood that my shame was so personal and groundless that the older kids would think I was stupid. Still, that's my strongest memory of those first few years at school: the slowly increasing sensation of my own family as something to be ashamed of.

Now my relationship to my mother became complicated by shame as well. It was in school, with my new awareness of other kids' mothers, that I first became aware of my own mother as a physical person. She was so much older looking, so much more used-up than the mothers of my friends. Their mothers seemed to be thinner, to have nicer clothes. I hadn't yet learned to calculate; I had no way of knowing that some of my classmates were the oldest child in their family, that their mothers might be ten years younger than mine. The mothers and housewives on television reinforced this sense. Donna Reed and Lucille Ball and Audrey Meadows were all attractive women, even if not sexually attractive, in my little mind.

But it wasn't just that. My mother was the one bringing the new kids home from the hospital. Since I didn't understand my father's role in that fact, there was no one to blame for the size of our family except her. My mother, it seemed, was the *source* of our family, and the cause of my shame. I already feared her; now I began to resent her.

I feel guilty when I try to write truthfully about my mother, because she died so painfully at the end. But the fact is, I wasn't crazy about her. I wanted to like her, and remember wanting her to like me. But by the time I was old enough not to fear her, long after she'd finally become too arthritic to beat me, it was too late to grow any love on the ground that separated us. Yet even as a little boy, my fear of her was diluted by sadness and pity. In my earliest memories she would have been in her late thirties (she was thirty-two when she had me), and already she was fat, depressed, exhausted by burdens I would never understand. It shocked me, as a boy, the first time I heard her stumble over two or three names trying to identify the kid she was scolding, a stream of half-names escaping her lips in frustration as she ran through the possible names. I was too young to guess what might be misfiring in her life, too young to understand that hers was a life without anticipation and joy in it anymore. Yet at the same time, I had this kid's sense that certain cards had been dealt her way, that some of what was going wrong for her wasn't her fault. And even a little boy can recognize that misery isn't a good thing, whether you bring it upon yourself or not. I'm thinking again about those lines from Genesis, about the pain in childbearing and the husband ruling over the wife. My mother didn't stand much of a chance with both God and our father lined up against her.

My confused feelings for her were weighted on the side of caution and doubt, and I withdrew from my mother so quickly I hardly even remember the act of pulling away. It must have started very early on, because I don't recall any period in my life of wanting her attention. Of course, as an infant, unconsciously or not I must have wanted and needed her love. But even before I started school I knew it wasn't worthwhile, or even possible, to get near enough to her to get it. There must have been a need for her physical attention in my infancy, but whether this need was met or not, I wouldn't remember. The evidence is that she did not have much "mother-ness" to spend on me, most of it having been spent on those who'd come before me. Somewhere along the line, I learned to not need her, then to not want her, then to stay out of her way. I can't remember ever asking for her help. In first grade, I was sent home a few days running with severe admonitions from Sister to get my blue Baltimore Catechism covered. One day she told me not to return to school after lunch unless this was done. I sat on the toilet shitting, crying for want of a brown paper bag to cover the book. My mother was in the kitchen. "Only five sheets," she called through the door; it didn't occur to me to wonder how she knew what I was doing. When I emerged from the bathroom, the book was covered. On some level it must have occurred to me she had covered it, but I only remember thanking the book for having made itself presentable. My mother had made a gesture of attending to my needs, but it felt to me like relief instead of attention. I had no idea what to make of her. I'm sure I didn't even thank her.

I clearly remember her sitting up in bed, trying to get going in the morning. She'd be in terry cloth bedroom slippers, a present she allowed herself each Christmas (her toenails rounding down over the sides of her toes like wild horn; I remember even then, because I could still bite mine, how she trimmed hers with a heavy steel instrument that belonged in a gardening shed). She'd be wearing the same shapeless housedress, sitting on the edge of the bed, as if her body could not respond to the needs, the demands awaiting her. She'd look blank; not staring, not even looking at nothing. Just blank, without will. As if waiting for animation to come to her from the ether. Because the demands on her were the same ones as yesterday and, even if fully satisfied today, would still be there again tomorrow.

I was one of those demands. We all were; every day, with or without intention, every one of us drained a few more drops of life out of her. I remember the Christmas when I was about five. Gifts would be taken from under the tree and passed to their recipients in no particular order. My first item was a cowboy hat, and then my name didn't come up again for quite a while. All the other kids were piling up toys, and I became very sad. Mom called me over and asked what was wrong, and I said, "Is this all I got?" I actually think those were my exact words, because I can still feel them from forty years ago. She pulled me in between her knees and comforted me and reassured me there would be more. How could I have known what they had to go through to provide us with Christmas? How could I have known what my mother must have felt while one of her many children was asking, crying to her, for more?

Yet I never thought of those questions back then. Just as I was beginning to understand how tired she was, I began holding her responsible for our circumstances, for how I *felt*. Blame and shame began to interfere with my budding compassion for her, with my unresolved need for my mother's love.

Because I was one of her many while she was the one mother, I had more of a relationship to her than she had to me. I had more to gain in capturing her attention, and more to lose when she withheld it, than she might have gained or lost either way through my presence. All the needing originated with me, while all the forces that could shrivel or nourish me were hers. This might have been different if she'd had me at twenty and stopped with two or three kids. But because of the number of us, all the influence and power flowed one way, from her towards us, even though we as a *group* overpowered her. Her moods changed rapidly, wildly sometimes, and she was unpredictable from day to day, from hour to hour. Mom would comb and oil my hair and call me her handsome son before sending me off to school, but I could not respond with affection for her because on her next approach I might get a scream or a slap.

(You had to look her in the face when she was yelling at you. But her teeth, which were rotten by this time, were too disgusting to look at. I stared not in her eyes, but at the lenses of her glasses. I would see myself paired in miniature on the tiny crystal screens. My mother would become reduced in size, aligned to the scale upon which I was seeing myself reflected in the lenses. It seemed as if a hummingbird were yelling at me; her voice would dim, and I would make a mental escape by commenting to myself on the absurdity of this miniature creature disciplining me.)

My mother, whose life was so unimaginably complex I could never presume to understand her mysteries. My mother, whom I both feared and felt sorry for; whose attention I didn't yet know I'd have to compete for; who was tied to a father I had yet to identify. Did she resent my very existence simply for what I'd done to her just through the fact of my birth? She and I were a pair of confused and broken magnets, unsure, if we got too near, how the laws of attraction and repulsion would affect us.

It would be a few years yet before I understood my father's role in all this. Then the boys at school were a little older, and the questions became a little harder. "Why doesn't your father just leave her alone?" "Why doesn't he use a skin?" I'd achieved that first woody, the actual receiving antenna for those first girl-rays of sexual desire. Although I now had some idea how babies were made (this thanks not to my parents but to my brother Marty and, to a lesser extent, dirty playground talk), and although I still didn't like or believe in the idea, I felt even more shame, because their words weren't merely vulgar, they were true: Why *didn't* my father just leave her alone? Because by this time, let's say fourth grade, my mother was fat and unattractive, with her teeth crumbling from all the coffee cakes, and there was another shame I could feel which, even if I did know how to put into words, I never would: How could he *not* leave her alone?

And attendant feelings I wouldn't understand for decades yet: resentment and anger towards my father. How could he not leave her alone, not because she was no longer the babe she'd started out as, but out of respect for the ravaged condition of her poor body? Had he allowed her any say in the creation of her children? Were the things I was ashamed of really her fault? How much of all that surrounded me was my father's doing?

It never occurred to me such questions might not have answers. All I knew at that point was that as early as third grade, I had the feeling of living under a microscope, a desire not to be from my family and our home, a fear of being noticed by my parents, a profound embarrassment about being trooped around in public with the rest of the kids. A collection of discomforts I've come, rightly or not, to call shame.

4
Hunger

All this took place in a three-bedroom house in the Ozone Park section of Queens that my father paid nine thousand dollars for. Our driveway was two tire-wide concrete strips straddling some brave and feeble grass, where I got the dirt to pack the nozzle of my popgun. I think we had a television. Down in the cellar was a wringer washer and many runs of clothesline. The oldest kids remember Dad installing a second bathroom off the kitchen, so in the beginning there must have been just one, but I can't describe either of them. Nor do I recall what changes took place in our sleeping arrangements as we increased in number. The only room I ever slept in was the one the five of us boys "shared," which looked out over 135th Street. Dad had carved the girls' makeshift bedrooms from the attic dormers. Mom and Dad's room was in the back of the house, facing the Van Wyck Expressway, and the door to their room was always locked. We had a very tiny fenced front yard, where I learned my first calculus; Paul would quarter it and beat me to the side door, which got me wondering how small zigzags would have to get before they became a straight line. I can't remember the back yard very well . . . a cinder block garage smelling of oil and old wood.

New kids arrived with mathematical certainty, filling up the fifties: Elizabeth Marie in 1954, Grace Marie in 1955, Rita Marie in 1957.

Down the corner, across from the park with the ball field, was the last frontier of urban wilderness, a vacant property that was simply called "the lot" by everybody in the neighborhood. The lot was a place to congregate away from the house, and took on some importance as a refuge, yet it was here that my nascent sense of anticipation of the outside world first began to decay. I'd found a rubber gasket of some kind, maybe from a washing machine or a car. I wasn't sure what I could do with it, but it was a nice-looking thing and I figured to hold on to it. Some kid came up and saw me with it. He said he could make a bow with it, that if I let him take it home he'd make a bow with it and we could shoot arrows in the lot. This seemed like a great idea, and I handed it over. I hung around for quite a while, waiting for him to return. Having no idea what being taken was all about, I couldn't figure out what was keeping him. Even as I felt the slow creeping tears and shame, I didn't understand; I waited until the last moment, when I'd have to be home for supper. Only then did I accept the fact that the kid wasn't coming back. Ashamed of having been fleeced, I never told anybody.

One day in the lot a neighborhood kid asked me to join his gang. This was something; any type of acceptance would be cool, but being asked to join a gang was best of all. Not that I knew what joining a gang *meant*, but I'd heard Marty talk about gangs once in a while, and they sounded important. All I had to do was rub dicks with this boy. I don't even remember if he *called* it that (we were calling it a "tutty" at home), but there was a bad feeling in me and I knew it was a wrong thing. I didn't do it; the thought of the mutilation I'd get if my mother found out froze me. I'm still astonished at the boy's advance; seven seems like an absurdly young age for such a suggestion, even if he never had sex in mind. The fact that it was boy-to-boy sex never occurred to me. Maybe what surprised me was the realization that other kids my age were already thinking about things I didn't even know existed in the world yet. After I rebuffed him, he lobbed a beer can filled with sand at me, cutting a slice into me just above the eye.

I saw my first fire at the lot, became intrigued by its possibilities, and earned my first beatings shortly thereafter. Martha took me on a walk to the store one day, and as we passed by the ball field, we looked in on the game. My hands were still small enough to pass through the grid of the chain-link fence. We could see across the diamond and out the chain link on the other side, where a fire raged in the lot. "There's a car on fire," she said, which puzzled me because I'd never heard of fire happening to a car before. There were black and orange flames and huge black smoke, and I recognized those things as the tiny actions of candles and wooden matches, multiplied a millionfold. But the thing about the car fire that scared me was the wiggly shimmering of things near the heat; it seemed like the fire was disturbing everything around it in preparation for destruction.

I took up matches immediately, starting small fires with my brothers. Aside from having a general fascination with flames, fire seemed to be a form of power. I had an urge to see destruction; a single match, carefully exploited, and I could destroy a discarded phone book. Mom and Dad both smoked, and matches were easy to come by. We boys received the worst of our beatings for fire damage wreaked at the lot, and for false-alarm pulls. Someone would pull the alarm just to see the trucks arrive. We soon learned that the beating would be so terrific, it would more than outweigh any possible thrill gained in seeing the fire trucks pull in. But we continued playing with matches. Later on, in Manhasset, we had a game called Statue of Liberty. The idea was to hold as many wooden matches as you could in the circle of the "okay" hand sign, light them off, and hold on. The winner was the boy who held the largest number without dropping them during the flare-up; the record was somewhere in the twenties. Tony stole a three-pack of kitchen matches from the store once, and we three boys each had a box of our own. This represented an army, aligned and uniform, ready to send into battle.

For me, the natural fear of a raging fire is linked with a small element of satisfaction or appreciation of its power, and a box of wooden matches brings that power within my grasp. Fire; one is surprised by the feebleness of the resistance it encounters. A book of matches levels the playing field, and even the weak become powerful. A fistful of matches in my pocket often felt the same as money.

It's obvious to me now where that need for power came from. Kids were getting beaten at home and were powerless to help themselves. I began learning about the power of violence when I was five, the first time I saw someone else getting it good. My mother had Marty standing up against the stairway, holding onto the bars as if he were in prison, and she was lashing him with a white nylon belt. It was a thin belt and moved quickly through the air, making a sharp sound when it landed. He had no shirt on and she was raising red welts on him. I had already been made to kneel on rice, had already been knuckled on the head and slapped across the face for lying and cursing, but I'd never seen anything like this. I must have been too young to fully register what was going on, too young to be afraid, and much too young to know why he was standing there instead of hitting back; I hadn't learned the true meaning of fear yet. I don't remember Marty crying out; he was a pretty tough kid and his silence paved the way for my misunderstanding what Mom was doing to him. I hadn't learned about the stick yet, either; that made *everybody* cry out.

We just called it the stick. It was maybe three feet long and an inch across; they kept it in the broom closet, a household utensil. It always existed, although it might have had twins or replacements over the years. It followed us from Queens to Manhasset in 1960 and migrated to New Hampshire when we ended up there. It was dark brown and nicely finished, but worn; it might have been one of the slats that made up the sliding gate on the baby's crib. Dad would say, "Get me the stick," forcing us not only into the few more seconds of terror we'd experience while fetching it, but into complicity as well, because we'd have to hand him the instrument he was going to beat us with.

It seemed as if kids were getting physically punished almost daily; sometimes, two or three kids would get it at once. There were many types of punishments. My mother would lift a girl off the floor by the hair, shaking the kid by her braids like a doll. We had the strap; kneeling on rice, sometimes with arms outstretched; there were ear pulls, vicious slaps to the face. Martha remembers Mom taking the meat fork out of a hot roast and whacking her with it, leaving three burning tine marks on her arm. For swearing, there was washing out the mouth with dense brown naphtha soap. Never punches in the face, never bruises where they'd show in school, and never anything as vicious as cigarette burns or beatings on the bottoms of the feet. But there was the stick, loud and public and humiliating, and this was the worst. I remember Catherine getting beaten for stuffing a hot dog down her pants in preparation for flushing it down the toilet. Tony first got the stick at six years old, for peeing in the upstairs bathroom drinking cup. The beatings Jimmy got with the stick were unspeakable back then, illegal today. One time, Dad beat the living shit out of him in our bedroom, with all five of us boys on our beds; the idea was to make the rest of us watch, as a deterrent.

There was something thrilling and compelling about watching the other guy get it, a sense of relief at your own survival. We would watch from the top of the stairs, from behind a door, until we were warned off. No false compassion here; you were glad it wasn't you, and you'd certainly lie to transfer your violence onto someone else. The hyena laughs before it eats because it has survived; the laugh is actually the nervous exaltation at the misfortune of the other animal. We took guilty solace in the beating of another, because it meant the infraction had been paid for, the score settled; that day's evil energy had been dispelled before it came our way. Our commiseration with the victim was defiled by the guilt of having ourselves escaped.

After the beatings, we kids never talked about what it meant or felt like to be utterly powerless. Perhaps the idea that the stick was about *power* couldn't come to us at so young an age. I didn't understand the meaning of power enough even to recognize that I didn't have any. All I knew about power was my father; most of us feared him more than we feared God. With all our religious training, there was no thought of sin attached to our crimes, only thoughts of punishment. "Heaven and hell, I've never cared," Louise tells me. "If I think of the things I was afraid of, the biggest fear element that ever existed in my life was my father."

I can't remember anything about my father from this time except in his context as authoritarian. We never did anything fun together, like go to the ballpark or fly a kite, but I didn't hate him yet, at least not consciously. When he beat me, the punishment was more on a purely physical plane. There was emotional damage to be sure, but the beatings were tied to things I'd done *wrong*; they were the same beatings everybody else got, and didn't yet turn my father into the towering psychological menace he would become. This began to change one day at the supper table. I was having trouble with my chick peas, because they looked to me like teeth and I couldn't eat them. But my father had seen me staring at them long enough; he squeezed my jaw open with one hand, shoved the chick peas in, and said I was going to eat them *because he said so*. I became aware for the first time of a new kind of fear: Here was somebody I was going to be afraid of, whether he hit me or not.

I already feared the physical pains inflicted by my parents; now I learned to fear confrontation, commands, loud voices, authority in general. Whatever nascent morality I might have possessed decayed as I learned to avoid violence by blaming others (if there'd been no witnesses) for my infractions. These are my strongest memories of Queens, when almost overnight, the world became a dangerous place. Even today, if I imagine killing somebody (my father being dead, the present rotation includes Howard Stern, Donald Trump, and President Bush) or bilking an insurance company out of a large sum with a false claim, wrongness has nothing to do with staying my hand: All I worry about are the consequences of getting caught.

Our section of Queens seemed pretty white back then, not in the color sense, although it was that, but in the innocent simplicity of day-to-day events. Our street was mostly Italians and Irish, working class; the few black kids were taken for granted and I never heard the word "nigger" from anybody. People's lives took place right on the block. The bigger boys whistled out bedroom windows to stop the ice cream truck, or hung off the taillights of the city bus for a ride. They wore wide black belts and hard black shoes (sneakers were for pussies) and really did roll packs of Luckies in their T-shirt sleeves. But they ungaraged the push mower every Saturday, and never missed Mother's Day. The girls wore pedal pushers and bangs and jumped double Dutch. The streets were chalked off for war and tops and boxball and other games that required a broomstick or some marbles, but no money. We played self-pitch stickball, one bounce, and stoopball. Some kids scaled baseball cards, a game of trading players by leaning and overlapping cards where the wall meets the floor. But not me; even if I'd liked baseball enough to buy the cards, I wouldn't have risked losing any by playing for keeps.

Money only came to me two cents at a time, when I was lucky enough to find a pop bottle under the stands at the ballpark, and I wasn't willing to spend it on anything I couldn't eat. I took up penny candy. Candy became a symbol; it was *mine*, purchased with my own money, and it was gratifying, because I could choose any type I liked. Whether I bought it from the store or from my mother, to purchase a candy bar was to exercise choice and gain a few moments of pleasure. After we started getting an allowance (two pennies a day), I became addicted. Candy buttons on paper, Pixie Sticks, whistle pops, Smarties. But it wasn't just about pleasure; it was about empowerment and control. For two cents I could pretty much dictate what the next five minutes of my life were going to be like. Even today, I mostly buy the stuff right after something else in my day has gotten away from me.

Social life took place on the street. Even little guys like me, meaningless Catholic-school cockroaches nobody would factor in when describing the streets of New York, played much more often in the street and the lot than in the park at the corner. I wanted to be boss like the big boys, to learn to whistle through my fingers and hit the spaldeen a mile with the broomstick, ride a two-wheeler down the street with no hands. I wanted a few coins to sound in my pocket or buy a Popsicle, to walk with a swagger, roll a pack of butts in my sleeve, maybe pen a girl's name on the cover of my notebook.

But becoming big in any significant sense was still a long way off. Before I even started school, I was already laboring under strong feelings of fear, frustration, insecurity, and a powerful inability to trust. The McCann family next door had a basketball hoop nailed up to a little building in their backyard, which we called the fish house, because the previous owner used to keep an aquarium there. The McCann boys used to shoot baskets there, and one day they let me try. The only way I could reach the rim was with a two-handed underhand heave. I'd never done it before, and after maybe ten tries, since nothing had gone in, I gave up. But it wasn't really giving up. I quit in a fit of pure and bitter frustration, perhaps the first such fit I can remember having. My sense of defeat was compounded by my wanting so badly to destroy the basket, which of course I couldn't even reach. It never occurred to me that sinking a basket might be a skill, that it would require height and practice; nor could I understand that, since I'd never tried it before, I was unlikely to succeed very quickly. My frustration was as strong as hatred and just as violent; I've come up against it many more times as I've gotten older. But even back then it felt like an *adult* hatred, already perfected and trimmed in a seven-year-old. Where had it come from in a second-grade kid?

One day Tommy McCann tried to get me to act out a scene from a western, wherein he was to knock me out with the butt of his six-shooter. No matter how many times he told me we were acting, every time he raised that pistol I ducked and cried out. I was a pretty simple kid; I remember watching westerns on TV and thinking they used criminals who were sentenced to death anyway, actually killing them. It was impossible for me not to think Tommy was going to knock me out. The source seems obvious today: I'd seen kids get hit plenty of times at home, and the beginning of the gesture was always carried through to its conclusion; there was never any acting about it. I was already so skittish around the gestures of violence I couldn't even act out a scene with one of our best friends from right next door. I'd used up my entire lifetime's supply of trust just getting to second grade.

❖   ❖   ❖

Once I was more exposed to the outside world and saw what existed beyond our four walls, the sensation of wanting things became very powerful. The memory of this wanting is still with me; it's manifested as collecting. I favor older things that, by coincidence or not, would have been new items about the time I began badly wanting stuff. Every kid who had a whistle ring or a new bag of marbles or a yo-yo caused in me a longing to simply *possess* something. It could be anything, as long as it was above and beyond things I got from home, and was dissimilar to things my brothers had, so I could know it was mine. A rubber book band, a different pen, a flashlight. This sensation, too powerful to resist and coupled with my lack of coins, soon led me to take things whenever I could. The first thing I ever took was a fountain pen ink cartridge from my mother's desk drawer. It was clear plastic, filled with blue liquid, and I took it because it seemed related to the Nickel-Nips wax pop bottles filled with sweet, colored syrup. You'd get four of those in a little paper carton for two cents. But the plastic cartridge proved much tougher than the wax, and the minute I got done sucking the thing out, I knew I'd made a mistake. I looked so awful my parents didn't even give me a beating over it; they must have already felt sorry for me.

Then I started taking stuff from the corner store, mostly candy, or a pack of matches if they were within reach. I never took gum or comics; anything you couldn't swallow wasn't worth the risk of a beating. You can't really call it stealing or shoplifting; I just wanted things so badly that the only sensation attached to the act of taking was the satisfaction of *having,* once the act was accomplished. The fears the nuns had drilled into us, of sinning and doing wrong and eternal damnation, were ineffective; the only thing I worried about was the stick.

My main occupation was scouring the gutters, the lot, and under the stands at the ballpark for returnable bottles. My desire for coins was even stronger than the desire for things. I would steal empty pop bottles from the cases outside the rear of the corner store, then run around front and cash them in. I asked my brother Marty for a few pennies once, and he sent me to collect BBs where he and his friends would plink tin cans, and streetlight bulbs, near the lot. He was just trying to get rid of me; I actually did comb the lot and come up with a few BBs, but he never paid off, even for a penny. The only other source of coins was under the stands at the ball field, but there were so many needy boys in the neighborhood that pickings were pretty slim. Once in a while, searching the coatroom for other kids' snacks, I'd come across a few coins and pocket them. A quarter seemed almost too big to steal; there'd be no way on earth I could explain it, or even spend it. As an adult, whenever I dream about money, it's always in coins—not bags of folding money, just a small stack of coins, or some loose coins on the sidewalk.

Back at home, Martha, Louise, and Marty had taken over Mom's work; they were looking after the rest of us, practically raising us. They too were overwhelmed, their adolescent years de-fined by *increase*: The family never stopped growing the entire time the four oldest were living at home. Martha, Louise, and Marty, and to a much lesser extent Jimmy, changed diapers, boiled baby bottles, did laundry, ironed school uniforms, polished shoes, bathed us, made lunches for the rest of us to take to school. I remember Marty polishing shoes, countless pairs set up on newspaper on the dining table: school shoes, Dad's shoes, Sunday shoes, my shoes, Mom's high heels, saddle shoes. There was something intoxicating about the smell of the polish. When it came to his own shoes, normal polishing wasn't good enough. He'd have to light the polish on fire with his Zippo (only when Dad wasn't around) to soften it up first, so it would really soak in.

"Down in that basement there was a pile the size of a fucking Christmas tree of laundry," Louise says. "That laundry was no joke. You'd come home from school and the first thing you had to do was diapers at three-thirty, and they were hanging everywhere, where do you even hang the other wash? We changed the first one right after school. It was smelly. . . . The babies had been un-changed for many, many hours. Kids were wearing the same blouse for five days in a row because there was no time to do this stuff." It was clear to Louise at a very young age that our mother, disabled by the workload, was already giving up.

"I never got over the sick old-cheese smell that came from the kids' bottles," Marty remembers. "One time I got so pissed at the responsibility, I peed in one of the baby bottles. I was just so angry, it was like, *that's* what I was going to do . . . that's how pissed I was. I couldn't take any more responsibility, you know? I'm through with responsibility, and I was only ten."

I'd never thought about how those oldest kids might have per-ceived the increasing family surrounding them, making more and more demands upon them as our mother slowly disintegrated. Only when I talk to them now do I get a glimpse of what had really happened to them: They'd lost childhood itself. "I kept thinking, 'Another kid? Another kid?'" Marty adds. "Every time she had another kid, all I knew was that more of my time was going to disappear. I got more and more depressed because I knew more and more time was just shot to shit."

It was a matter of scale. With so many kids, our family consisted entirely of itself; that's all it could be. There was no outside world. I was too young, too much inside the thing, to see what that meant to those older than me, those who were responsible. I never imagined that *people* were necessary to run such a machine, that all their time and energy were directed towards the maintenance of something of which I was only a tiny part. My school shirt materialized in the morning, ironed; food appeared on the table; diapers got changed. Martha, Louise, and Marty ran the machine, a full-time job. It never occurred to me that their lives could have consisted of more than looking after the rest of us, that their classmates were in the Scouts, in Little League, summer camp. I'd hear a ball game on the radio, yet I never figured out that the crowd was made up of fathers who'd taken their sons to the stadium. I didn't realize it wasn't normal for my mother never to have spent time alone with me at the swings. The family was so big that all my parents and older siblings could do was take care of it, manage it. There was no spare time or love or money for anything else.

When I listen to those oldest kids talk about the past, I feel lucky I wasn't born any earlier than I was. As much trouble as I was going to run into when I got older, at least I had time of my own as a kid. By the time I was a teen, my responsibilities were limited to getting decent grades and staying out of trouble; we had machines at home for doing most of the things that had sapped the vitality of the older kids. When I talk to them today, forty years later, they are still bitter about having had their childhoods confiscated. And, although I dislike their assumption that because we didn't have problems like theirs, we hadn't had *real* problems, I understand their bitterness. My teen years included listening to the radio, swimming, spending time after school with a friend at the library. Their teen years consisted of taking care of my needs.

Marty tells me of the time he and Jimmy tied up some clothes in little bundles on broomsticks and ran away from home. They got as far as the lot, where the carnival used to set up in the fall. They couldn't get very far without food or money, and a few hours later they were back home in tears, doing their chores. But that, Marty said, was when he first understood something was wrong. What was happening at home, he realized, was not what he wanted his life to be like. Louise was not far behind him. "I never felt that my existence counted outside of my usefulness to the group," she says, "what chores I did, the part the family needed."

I was too young to have chores assigned to me, but not too young to have my own experience of the taxing crowd around me. I moved further away from any sense of my siblings as individuals, as my family, and came to see them as a crowd. There were so many people to respond to; if I found one or two negative traits in a kid (such as snitching, nose-picking, too loud a voice, wetting the bed), I'd just sign that kid off, since there'd always be others to play with, until finally there was no one left who didn't irk me. This was especially true of the boys. Because we were all packed together in that front bedroom, their habits and needs weighed upon me, as I'm sure mine did on them. Another factor was noise. Since at any given moment someone was usually talking, there was never much peace and quiet; the vocal sum of all those kids was a pervasive and disturbing white noise. And there was never any place for your eyes to rest as long as they were open—nothing but motion. But my distance from my siblings had a more fundamental emotional cause as well, one that would be obvious to a psychiatrist. Perhaps, in order for my parents to see me as special (and perhaps worthy of love), in order for me to stand out, I had to be something other than just another one of their kids. To achieve this, I would have had to dissociate myself from the others. And once I started seeing the sibling dynamics in terms of me in conflict with the others, me as *separate* from the others, it'd be only a short step for those "others" to become "them," the crowd.

There were maybe a dozen instances where I spent time with one of my siblings as an individual, with just two of us engaged in some activity. I recall helping Grace learn how to read, working over the alphabet with her letter by letter, starting her on Golden Books. Later on, when she was at college in Middlebury, I'd visit her up there in Vermont. We'd piss away entire weekends without even walking the grounds, just eating pistachios by the bag in her dorm room, reading Sherlock Holmes.

I recall a few moments with Tony, playing with matches in the lot; we got in most of our trouble as a team, and he became the boy I got beaten with most. There were a few times with Jimmy, when he had that broken leg and was laid up in our room for a while. I spent most of my time with Paul and Tony, because Mom always made us play together, and because we were surrounded on both sides by girls. We played with matches together, started smoking together, compared feats of shoplifting. Tony might have been the first person I trusted to talk to about hating my parents. This would be early teens, though, closer to the end of our stay in Manhasset. Sometimes we three would get beaten as a group for things we'd done together, such as starting a fire or shoplifting. It was almost funny . . . if one of us got caught with stolen goods, the other two were searched immediately, the assumption being that we were all of the same cloth. We could talk among ourselves about Mom and Dad without fear of betrayal; I could feel sorrow or anxiety for my brothers if they got caught stealing and I was clean, or if one of them wet the bed. We hadn't learned yet to trust Marty; he was just enough older than us to cause suspicion, for us to question his allegiances.

But in spite of some moments of closeness, there was something brewing, a feeling of being lost, of having nothing for myself, of not knowing how I fit in, or even if I was supposed to fit in; feelings not quite clear enough to name. Gradually, my siblings became reduced to their final category: *other people*. I don't remember feeling special attachments to them because they were related to me; I would steal money or candy from my brothers as readily as I would from the corner store. I never thought about my siblings' problems being the same as mine, how that was linked to our parents being the same. I didn't care about their problems. I'm not proud of this, but I don't feel bad about it either. It must have been necessary; something about the crowd wore down any compassion and attachment I might have had or felt for those who should have been closest to me.

Although my brothers and sisters are in their forties and fifties now, and although we still refer to ourselves as the kids, that word doesn't help me feel like one of them. The word *siblings* gives me the jim-jams. It derives from the Old English word *sibb*, which in turn comes from the Germanic *sibja*, meaning "one's own" people. It suggests to me something small and helpless, almost pathetic, and causes certain calendar images to swim before my eyes: litters of puppies and kittens wallowing in plaid-lined wicker hand baskets. I've searched for alternative words to describe my parents' other children, neutral-sounding words lacking implications of weakness and dependency. I wanted to write about them just as people, not as people connected to me. But there aren't any other words that mean the same thing, except *kin*, which nobody uses. And as I probed J. I. Rodale for synonyms, I realized that even as I enter middle age, I'm still trying to separate myself from them, from "those guys," the Zanichkowskys, in an attempt to remain or become an individual.

Grandfather and my aunts and uncles were only slightly better off. I never saw them as fully realized people, entire, complete with wives and husbands and children and problems of their own. And that in itself is too bad, because only as an adult did I learn how completely they had been on our side, especially Mom's siblings, Leon and Helen. They always brought gifts and treats, and often became embroiled in bitter arguments with Mom and Dad about how our parents were mistreating us. They, and Grandfather, were my first experience of adults who weren't my parents. They took the pressure off just by their presence; they created a buffer, because Mom was in her glory while preparing a spread when company was coming. The world became a little safer with relatives nearby.

Still, I didn't know them as individuals; I didn't even know until I was in my twenties that those aunts and uncles were Mom and Dad's brothers and sisters, that they shared the same relationship with my parents that I did with Paul and Tony and the three girls. I'm sure I was told this by the older kids at some time, probably many times, but somehow it never sank in. Maybe I just couldn't imagine my parents having brothers and sisters; maybe I couldn't imagine it because I never met my parents' mothers. It's possible I couldn't imagine it because Mom and Dad seemed so powerful to me that I couldn't imagine them "coming" from any place. Mom and Dad had always existed, and they were all-power-ful; why would they even *need* brothers and sisters?

I never did find my place in the crowd. Forty years after leaving that tiny house in Queens, I have learned to insulate myself from unwanted intrusion. I seldom listen to the radio or television, I almost never answer my telephone, I rarely read the papers or do activities that involve more than one other person. Forget raising a family; the thought of having children gives me a bigger case of the jim-jams than the thought of having siblings. I see in group activities a loss of something about myself, a denial of separateness or identity; I fear the loss of my right to choose my own direction, even for an hour. I can't surrender to the idea of *community*, to the idea that the group as a whole might benefit if I were to give a little somewhere. It's gotten to the point where I don't even understand, and actually mistrust, ordinary social interactions such as dinner parties, because somewhere during the transaction, I might be required to *give* something.

Almost every day, I experience things that drag me back to the alienating pains of childhood; it's funny to think now that these could be the pains an only child might feel, a kid who'd have a good reason to fear a crowd. For example, I recently passed some kids at a playground; they were happily kicking a ball around until it escaped their bounds. "Hey, Mister, can you get our ball?" Their joy caused me a regret I'd rather not have to face. Is this because I don't remember having such experiences with other kids? Not directly, no, because I played similar street games when I was their age. But I carry too many feelings of being chastised, and kids today serve as a reminder that I should have felt *joy* during my childhood, that kids are entitled to that. I remember chalking out a boxball court on our cement one day, and right away losing a game to Johnnie McCann. My mother was watching the game,

and after Johnnie's victory, she said to me, "You stink." I know
she meant it in jest, but it was just one more in a hundred such
jests that had never been counterbalanced with praises. And because she said it within earshot of others watching the game, the
power of her remark was multiplied, and the incident came to in-
clude more than just the two of us: My shame, my desire to crawl
away, now involved all the observers, and the game itself. Thus
the sight of kids playing ball today returns me to a place of regret
and unhappiness.

Something else I have all wrong and find unbearable is the
sight of restaurant help sneaking out of the kitchen with a candled
cake, surprising some diner with a chorus of "Happy Birthday."
Just witnessing this spectacle gives me the willies. It brings back
memories of the hollow rejoicing we'd force upon ourselves on
birthdays, when the whole family, still seated on those benches,
would sing "Happy Birthday" to the celebrant. There would be a
cake and a block of ice cream cut into sixteen cubes. But there
wasn't happiness, not that I felt, and in spite of the attendant flash
of birthday joy, it remained impossible for me to sweep the day's
yellings and anxieties under the carpet. Those waiters don't really
care for whom they sing; I sense a hollowness in their song, the
same hollowness I felt at home at the singing of my siblings, a
thinly veiled indifference, in both cases, as they sing for the happiness of someone they'll never know.

5
My Two Afflicted Children

*I*t was around 1960, towards the end of our stay in Queens, that I began to sense a difference in how our parents were handling Annie and Jimmy, compared to how they dealt with the rest of us. Actually, it wasn't just our parents; the older kids were treating Annie and Jimmy differently as well. Neither of them was fitting in, either at home or with other kids on the block, and both seemed to be magnets for Mom and Dad's negative attention. Jimmy attracted much more violence than the rest of us, and the house often seemed filled with a sense of negative anticipation when he was around. Mom's impatience with Annie was palpable, and Annie confesses to disliking our mother from a very young age. It seems to me those two kids' troubles had much more to do with Mom than Dad, but that could be because he wasn't home all day with them like she was. There was no ignoring the price Mom was paying for days spent with Jimmy and Annie. Marty says of her at this time: "I saw the joy of life leave Mom in a steady decline."

My most concrete memory of that time is undoubtedly the day Mom and Dad took Jimmy out of our bedroom and put him in the psychiatric hospital. I was seven, and Jimmy was thirteen. Even though I was too young to know what had really happened to him, and strangely, even though I barely felt I was part of the family, still I felt something was wrong with us *as* a family when he was sent away. That's because we were not told where he went, nor why. He was just missing from our bedroom one night. As I got older, I came to understand that Jim's behavior had taxed our parents beyond what they could endure. But at the time, I didn't see it that way. I saw it as this: If you made trouble, there'd be an empty bed. His going away so suddenly (and, as it turned out, permanently) was the origin of a disturbing feeling I've had ever since that time: that I am essentially alone in the world. Not necessarily that there were forces conspiring against me, but that, if things started to cave in, no one would come to my aid. My parents had abandoned my brother, and no one had rescued him; why should anybody be there for me?

At this same time, Annie's difficulties, which had been mere threats earlier, were now becoming unavoidable; the invisible damage of those few backwards minutes before her birth was now becoming apparent. As she repeated third grade, it became obvious Annie wouldn't get much beyond there in terms of academic and social skills. Elizabeth tells me a story about her first encounter with Annie, when she was six and Annie was twelve. Annie went into the three girls' room and lifted up her shirt to show Elizabeth her newly forming breasts. "I was fascinated and spellbound and horrified at the same time," Liz says. "Somehow I knew she wasn't supposed to be doing that."

Why would Annie show her new breasts to a six-year-old who couldn't possibly understand them, rather than to Catherine, the nearest chronological sister, and one experiencing the same physical development herself? Did Annie perceive Catherine, who was almost two years younger, as a superior who might chastise her?

Late in her own life, Mom told me she'd always worried about what was going to befall Annie when she got to be an adult. For as much grief as Jimmy had caused her, she knew he'd be able to make his own way, even, one supposes, if it meant a life of crime. But she felt, way ahead of time, that she and Dad would have a difficult time preparing Annie for adulthood, because doing everything they'd be able to do for her in the eighteen years they'd have her wouldn't be enough. She would never become a responsible adult by their definition, and they weren't equipped to prepare her for anything else. So perhaps the shortness I saw from Mom and Dad was just the throwing up of their hands in surrender as they were forced to recognize, so early, just how much work Annie was going to be, and that there was nothing they could do about the dissatisfaction that their work, and Annie's life, would bring to them. It must have pained them, my mother especially, to work for years on a child, the second in a row now, who they knew in advance was in for a life of struggle.

But it's their first difficult one, Jimmy, who haunts me more, because he shared that front room with the rest of us boys, and it was immediately obvious when something finally went wrong.

Maybe the earliest thing I remember about Jimmy is not liking him. Although it's hard to pinpoint where this dislike originated, it gradually but clearly became a callous indifference bordering on meanness. One day, I discovered Jimmy searching around in Mom and Dad's bedroom for stuff to steal; variations in the pattern of light under their door gave him away. This was a big deal, because our parents' door was always locked, which meant Jimmy had gotten a key from somewhere. I had him trapped like a rat and kept watch on him until Mom got home and beat the hell out of him with the stick. I felt pretty bad afterwards, watching him get it, but even that guilt was compromised by my sense of having "helped" Mom. Would I have squealed on Marty or Paul? Hard to say, because there was also an element of self-empowerment to my act: In a world of chaos, in which I held no power, I had *controlled* something.

(Snitching and blaming others were despicable, but both were useful for deflecting attention from your own sins, and we all did it. More important for some of us, if a kid stole something, he then had *more* than you, and the inherent unfairness in that might make you want to even the score. Just the thought that Jimmy owned a key to Mom and Dad's room was enough for me to want to take him down a peg or two. Mostly, in my mind, squealing was an exercise of power, and we snitched, as the joke goes, for the same reason dogs lick their cocks: because they can.)

Every morning at our house, there was a mass exodus of kids going off to school, and every afternoon a slow but certain reassembling of the crowd. We came and went in twos and threes, depending on which schools we were in. One day, at the end of the school year, Jimmy was no longer there in the coming home. I didn't notice it until bedtime. I got up to our room, and at lights out he wasn't in his place. I didn't know what to make of his empty bed, because I'd never seen one before. This change didn't develop over time; all of a sudden it just happened. It hadn't occurred to me yet that people left homes for school and marriage. I don't remember asking about it, and Marty didn't say anything. It was a couple of days before I figured out his absence might be permanent. I looked around to see if he'd had any candy hidden that he'd forgotten about.

Jimmy was thirteen when he went away. The day after he graduated eighth grade, Father Kruzas came over in his car and, along with Mom, took Jimmy to a private psychiatric hospital in Westchester. Dad had gone to work as if nothing were out of the ordinary, and Jimmy had no idea where he was going when they got him in the car. He spent the summer at that institution, and in the fall put in a few months at Thomas Edison, a trade high school. But something went wrong halfway through freshman year, and they put him in Creedmore, the state hospital in Queens. Our parents must have known they weren't going to be able to afford a private hospital for as long as Jimmy was going to be away. Creedmore was his home for the next four years; he never even finished out his first year of high school. I didn't know any of this back then. Some of it came down to me from the three oldest kids, after Mom and Dad were dead, and some came from Jimmy.

I didn't ask questions as a kid (mind your own business was the rule) and don't remember worrying about Jimmy. I suspected it had something to do with Mom and Dad. Kids understand the heat of dislike; they understand silence and loud voices, certain kinds of looks. But I didn't understand enough to connect their violent discharges against him with his actual going away. There was not a feeling of crime about it, of that I'm pretty sure. The police hadn't come over, nobody from the school or the church. Jimmy was just missing. And because Mom and Dad revealed nothing about it, and because he was gone for so long, Jimmy was lost to us as a sibling. He was out of the house before I got a chance to know him, before our two youngest sisters were born, and almost before the three girls could speak. By the time he got out of Creedmore, the rest of us were getting ready to move to New Hampshire.

"My guess would be that Jimmy was intelligent," Martha says. "But I think his behavior probably got in the way of that intelligence. Jimmy always seemed to be in trouble. He was one of those kids that's always a nudge."

"He finally figured his way around these knots they used to put around him," Marty recalls. "He and I worked his way out of the ropes one day, and we were on the second floor and we decided to play this daredevil game of going out one window and crawling in through the next one. I made it across . . . no, I don't think I had the balls. But Jimmy crawled out the window and fell off the ledge and hit the ground. He was bounced around pretty good."

This is something I'd never heard about before, but Martha confirms that Mom and Dad had started tying Jimmy to his bed by the time he was three or four; they must have stopped before we younger boys came along, because I never saw it. And who knows what might have happened to Jimmy if he had landed on his head when he fell out the window.

The three oldest tell many stories about Jimmy, not so much things he'd done, but how early and badly Mom and Dad had started abusing him. He'd been singled out to such an extent that those kids had begun to fear for him. "I remember one time," says Martha, "where Jimmy was getting a real beating, Mama was doing it with the stick, a real beating, laying across two chairs and he was screaming and hollering. And I had the phone in my hand and I turned around to Mama and said if she didn't put it down I was calling the police. Because she was enraged, out of control, in a rage. I was scared to death. And she stopped. I think she probably realized what she was doing. I didn't even get a beating because of it."

Martha, Louise, and Marty all talk about confessing to crimes they knew Jimmy had done, in the hopes of saving him from the next beating. I saw it happening too, of course, we all did; the house was just too small not to see such things, and even if the beatings frightened you into hiding, you'd still hear them. But even though the sounds of violence at home were common, it was a while before I made any cause-and-effect connection between my parents' beating Jimmy, and his disappearance.

According to Jimmy, it was always Mom who administered his discipline. When I last talked to him about her, his eyes glazed over. He felt very strongly that Mom, in conspiracy with Father Kruzas, had talked Dad into allowing her to send him to the institution. He wasn't close to either parent, but he was willing to see Dad as a weakling overpowered by a henpecking wife. When I asked him what he'd felt at Dad's funeral, he said, "I didn't love him and I didn't hate him." But about Mom's he said even less: "There's number two."

Only at the very end of my mother's life did she make even the slightest reference to me about Jimmy. It was during my last visit with her before she died. I'd heard stories about Jimmy's going away, but never anything from my parents; it would be a few years before Jimmy told me anything. I wanted to be cautious, and asked my mother in a very general and innocent way what Jimmy had been like as a teenager, suggesting I couldn't remember him from that time. Her voice took on an even, distant quality. She said he'd been a troubled boy, that they'd sent him to a special school. She offered no details, but I didn't press her. She had that look of memory-film scrolling on her retinas, like when you tell someone it would take too long to explain the book if you hadn't seen the movie. This was in 1992. Jim was forty-five then. Mom was seventy. I was forty.

Maybe she was scrolling back to a scene in the kitchen in Manhasset (where we'd moved, after Queens) that even I remember. Marty drove out to Creedmore and brought Jimmy home for one of his Sunday visits. There were no overnights; he was driven back every Sunday evening. Louise remembers this particular visit. "What they did to him was extraordinary," she recalls. "I remember this very vividly. Mom was at the table reading pieces of the Sunday paper, it was after dinner, I was still at the sink cleaning up. And he came in and they had some words, and Jimmy said to Mom, 'You don't like me, do you?' And she stopped reading her paper and she looked at him and said, 'God says I must love all my children. Nothing says I have to like you.'"

Marty didn't help much, at least as far as my take on Jimmy was concerned. He carried a lot of weight in our room, and anything he said about Jimmy I took as gospel. There was no love wasted between them. "Jimmy was supposedly under my control," Marty explains, "so what he did, I became responsible for. I used to hate him, I used to call him the poison in my life. If he was sleeping in bed and we were both facing east, I would turn to face west so that we wouldn't even be facing in the same direction. And then I'd think, 'Oh, we're facing back to back now, and that's symmetry too.' You have no idea."

Stories like these convince me I inherited my attitude towards Jimmy, that it was passed down to me fully formed. I learned from those above me not to drink from Jimmy's glass, since it was poisoned, not to steal candy from him unless it was unopened. I'd hang back with casual deliberation when filing into church, so as not to have to sit next to him, and wouldn't sit next to him at the supper table either, if I could help it. Forget taking a drag off his cigarette. And forget the car, especially in the car where the seating was too close and the window cranks strictly off limits. I didn't know I was being hurtful. I can remember feeling guilty, wondering if Jimmy understood my dawdling while we all piled into the station wagon. Maybe the first stirrings of conscience come when you're old enough to know you've done something wrong but still too young to know what it is. But that takes time, and by the time you've inflicted meanness often enough to understand there's something wrong with it (if you get there at all), you could destroy somebody. As I look back on it now, I realize I wasn't too young to hurt Jimmy. I just did it more slowly as a kid, with stings instead of stabs. All I can hope for now is that the stings from a much younger brother didn't hurt him too badly.

Anne Marie was born two years after Jimmy, in 1948. Since her troubles apparently began in the hospital with that oxygen-deprived delivery, her misfortune took root before my time. My earliest physical memory of her, from when I was four or five, is that her eyes operated independently, which caused me a faint apprehension. Her thick glasses magnified this defect, and my intuitive response was to keep my distance. Annie shared a room, and a bed, in the attic with Catherine; since I seldom ventured past the top of the attic stairs, it only added to her mystery. She approached the world at a tangent; she'd read a comic with her head slightly turned, as if she were listening to it with one good ear, and she walked askance, quartering the room like a three-legged dog obliquely approaching its water bowl. In a word, she spooked me, and there was already something misfiring between us long before I learned that anything was actually wrong with her. She was four years older than me, tallish and skinny and not unattractive. She had rich, black hair and a nervous kind of energy that made her every movement seem animated and spidery, as if she weren't responsible for her own propulsion. Hers were the first breasts I ever saw, when I was an eleven-year-old spying on her under the cover of darkness from out on the upper porch. It was a mystery, like gravity, because there was nothing I then understood that could connect her plump, nippled tissues with the wetness that came upon me. But, also like gravity, it was action at a distance, because I'd never get any closer to her than that. There was something wrong with watching Annie undress, a feeling not present when I watched the other girls; it felt just like what you'd expect a sin to feel like.

We always called her Annie. In one of his novels, Thomas Mann describes "a certain sort of old woman who used to be suspected of witchcraft simply because she looked queer, though her appearance may well have been in the first place nothing but the result of the suspicion against her." This is my sister; because she looked queer, I took her as such. Somehow, I had learned to feel sorry for her because of her poor grades, even though I got poor grades myself. I'd learned to not want to sit next to her. As with

Jimmy, I was influenced by the actions of others. The distress of my parents was tangible, even if it wasn't the active dislike they showed Jimmy. The other kids, although tolerant of her, weren't warm towards Annie; she played with Catherine's friends but couldn't seem to make friends of her own. It was obvious to me, even at seven or eight, that Mom and Dad had no patience for her, perhaps felt burdened by her. They didn't use the violence on her they used on Jimmy, but there was a short-tempered frustration that became despair as they came to understand her disabilities and their permanence.

I can't recall a single day of playing with Annie when we were kids, nor her playing with me. She was not one of the kids who showed me the crayons, or how to tie my shoes, or where to walk to school. I can think of only one instance of being alone with Annie, and I couldn't even say for certain there wasn't a third person with us. We were walking to the store on an errand. The store was closed when we got there, and somehow we got lost on the wrong side of the Van Wyck Expressway on the way home. I didn't worry about getting in trouble when we got home, because a "big kid" was with me and therefore I was not *responsible*. (Strange to realize as I write this that relief from accountability would already seem like a godsend to a seven-year-old.) That's all I take away from time spent with her. But then, she was a girl and I had my brothers. The only other times I saw her alone I wasn't with her; I was spying on her as she undressed.

Louise describes her as a girl always underfoot, trying clumsily to help with the laundry or cooking, like any other kid sister. When Annie was still underfoot at ten and eleven, Lou found herself wondering why Annie wasn't out making friends, or playing board games with the other kids, or reading at her grade level. Mom and Dad slowly began to realize Annie was going to need

special attention. Father Kruzas, who had found a doctor willing
to uncross Annie's eyes as an infant, came to their aid again, finding psychiatrists to help Jimmy and Annie. Annie, unable to keep
up with her classmates, was put in special classes at school. She
would continue in special classes right through high school.

"I don't think I had much trouble until I got into third grade,"
Annie tells me, "nothing that would surface any telltale major
concern. I got reasonable grades in first and second grade, and I
repeated third grade, and from fourth grade on it was kind of
touch and go."

By sixth grade, Catherine had caught up with Annie academi-
cally, then passed her, then pulled away. Paul, right behind
Catherine, did the same. Maybe that's when we began to notice
that Annie had few friends, that she had poor communication
skills, that she'd receive dimes from Mom and Dad for the C's on
her report cards that the rest of us would get scolded for. She
wasn't sent on errands, was never left in charge. I'm not sure these
observations left me with any particular feelings about Annie one
way or another. I'd seen "Jerry's Kids" during the telethons, and it
never would have occurred to me to apply the word *retarded* to
Annie. Maybe I just don't like that word, because back then, to an
eight-year-old boy, it was more of a swear word than an assess-
ment. But you can retard a person's advancement, or slow an engine down, in increments. And in the sense of having been slowed
down in relation to her peers, the word applies.

Newtonian time, where events occur sequentially and only
in one direction, seems to have bypassed Annie completely.
When talking with her, I get the impression that everything
that's ever happened to her happened in the past few days. She
reminds me of Faulkner's Benjy Compson, trapped in an eternal present. Her time line lies on the rim of a wheel, and any

place she touches down is as much "here and now" as any other. During one conversation, it took her some moments to determine how old she was in 1961. Yet I didn't get the feeling she was simply having difficulty making a mental calculation. It was as if the year of her birth and the year in question were just two among dozens of overlapped transparencies on an overhead projector; all the information was there on the screen, but with no page numbers for sorting it out. Like Benjy, she is doomed to see her entire history at all times, galley pages pinned at random to the wall.

As with Jimmy, our mother was the central figure in Annie's life. When asked about Mom, Annie will recreate (or perhaps just create) both ends of a dialogue from confrontations that took place decades ago. Within moments, she becomes bitter at being disliked, misunderstood, and mismanaged by her mother, a theme she returns to constantly. The snippets of dialogue have an energy and insistence that convince me that Annie is talking to Mom in real time. And perhaps she is, saying to her mother now those things she would never have had the courage to say to her in person. (Of course, Annie is not the only one of us who does this; she's just better at it.) It is dialogue from a neglected drama written when she was eight years old; like the ink in a first edition, the words have remained the same ever since.

And there's something else. I get the feeling while talking to her that those words belong to someone else. It has something to do with her syntax:

"By the time third grade came along, Mom and Dad knew I was having a little trouble." "My concentration span wasn't what my teachers expected it to be." "By the time I went to junior high. . . I don't know why, but there were some telltale problems getting along with Mom and Dad."

Annie's usage gives me the impression she is somehow detached from her own experience. "Mom and Dad" know she's having trouble, and "her teachers" are concerned about her concentration span, while Annie herself seems to have no self-reference to the
issues. She seems not to have her *own* knowledge of the trouble
Mom and Dad finally recognized, trouble in which she was the
central character. Her usage suggests that the concentration span
doesn't belong to her, or that it came with a preassigned value that
was more important to others than to her. I get the impression Annie isn't describing herself, but someone *like* Annie. It's almost as if
she had heard about Annie's past, but had not experienced it firsthand, or as if she'd been given Annie's past to inhabit.

It makes me wonder if Annie was more susceptible to the input of our parents than the rest of us, that she believed in her difficulties more strongly because she'd been constantly reminded she
had them, but not because she felt them. If our parents had told
us of Annie's difficulties, even if they limited their trust in us to explaining only Annie's learning disorders, might we kids have been
more patient with her? And this makes me wonder further: If
Mom and Dad had had fewer kids, and more time and patience
to devote to Annie, might she have fared better? Might they have
tried to hold on to Jimmy, work with him a while longer, rather
than send him away?

I say "Mom and Dad," but my father's role in Annie's and
Jimmy's lives was limited. Right after Jimmy died at the age of fifty-
two, I wrote to Creedmore because I wanted to find out why our
parents had sent him there. I was astonished to see only my
mother's name on the papers admitting him to the hospital, a stay
our parents must have known would be for years. Where was my father's signature? Was he so detached from his kids that he could
leave such a decision in Mom's hands? Not take a day off from work

to drive his son to the hospital, reassure him in any way? When I saw the one signature, I didn't even get pissed at my mother for signing. I just looked up at the sky (where *is* my father?) and asked my father, "Where the fuck were you, and how come your wife had to do this by herself?" Just one more piece of evidence that we weren't his kids, just hers, and that she was in it alone.

By the time Annie and Jimmy were fully emerging as difficult children to manage, our mother had ten other kids to worry about. Her back was shot, her arthritis was setting in, she was up to two packs of Tareytons a day. She was not even forty years old. Her next two children were born dead. It was 1960, and her life was spinning rapidly out of control. Had she institutionalized Jimmy simply because she'd lost control of her family? Did she pick on Annie more because Annie couldn't fight back, because Annie's slowness gave Mom *justification* for being short with her? Was our mother so completely overwhelmed, our father so lacking in understanding and support, so emotionally absent, that it was just easier for Mom to remove Jimmy from the house?

I never understood just how much of a burden Jimmy and Annie had posed for our mother in those days until Louise told me about a note Mom slipped her to read on the plane, as she and Martha prepared for a trip to Rome. It said: "Please say a prayer on the altar of Saint Peter for my two afflicted children."

Annie has told me on several occasions that when she was eleven or twelve, Jimmy began to ascend the attic stairs to her bedroom and sexually molest her. This would be right before Jimmy was sent away, and right before we moved to the big house in Manhasset. The first time she talked about it was at Dad's funeral, where she, Mom, and Jimmy came together for the first time in maybe ten years. Annie was terribly upset at the sight of Jimmy, and I didn't know just then what to make of her accusations. Annie is so hungry for love and attention that at the time I thought it entirely possible she'd made the story up, just so I'd pay attention to her. My suspicions were triggered by certain phrases she used, such as "there was inappropriate touching, inappropriate penetration." It was the kind of language one hears on television talk shows or reads in self-help books. Again, it made me feel she inhabited the body of someone she'd heard about, someone named Annie. But then she told me the same story in more detail eight years later, and I began to wonder if there might be some truth in it after all.

In a family so bent on control, the truth is often hard to come by. Catherine was linked to Annie with a ball and chain; she shared a bed with Annie, and she remembers no such episodes. Martha and Louise were in the other tiny attic room, and they remember nothing. Marty and Jimmy weren't pals, but Marty and I were; if anything had happened between Jimmy and Annie, I figure Marty would have told me about it by now. I'm left wondering how Annie's molestations could have occurred in a tiny house with fifteen people living in it. Annie says that Martha encouraged her to go to Mom with the story, and that when she did so, Mom dismissed her, saying that if anything had happened between Annie and Jimmy, Annie must have instigated it. But having parents capable of beating a kid senseless for smoking a cigarette, parents who had it in for Jimmy, I'm left without much faith in Annie's story, at least the part where Mom is concerned. In spite of my mother's obvious inability to relate to Annie, such a dismissal would have been impossible from Mom.

Nevertheless, it has occurred to me since then to believe my sister. One reason is that the three oldest kids couldn't remember convincing reasons for Jimmy's being sent to Creedmore. Also, my parents would have been too ashamed to mention the story Annie tells, even if it were true. I mean mention ever, to anybody, even to the doctors admitting Jimmy to Creedmore. They were so morally uptight they just wouldn't have been able to do it; the public shame of it (because with so many of us such a secret would have been impossible to keep) would have been unmanageable. In the end, Annie did not attend Jimmy's funeral. She tells me she finally reached a point of closure, where she never wanted to see Jimmy again. When I remember our parents' funerals, the anger and fear Annie expressed over Jimmy, I'm more willing to believe her. The intensity of Annie's emotions has to come from somewhere.

During my final conversations with Jimmy just before he died, I never asked him directly about Annie. Frankly, I was scared to. Anyone left in a room with him for an hour could tell he was capable of extreme anger and violence, and I didn't want to put myself on the wrong side of all that. When I mentioned Annie even incidentally, Jimmy's manner became keen and suspicious immediately; he grilled me about anything Annie might have said about him, but I was evasive in my answers. The world he'd created for himself after Creedmore had seen him through to fifty years of age, and I wasn't interested in dismantling it. I'm not sure which idea scared me more, pushing him to reexplore old territory he'd spent years burying (if he'd ever been there in the first place) or what he'd do to me once I'd taken him back there. The only comfort I can take against my loss of nerve is thinking that even if I'd asked him about Annie point-blank, he would have denied it point-blank.

I never did learn the "real" reason our parents sent Jimmy to the institution. Martha says it's because they feared his burning the house down. Louise can't remember anything drastic, just a slow accumulation of lesser juvenile misdeeds. Marty says it was because he pulled his pants down at school, was feeling up neighborhood girls, exposing himself to the girl next door. It could have been any and all of those things, or it could have been for molesting his sister. The Creedmore record gives the vague and harmless-sounding diagnosis of "childhood schizo-phrenia," which, without any examples of serious violence or per-version, hardly seems sufficient to lock a kid up for five years. The only words Jimmy would apply to himself during those last visits were "rambunctious" and "outgoing." How much would a kid have to do before his parents tied him to his bed? Gave him up to the care of the state? It depends on the parents, at least until the kid is old enough to be wise to the trouble he's causing.

Jimmy takes no responsibility for his being sent away, nor for any of his beatings, and I don't know what to make of that. I know our parents beat the stuffing out of him constantly, but some of those beatings must have been "earned" in the same way the rest of us had earned ours, by smoking cigarettes or shoplifting or swear-ing. We kids cry about the unjust severity of our beatings, but not about getting beaten for no reason whatsoever. My own belief is that many partings, including most divorces, are to some extent both parties' fault. Perhaps Jimmy became so bitter at having spent his high school years in the loony bin that he came to see himself as completely innocent. Maybe he *had* to, so that he wouldn't have to see himself as an accomplice to the loss and waste of his own child-hood. I try to imagine what he might have been doing at eight, nine, ten, how he might have spent the spare moments I'd spent lighting matches, shoplifting candy, smoking stolen cigarettes. The worst thing I can remember doing at twelve was taking Marty's BB gun and popping a shot at the electric meter on the pool pump house, from point-blank range. The BB made one of those curious little roundels in the glass, and my career as a vandal was over. Jimmy was only six years older than me, but those years turn everything Martha, Louise, and Marty have told me about him into hearsay. I personally never saw him do anything against the rules, except for that one time I found him in our parents' locked bedroom. I don't think he's ever had a drink in his life, and he couldn't swear for shit. One saw filaments of ugliness and violence in him as an adult, but had they been there at twelve?

Jimmy's reluctance to describe childhood misdeeds of any severity makes me uncomfortable, and brings me once again back to him and Annie. What had he done that he couldn't or wouldn't talk about even forty years later? I kept waiting for him to tell the true story of the horrendous adventure that led to Creedmore's doors, but the story he told just didn't convince me. What finally did it, he said, was another beating with the stick, this one over a red rubber band. Mom was at the helm when Jimmy took the stick away from her and, in his words, tried to kill her with it.

"Something of hers was missing," Jimmy explains, "one of those big red rubber bands. And I had found a big red rubber band. That's what led to that big beating, this stupid rubber band. I would not say that I stole it from her. Because I didn't and I wasn't going to say it. I'm not saying I didn't steal stuff from her. But I did not take that rubber band from her, and I wasn't going to say I did. And she was intent on beating me with that stick until I did tell her I'd stolen it. The action I took then put a fear in her . . . showed her to the point where, hey, she's finished. Because I took the matter into my own hands at that point, something I'd never done before.

"What got me into that rage was that she was wildly swinging that stick, not just over a chair at my rear end . . . after I fell off the chair she swung and hit me in the head. At that point, I snapped because I didn't know where she was going to stop. I grabbed the stick. I didn't lose it to where I didn't know what was going on, oh no, oh no. I knew what was going on. I knew what I was doing, and when I had the opportunity to hit Mom, that would have been a deliberate wanton act. I was already in the downswing. Oh, I would have definitely done it, no question about it. If that stick wasn't taken from me, she would have been wearing it. I would have taken her out.

"It was very shortly after I took the stick to Mom that I was gone to the institution. They could not take the chance of my staying there. I never saw the Queens house again, not since the day after graduation when they got me up at six o'clock in the morning, put a bunch of my stuff in a little bag, and ushered me into Father Kruzas's car with Mama."

What happened in the middle there is a little sketchy. I know now Jimmy *was* a victim in the larger context, but his insistence on his own innocence in the daily context makes me want to discredit him. His story had the ring of a story that would qualify a guy for a trip to Creedmore, but not the ring of truth.

But I have bigger questions than that. Like who took the stick away from him? Jimmy said it was either Marty, or the Man Upstairs. But Marty doesn't remember this story, and I don't believe God comes down to earth to meddle in such trifles as domestic violence. And why was Dad, no stranger to violence, sitting idle while someone threatened his wife's life? Jimmy places him in an easy chair during the whole thing, paralyzed. "I swear to this day that Dad went up and changed his underwear," Jim says. And why, in a house with fifteen people in it and where beatings were routinely watched because we were often beaten in groups, why doesn't anyone else remember this one? His story is as incredible as Annie's story about being molested; not that either couldn't have happened, but how could either have happened unnoticed in that house?

I guess if Jim's story has a few holes in it, it doesn't matter. It's just a story. Not a story in the bullshit sense, although even if it is that, it still approximates the truth about his relationship to our mother. And it's a story that ends with a true fact: He was out. The only part that needs to be true, that is true, is that Mom and Dad had him carted off. I can't know with certainty about anything that might have led him to Creedmore's doors. But the house never did catch fire, no drugs were being dealt, and he didn't hold anybody at gunpoint, so how bad could it have been? Annie's story, in this context, weighs quite a bit.

And if he was carted off not for molesting his sister but for taking that swipe at Mom, there's a miscarriage somewhere. Not that Mom would have deserved, in Jimmy's words, to be taken out. But based upon my own experiences with home discipline, it's clear to me that Mom and Dad were capable of bringing someone to the act of retaliatory violence and, in Jimmy's case, probably had. I'm not saying I can justify Jim's action, I'm just saying I can understand his rage.

But I'd still like to understand what had transpired with Jim up until that day he swung at Mom. Not actual deeds, but emotions. How much had my parents distanced themselves from him emotionally? How much had they hurt him? Because you wouldn't take the stick to her all at once; whatever it was that got him to swing that stick had to be built up piece by piece for some time. And that buildup had to make him not only rage-filled, but fearless, heedless of what the world was going to look like the minute he was done swinging. Because once you were done with the swinging, your life was changed whether you connected with her or not. I would only daydream about it. I was too afraid to hit back, and as far as I know, not one of the rest of us ever took a swipe at either of them, no matter how bad it got. Many people

have asked me why none of us ever fought back, but that's because they don't understand real fear.

If Jim's story is true, then he'd snapped in a clear and deci-
sive way at thirteen, in a manner that paved the way for action,
something that had never happened at home before. I wish now
there was some way to know more about him, but I suspect the
"facts" of his past are as securely buried as Jim himself is today.
I'd like to have gotten him on the couch as a psychiatrist, even
though, because of my firsthand knowledge of him as a bullshit-
ter, I'd have dripped him with truth serum right off the bat.

I didn't know it then, but Jimmy's going away changed something in me I wouldn't begin to understand for many years; it
caused me a lifelong fear of authority. It wasn't like Martha, who
left for nursing school, or like Louise, who married out. Jim just
disappeared. When he fought with my parents, he ceased to exist.
It only took one day. From this I learned at a young age to associate conflict with defeat. I became afraid of the power and effects
of Mom and Dad's authority. I never once argued or fought with
them, never tested their might or their will; I was already beaten.
And long before they died, I learned to transfer that fear to any
priest or cop or boss or girlfriend who happened to be in a position of influence over me.

Jimmy's going away changed something for the rest of the kids
as well: It made us aware that we were not a supportive family.
There were no loyalties, only fragile alliances of expediency. There
was no devotion, no dedication. Our parents would not support us
in times of difficulty, and we kids weren't learning to look after each
other. Although the three oldest told those stories of taking the rap
for Jimmy on occasion, the general response around the house was
that, since Mom and Dad had it in for him, he was therefore
doomed and you might as well stay out of it. Why associate with

someone who's always in trouble? In fact, why not blame your crime on Jimmy, since he's always getting beaten anyway? The fear of the stick turned us into the very liars and sneaks our mother always accused us of being. I remember one time when Jane, who was about four, got caught writing on the walls with crayons. When confronted, she pulled herself up to her fullest possible height and said, in her deepest artificial voice, "I'm Gracie." Too young to know that the rest of us knew who she was, she was still old enough to understand blaming somebody else for her work.

❖   ❖   ❖

The summer of 1960. What was Mom thinking as we prepared to move from that little house in Queens? Did she expect to see Jimmy at the new house occasionally, or did she already know he was finished as a member of the family? Perhaps the move meant her family was now complete, that with thirteen kids she was all done having children. Did she anticipate privacy, having a whole suite to share only with her husband? Was she worrying about where the money would come from to support a new house five times the cost and ten times the size of their old one?

Or was she relieved? Perhaps she felt safe. Perhaps, for the first time since their wedding day, she felt hope. She was taking her children to a big, comfortable house on the North Shore; she was leaving behind the house in which she'd endured the deaths of her parents, the loss of her figure and her health, and the loss of two children to miscarriage. Whatever darkness might have transpired between Jimmy and Annie, well, Jimmy was gone now, and they'd see what they could do with Annie. Maybe she was leaving that behind, too.

6

The Expanding Universe

The photograph on the cover of this book is one of the two family portraits I mentioned earlier. My brother Tony found it among our parents' stuff after they died. We call it "the family photo" because for decades it was the only picture we knew of in which our whole family was present. It was taken by a North Shore society magazine right after we occupied the Manhasset house; they ran a story about the huge family that had finally purchased the neighborhood's white elephant. It was a mansion, and we kept hearing rumors about famous people who'd lived there, that it was the inspiration for Gatsby's mansion, but who knows.

I forgot this picture existed. I never saw the magazine article, but I remember sitting for the picture, because there weren't many occasions when the kids would wear dresses and neckties at home. It was not displayed at our house. Not for any reason that I know of, we just didn't have photo albums, and we never hung pictures of family or friends on the walls. Tony says he found it in one of the shoe boxes full of crinkle-edged snapshots that doubled as bookends. I hate to think about it now, but when I was a kid I used to raid those shoe boxes for negatives; I'd roll them up in newspaper, to make smoke bombs.

My mother was pregnant when we moved, and Stephanie Marie was born on October 25, 1961. There were fourteen of us now, and at last we were done. Mom fussed over the new baby the same as she had all the other kids; you'd think she'd never seen a baby before. She loved infants, their newness and delicacy; she'd decorate the carriage with ribbons and parade up and down the street. Inevitably, she'd lose interest in the new child the same way some people who love kittens can't tolerate cats, but not before she exercised exclusive right of care for ten or twelve months. For me, even more than with Janie, Steffie's appearance on the scene was disturbing; it meant that Janie wasn't an aberration after those blank years following Rita. I became so disinterested in the new kid my distance became noticeable to others. I remember one day in the dining room in Manhasset, around 1964, when Stephanie walked up to me and asked me something. She had taken me utterly by surprise. I said to Marty, "Since when can Steffie talk?" And he replied, "Where have *you* been?"

At number 6 Gull's Cove, we finally had a living room that could hold all of us at once. When Louise got married in 1964, the reception was held in that living room, and there were almost a hundred people seated for dinner, with room left over for a dance area and a band. Carved plaster embellished the ceiling; silver candle sconces adorned the walls. The Christmas tree would be set up in there, and the good furniture installed. But the room was generally off limits, the doors frequently closed. Very rarely, I'd sneak in there at night, pop open one of the big picture windows, and escape for a clandestine sojourn around the neighborhood on my bike.

Mom and Dad had bought the new house a year before we moved, because it had been empty for eleven years and needed a lot of attention before it would be livable. I was eight. The older kids who'd been out working on the house would return Sunday evenings with tales of the size of the place. Even Jimmy had gone out there to work a few Sundays, from Creedmore. I was too small to be allowed to go out and help, and I never saw the new house until we moved. But I remember listening to Paul's descriptions of helping repair slates on the roof, replacing rotted floors, setting up for laundry in the basement. I was envious of his excursions, confounded by his attempts to explain how big the house was. My imagination failed me: I couldn't picture a "much bigger house," near a bay, with more than an *acre*. All the houses I'd ever seen were the same size, and I'd never heard of an acre. Even as he described twenty or thirty rooms, I couldn't imagine one of my own: My "self" had either failed to materialize, or was not worthy of a room of its own.

The scale of the new place was entirely beyond the range of my experience. It seemed as if our old house might have fit in the garage of this new one. We decompressed, expanding like Crazy Foam into the eight or nine bedrooms, each with its own bath; I marveled at the six actual fireplaces, never having seen one before. There were screened-in porches upper and lower, a slate terrace facing the bay, that huge living room, a library, a den, chimneys, and leaded windows. We had a pool at least fifty feet long, in-ground, bigger than any pool I'd seen up until then even in the Queens park. The place was unavoidable, a big lawn with huge trees, rolling slowly downhill and ending on the shore of Manhasset Bay. Boats rafted together out in the bay, cocktail glasses and laughter drifting in toward the shore like fog. Lawns manicured to mysterious green perfection, roses and carved hedges, exotic-looking trees, weeping willows and flowering dogwoods and miniature red maples. This was Dreamland.

We'd moved up a notch in moving to Long Island, several notches, and I knew immediately that our circumstances were different. There were no mom-and-pop stores at the corners now, because there were no corners; we'd graduated to a private, closed street with huge houses on great expanses of lawn. More than that, ours was now the most grand house, the most expansive lawn, a complete about-face from 135th Street. There were no more street games involving the tops and marbles of allowanceless kids, no ring-a-levio, no hopscotch or kiddie amusements like at the Queens park, where each day they'd unlock the park-house doors and distribute the Ping-Pong and the shuffleboard and the sporting goods. We were on our own now: no park, no black kids, no scooters, no young Italian hotshots running to tag a ride off the taillights of the city bus. The bikes in the neighborhood were nicer; there were fruit trees on people's lawns. The young boys were mobile; they tooled around the bay in little motorboats and welded lawnmower motors to their bicycle frames, creating makeshift motorcycles. There were no skate keys anymore; what few roller skates I saw now came with their own lace-up boots.

Although I didn't realize it yet, I was coming into contact with money for the first time. I'd seldom seen a dollar, and my experience of money up until that time had to do with coins. Even at Christmas, although I knew where the presents came from, I never thought about where the money for them came from. The whole concept of Dad leaving for work every morning, the idea of salaries, bank accounts, food bills, a paycheck being divided sixteen ways, I'd never thought about any of it. I don't ever remember connecting our material circumstances to Dad's salary. I had no idea how much he earned, and hardly understood that I lacked certain comforts because the family operated on one simple formula: money divided by kids. It was a miracle that our family got by through the relentless industry of a single individual and the niggardly scrimping of his wife, but I'd never once, at least as a kid, given that miracle any thought. Thus I could hardly figure out how and why my new circumstances differed from my old ones.

Life became a little looser in the new place. Although Paul, Tony, and I still shared a bedroom, I could always find an empty room to hide in. After a while Paul was bunked up with Marty, and Tony and I had a room for ourselves, with our own bathroom. We were on the third floor, overlooking the bay, and there were no sisters up there; to us it was a fortress. Even absent Jimmy had a room, although he never lived there. Martha says that when Jimmy came home from the institution on Sundays, the girls' clothing and makeup would disappear; Louise figures he was bringing the stuff back to the hospital to use as gifts. Mom gave the girls keys to lock their doors against his stealing. Tony says we boys had keys for the same reason, but I don't remember that. Unlike in Queens, Mom could no longer just shout a name and expect to be heard throughout the house. If I heard her call me I'd just yell, "What?" and she would scream in response, "Don't 'What?' me!" She soon took to sending someone to chase down the kid she wanted to see. This allowed the victim to query the messenger about Mom's mood, and we felt much less within range of the evil eye as we scampered about. Tony and I would take little blocks of wood and stash them around the house, pretending they were tape recorders. We played hide-and-seek. We made flashlights from paper towel tubes and explored the attics and eaves and all the dark corners of the third floor. We made slingshots from tree branches and inner tubes (and leather cut from my baseball glove, which led to another beating), and held chestnut wars against the other neighborhood boys.

For the first time in their lives, our parents had a little something for themselves: privacy. Their bedroom was at the end of the house on the second floor, with windows overlooking the water.

They had their own bathroom and a small sitting room with a fire-place and bookshelves. They installed a second television there. Once the chores were assigned, Mom could close the door to that little wing and allow herself the pleasure of reading or television, for the most part out of earshot of the rest of us. I remember Mom and Dad relaxing on the screened-in porch, or sitting on the back terrace, a pitcher of Manhattans at the ready. They just seemed more at ease. Whatever it had cost my father (and it turned out to be only $50,000), that place was worth it.

As with the great hall at Annunciation, when we left that house five years later, I had dreams of it for many years afterwards. Dreams of it burning down; dreams of all us kids renting it from newer owners after our parents died, with all of us in our old bed-rooms; dreams of living in it while it decayed from rain and ne-glect until I could see stars through my bedroom ceiling.

The pool was the most liberating thing about the new place, and I looked forward to that first day each season, when they opened the tap. The water would drop eight or ten feet into the deep end, creating a continuous crackling-cellophane sound I could hear from my bedroom; it'd last the entire day, until enough water had accumulated to change the sound into something more like a bathtub. Only the ten or so families on our closed street could use the pool; we all chipped in for its upkeep. That pool saved our lives. We kids could hang around the water all day, every day, at no expense, no questions asked. I can't imagine what this meant to my mother, what a relief and blessing it must have been for her. She could now get out of the house, sit in the sun, and keep all her kids in sight at the same time. Even if one of us got in trouble, there was a lifeguard, whose single responsibility was the kids' safety. Techni-cally, he was the first person ever paid to look after us, even if it was only while we were inside the cyclone fence.

That pool was going to be the launching pad for my big-boy-hood in a couple of summers, once I became old enough to appreciate those sleek and glistening teenage girl-bodies emerging from the water like Barbie dolls.

❖   ❖   ❖

After a while I made another discovery about money. Not the serious money of privilege that those in Plandome Manor possessed (although that would come soon enough), but the fact of money as an ingredient in the machinery of our expanding household. This discovery came when I saw Louise and Marty folding twenty-dollar bills into small aircraft and flying them over to our mother, seated at the kitchen table. In an instant, I understood what was happening when they left the house in the morning: They were going to work, just like Dad. That's what a job meant. This was my first bit of worldly knowledge since the discovery of matches: A time comes when you finish school; you get a job, work every day, and bring home money. Of course, I was too young to know why they were giving the money to my parents. I hadn't yet learned that, in our house, earning your own money and having money of your own weren't the same thing. But I knew how miraculous a quarter was, and seeing that much cash all at once shocked me into the realization of the position money held in the world. I was amazed by the sudden factuality of money, at least as much as a nine-year-old could grasp the significance of wealth.

My older siblings revealed why our parents could afford Manhasset in the first place. Martha, Louise, and Marty had to fork over their entire earnings to our parents. In exchange, they got carfare and a bit of spending money. Our parents became addicted to those sources of income. Louise says when she was planning to get married, she told Mom she wanted to keep her last two paychecks before the wedding, so as to prepare for her new life, and that Mom told her, "If you don't have enough money, maybe you shouldn't be getting married."

"The whole paycheck went into the house," Marty says. "I think that's the reason I started taking stuff from Gertz. I was working so fucking hard, and I had nothing to show for it." Marty attended the Fashion Institute of Technology, not far from where Martha was a nursing resident at Saint Vincent's Hospital in Manhattan. His first jobs included installing window displays at department stores. "Even when I was at Lane Bryant's, the check came home and I was given an allowance, and the allowance wasn't enough to piss. And I think my resolution to that was . . . 'Okay, I'm in this huge fucking store, surrounded by all this shit, you know, and they're not going to miss it.' It wasn't like right or wrong, it was like . . . I'm working this hard, I've got to have something to show for it."

This was something new and important for me. Marty was coming home with clothes, cigarettes and lighters, shoes, imported chocolates. This was a lot more stuff than he needed to justify having a job, but all I saw was the material improvement. Dad's money had been going for insurance, mortgage payments, tuition, money invisibly coming in and invisibly going towards intangibles I didn't understand. Marty was the first of us to have *possessions*, things that didn't originate under the Christmas tree. For me, this wasn't about chocolate and cigarettes; it wasn't even about right or wrong. It was about control: Marty was taking charge of Marty, shaping his world and separating himself from the rest of us. If our parents taxed him too heavily, he'd make it up elsewhere, but he wasn't going to suffer. I began to see money and stealing as two solutions to the problem of need, and the option of doing without began to fade. My brother made no excuses for stealing a pair of shoes. "It wasn't like a theft thing to me, know what I mean? It was like: 'These are here, they don't need 'em, and I do need them.' I was just moving them over to where they needed to be."

Stealing had never been explained to me with reference to necessity, but only in strict terms of right and wrong. Now there seemed to be an inconsistency between life's fairness and the textbook honesty we'd learned. Marty brought to my attention the idea that "taking what doesn't belong to you" had to be weighed against need, something our nuns, priests, and parents had never allowed us to consider. I know now that many of his wants were not actual needs. On the other hand, when you're young and don't have much, and all your schoolmates are better off than you are, wants and needs can feel like the same thing. Maybe stealing wasn't the solution, but it was something like fighting back; at the very least, my brother pointed out that the problem of want existed, and that the problem had solutions. I began to lose whatever residue remained of the original Catholic guilt I'd felt since the beginning of my own shoplifting career down at the corner store in Queens, and my shoplifting increased accordingly.

Operating behind our parents' backs was a solution to other needs, and my brother began taking some small measure of control over the quality of his daily experience. "I was getting my shirts laundered," Marty tells me, "and Mom thought I had too much money, because I'd come home with these blue boxes with my shirts in them. Well, yeah . . . I'm getting home at 11:30 at night from school, I'm leaving at 7:41 in the morning to get to work at whatever time I was starting. . . . What was I going to do? Press 'em in Central Park between the end of my workday and going to school at night?" Marty took to de-boxing the shirts and sneaking them past my mother in a briefcase, disguised as work. Even a twelve-year-old could see that my mother's favorite descriptive phrase, he's a *sneak*, couldn't be applied to Marty in this case. (She'd get pissed at him, but that's all she could do now; Marty was six foot three and had constructed makeshift but efficient bodybuilding equipment: stacks of glossy magazines bundled with clothesline running through pulleys in the ceiling.)

Marty had introduced me to selfishness, to the idea of healthy self-interest: I had needs, could name them, and was entitled to look for ways to satisfy them. All it took was accepting that my needs were valid and that other people's demands didn't nullify mine. Marty's actions illuminated this truth: He couldn't possibly fly enough twenties over the kitchen table to fix everything that was wrong for all of us, and he shouldn't have to. In this way he planted in me the idea of self-action. I began to understand the value of putting myself first; it'd be a while before I'd learn not to cross others in the process.

Thus began the slow fuzzying of my ingrained Catholic absolutes; the first signs of rust began to appear on the iron authority of my father, my teachers, and the Church. There seemed to be things that might be true (or false) that had nothing to do with what those powers dictated; gray areas began to occur in the spaces between the black and white certainties of the Ten Commandments. I didn't acquire a sense that those authorities were wrong, only that the world they described was incomplete. The incompleteness of my father's world would catch up with me again later, during Vietnam, when I applied for conscientious objector status with the local draft board. Dad tried to argue me into fulfilling my "duty" towards my country. Although I lacked the words and perspective to debate him, not to mention the courage to defy him, I could sense that the definitions of words like *duty* and *patriotism* were contrived against me, against anyone who didn't want to be a soldier. But in spite of his dire physical threats and bleak prospects for a Communist world, I filled out the paperwork anyway; the seeds Marty had planted ten years earlier were beginning to produce.

❖   ❖   ❖

In the looser Manhasset atmosphere, I began to recognize my mother as a person in her own right. I especially noticed her physical agonies, her interactions with the other kids, the stresses we caused her. At times it seemed as if her days were without purpose or plan, that all she really did all day was react to her surroundings, and I wondered just how much might be wrong with her. One morning, a neighbor brought over an egg, to replace one she'd borrowed. I had to examine this replacement, to see how it compared with the ones we had, and dropped it in the process. Mom didn't even yell at me, but when I saw the tears well up in her eyes, I knew there was something much more wrong for her than the loss of an egg. Another time, Elizabeth scrubbed Mom's wedding silverware with a Brillo pad, destroying the soft and ancient polished finish. I thought for sure Liz was in for the stick, but Mom just started crying, picking up spoons and knives from the mahogany case one at a time, as if they were burn victims. She appeared to be talking to them. I began to recognize in my mother a sorrow I'd thought belonged only to myself.

For the first time, I recognized my own isolation within the isolation of another, and I began to acknowledge my mother's struggles, the fact that she *had* them. I became aware of her as deserving not actual pity, but some form of compassion. She told me a story from that time, how she'd been reading a mystery one afternoon and realized she'd devoured half a coffee cake along with half the book. Feeling shame and guilt at the thought of Dad finding her out, but unable to lie to him by hiding the cake, she ate the other half and threw the box away. I still remember the time her doctors warned her to quit smoking. It was their final warning, but she'd just bought a fresh carton of Tareytons; she smoked all ten packs in five days, and then quit. She reminds me of Quentin Compson, who wouldn't commit suicide until he finished out that first year at Harvard, so as to get the full value from the land his father had sold to cover the tuition. Today I find in such stories, in addition to evidence of her frugality, touches of her dark humor and her own shameless acceptance of her weaknesses.

But feelings of compassion were new to me then, and I didn't understand how they applied to someone I feared. I would wait by the big picture windows while Mom was out shopping, keeping a sharp eye on the entrance to our little private street, hoping her car would never reappear. (The three girls did the same thing, except instead of keeping an eye on the driveway, they'd climb the swing-set down by the seawall, and scout for Mom's car while it would still be a mile away.) What thoughts I gave to her efforts as our caretaker were diluted by a generalized fear of her, a fear all the kids shared. Still, my fantasies of her death made me sad because, although I feared her, I wanted her to love me. I felt sorry for her but never volunteered to help her; although I seldom even showed her kindness, I wanted her to take joy in me just for being one of her creations.

There were times when she'd grant one of us the benefit of the doubt when Dad's back was turned, signing a note from school before he got home, or just not telling him about some infraction that might cause him to go overboard. I'm thinking of the day we boys found a bullet on the shore and tried to set it off by flinging it against the seawall. Mom must have seen us from the back terrace taking turns at it, because she was white as a sheet. But instead of reaching for the stick, she told us to kneel down right there in the hallway and thank God we'd not been killed. Whether she said her own prayers or not I don't know, but she didn't mention anything to our father.

But she was not repaid in kind even for those reprieves, and there were times when, finding herself alone with one of her children, she left herself open to affection and was denied. "One time, I happened to be alone with her," Grace says, "driving in the car. It was warm inside the car, and it was really quiet, and she was in a good mood. And I remember the trip being an agonizing struggle inside myself. I kept thinking: 'She's quiet, she's in a good mood. This is nice. If I were to move over there and sit next to her . . . and touched her and told her that I loved her, she'd probably respond.' And I couldn't do it. It was agony, because even though I knew she would respond and that it would be heaven, Mom and I having five minutes of bliss, the fear was too great, and I was paralyzed. By that time fear was such a habit, it was automatic, like drooling. God had sent me a perfect chance on a platter, and I couldn't do anything with it."

A similar chance came to a roomful of us one night, when Mom tripped and fell coming into the dining room. We were all seated at the supper table, but although several kids asked her if she was all right, no one made a move to physically help her to her feet.

Because we *were* afraid of her. There was no predicting when her touch would be hard or soft. It was like that with all of us: Once you got within the range of her arm, you became skittish, like an old horse suspicious of the hand of a new trainer. It's depressing to imagine, or actually remember, that the apprehension and uncertainty had become so ingrained that even offering kindness to our mother was risky. But with Mom, there was just no way of knowing. Sometimes she'd beat the shit out of you, other times she'd try to talk you into understanding why the thing you'd done was a bad thing. On those occasions, it wasn't an undercurrent of mercy you experienced, or even relief: There was an actual belief, however short-lived, that she cared about you, that she just plain wished you hadn't done the thing, whatever it was, because it wasn't a good thing, and a beating wasn't going to help you learn that. Rita told me several stories about Mom beating her to a pulp one day, and the next day talking to her calmly about the responsibilities of knowing right from wrong.

I can't imagine how complicated her life must have been, and as long as she lived, I learned almost nothing about her beyond the strength of her religious faith. It depresses me to recall how badly Mom relied on the promise of an afterlife in order to make this life bearable. In Manhasset, we kids drained her of everything: love, patience, kindness, food, attention. We even drained her of violence, and she finally just ran out of the energy necessary to beat us. It was sad and pathetic to watch her become powerless, to see one more thing taken from her. Yet even this understanding of her brought me no nearer to her, and I never once told her I loved her, not even at the end, while she was in the hospital, when I should have lied to her.

As far as I could tell, God was my mother's only comfort. Perhaps it started in 1946, on the day her parents died. Suddenly, her children lost any position of importance they might have held with her and became simply the work she'd have to do to qualify for God's greater reward: eternal salvation. On my last visit with her, right before she died, I asked her about the distance that existed between her and us kids, the lifetime of troubled relationships between children and parents. She looked straight ahead with one of those looks that stops right in back of the eyeglass lenses and said, "If I had to choose between the love of my children and the love of my God, I would choose that of my God."

7
Satisfaction

Y ou could say our family started coming apart even before it
  had been fully assembled. Except for holidays and the
occasional Sunday meal, when somebody would drive out and
fetch Jimmy from Creedmore, we sixteen have almost never
been together as a group since the day that black and white picture
was taken for the magazine. But we treasure the picture anyway,
because it grants us the illusion, or promise, or memory, of family. When Martha and Jimmy were home, though, even that
huge house seemed full. Any pleasant family memories the kids
express as adults today come from that five-year period of North
Shore luxury. Especially during holidays, when a bunch of relatives were there, that place felt like our home, our center. That's
when Mom was in her glory. "I think she loved having people
over," Liz remembers. "She was much more social than Dad,
more willing to be social, and she went all out, a tired old woman
with a million kids. She just dove in, and the whole atmosphere
of the house felt different."

The words "company's coming" changed everything. There'd
be a tablecloth, plates of cheese and crackers, bowls of black olives,
kielbasa with horseradish, all before the serious eating began. The

mood would brighten considerably once the martinis and Manhattans got flowing. Our aunts and uncles, even Father Kruzas, served as a buffer between us and our parents. The guests paid a lot of attention to us, sometimes tucking us in to bed, and often incurred Mom or Dad's wrath by "sticking their nose in" where it didn't belong. These were the days when, if you didn't finish what was on your plate, it would reappear at the next meal exactly as you'd left it, only colder, and all by itself. Catherine tells me a story about some lima beans that she'd looked at for four straight meals before Aunt Helen intervened. "She took the plate and threw it into the trash and said to me, 'Catherine, go make yourself a peanut butter and jelly sandwich and then go to bed.' Well, Mom and Helen didn't speak for months, because her sister dared to interfere."

We were required to play in our sibling groups whether or not neighborhood kids were involved. This was a rule Mom enforced to make sure the neighbors didn't play favorites and to make sure none of her kids were left out of the local scene. Catherine had to play with Annie; the three girls had to play together; Marty with Jimmy when he was around. I could play with Bobby Izzo down the street, so long as Tony and Paul were part of the package. I doubt my mother understood how or why this could cause resentment, or maybe she did, but figured it was the best she could do. Bobby wasn't crazy about my brothers, and when he chose to ignore the three of us because of that, I resented my brothers for it. Even my friends didn't belong to me; they were "ours." Some of my classmates were friends, but none lived in our neighborhood, and my best chance for hanging around with them without my brothers was to go to the library after school. And yet, because of the size of the house, and with the shoreline being right there and having my own bicycle, escapes were possible. Also, my brothers were not needy hangers-on. They were independent; they weren't any crazier about me than I was about them and would often do things with each other, or alone.

The world had become large enough that my existence didn't take place in my bedroom anymore; I was discovering things outside the home. And even in my room, which I still shared with Tony, my mental escapes became more elaborate. I'd take my blanket and fix it to the four corners of the bed frame, then take the Monopoly board from the game and jam it in there at the lower end, creating a house. I'd make a flashlight from a paper towel tube and some batteries and spend all my time in my tent; that's when I took up reading. I read the Hardy Boys, comic books, the James Bond books from Marty, the Arabian Nights, radio magazines. There was little else I could do to occupy myself in my new home, as I was still a year away from discovering my johnson.

I would go on long bike rides by myself, a transistor radio strapped to the handlebars. The crackling signals coming in over the torn speaker reassured me of a world separate from what existed at home. I'd fish off the end of the dock by myself for hours, catching flounders by the ton and bringing them home for Mom to cook. It felt good, her being happy with the free fish. But I'd feel sad while catching them; my dock time was spent in violent fantasies, daydreaming about escaping . . . what? Fishing wasn't about fish, it was about hours spent in the senseless cold wind, with nobody else stupid enough to be out there with me. One day I found a section of wooden ladder washed up on the beach. I thought to stand it up in the sand and see if I could climb it, like a circus performer. After getting up three or four rungs, I'd topple over. Frustrated beyond speech, I took a huge rock and smashed the rungs, one by one. Then I started crying.

Another time, we three boys got tennis rackets for Christmas. But we didn't belong to a club and there was no park, so we had nowhere to use them. I'd go down to the seawall and take rocks of an appropriate size; I'd smack them with the racket as far out into the bay as I could. The racket was quickly destroyed. Again I was crying; all I could feel was the desire to destroy something more.

Things were changing too quickly. Impulses and motivations I'd never imagined were coming to me almost daily: anxiety, curiosity, doubt, anger, hatred. But mostly I felt a sense of not belonging to anything, not being attached. Maybe my first concrete step in walking away from the others was erecting that shelter with the Monopoly board in my own bed, against my own brothers. It wasn't just about wanting to do things by myself because other people bored me: I was unhappy. I spent more and more time by myself, unable to talk to others. I felt no sense of anticipation or adventure; I was joyless and disconnected. Occasionally, Tony would join me on a bicycle escape, but there was no fooling myself that I was living inside my own head.

What had the crowd meant to my brothers and sisters? I never asked myself that question, not back then. Not even after I had twenty nieces and nephews and found myself still single and childless at forty. How had the others, raised with the same parents and on the same food and with the same degree of compression (for each of them had thirteen siblings), managed to get married and make whatever compromises were necessary for raising a family? It never occurred to me I might be afraid of those things, or that I might have become so selfish that the thought of making room for another human being was out of the question. Nor did it occur to me that getting married and having a few kids was the standard course of events, that my siblings were just following normal human biological impulses. Instead, I concluded that my siblings were chickens; they were taking the easy way out and getting married because they couldn't think of anything better to do. It would be some years before I learned some of them were as paralyzed as I was, that many of the girls had married just to get out of the house as quickly as possible, to cause an instantaneous change in an unendurable situation: living at home.

But for the most part, their anxieties were more about our parents than about how they felt about the number of kids; the crowd itself didn't seem to bother them. "I was both fascinated and disturbed by the fact that the number meant something," says Elizabeth. "Some of them say, 'I'm one of fourteen, and it would have been sixteen but two of them died.' As if the stillborns counted in the family count. It was all about counting." What Liz calls the "fourteen-ness of everybody" created a sense of entitlement and power based strictly upon chronology, with any kid having what we called "authority" over all those younger. "One's number had to do with who could say what goes," says Elizabeth, the tenth child, who carried this strange numerology over into adulthood by choosing "ten" as an early e-mail password. But the crowd hadn't bothered her. She'd figured out early on how to take the kids one at a time.

I am almost alone in my inability to find a place among the fourteen. Most of the kids, when I talk to them today, say they enjoyed coming from a large family. Yet my disbelief in them is so great that my first reaction is to assume they're lying, sweeping away childhood unhappiness too painful to drag along into adulthood. I find myself asking what they're hiding, why they need to construct happy memories from a childhood I remember as depressing and grim. I then have to ask myself what I'm carrying around that prevents me from believing them. Must my own sense of melancholy be universal among us in order for me to validate it? Or do I need them to verify my experience so that I might not have to look inside myself for the source of my own dissatisfactions? How is it they retained a sense of family, created families of their own, while I became a loner? Maybe all my questions come down to one, not even for them, but for me: Why, as an adult, do I feel alienated from my family? I assume it's because I could not then, and cannot now, handle the fourteen-ness of everybody; I feel we kids were merged into a hash at the expense of our individual selves. But the other kids didn't see it that way, and here I made a big mistake: Rather than listening to them and perhaps learning another way of seeing our family experience, I assumed they were deceived, that only I myself really understood the true meaning, the *impact*, of the crowd. Even today I can hardly understand them, can hardly help dismissing them, as if it would be too much work for me, this late in life, to accept the idea that we'd at least *tried* to love each other over the years, in spite of everything.

❖   ❖   ❖

The money I was stealing from my classmates' pockets in the cloakroom, and the twenties the bigger kids were giving to Mom on payday, soon gave way to the concept of really big money, that is, money as a way of life. Sometimes I'd skip the school bus and walk the few miles from Saint Mary's, on Northern Boulevard, down Plandome Road to where we lived in Gull's Cove. This would normally take half an hour, but some of my classmates lived on the side roads, and I'd extend that half hour visiting their streets. I was shocked by how different it all was. Cars with names I'd never even heard of, marble sculptures where the houses in my street had painted Negro lawn jockeys, elaborate brick houses with electric garage doors and copper gutters and hired help in uniforms to answer the door, and one or two houses (Jesus!) with pipes carrying hot water under the driveway to melt the snow. In thinking about money, I'd missed a turn somewhere. For me, money still meant the ability to buy things. Now I began to see that money wasn't about that at all. Even a small amount of money would buy anything I could imagine wanting. But I had no imagination. This kind of money wasn't about wanting; it was about occupying an entirely different location in society; it was about separating yourself from the others. Real money wasn't about the power to purchase; it was about having the power to turn your back.

Things were much more complex than my parents had let on, maybe more complex than they knew. People weren't created equal, and the means of leveling the playing field were limited. Some people lived in an entirely different universe than others, and (this came to me later, as intuition) always had. I saw, for example, that black people worked for white people along Plandome Road, but never the other way around. There weren't any black people on the boats at the yacht club either. But it wasn't just about black and white people, it was about social *order*: How come these people had other people doing their chores? Never mind that we didn't have the money to hire others; we didn't even have the brain wiring to think of it. Some of my classmates had been to Europe with their families, to places I couldn't even find on the globe. There seemed to be a system out there, putting certain people in certain places, while limiting the range of others. People's paths crossed every day, yet many of those people never met. The Jews, it was whispered in my school, lived in Roslyn; so-and-so is a *Lutheran*; Johnnie Fowler goes to *public* school; you should pray for Mary, her parents are *divorced*. It was more than money that was making me dizzy, it was the scale of what the world contained. There were other kinds of people, living entirely other kinds of lives. So *that's* why there weren't black kids in my neighborhood anymore.

I'd had no idea there was so much more "more" out there. With a few trips down Plandome Road, our giant house, which I already knew wasn't big enough because I didn't have my own room, had been reduced not in actual size, but in meaning: We were not like those others. We'd leveraged our way into the house on the private street, but that was as far as we were going to get. I could already tell it had to do with other things besides money. It would be a while yet before I learned that's what was meant by class.

My early need in Queens to shoplift measly, self-gratifying snacks was swept away on a tide of pure, envy-fueled desire. I didn't even know what I wanted, but I knew now there was a better life out there. How one got to it remained a mystery. Stealing was empowering in its own way, but it would never get me from what we had at home to what I saw outside. Some classmates had fountain pens, nice jackets, wristwatches, more refined shoes, which you could tell just by the fine stitching. I began to sense how the system worked: They'd always had plenty, and that would never change, while I had little, and that wouldn't change either. I'd never be able to steal or earn enough stuff to make my circumstances look like theirs. I could get a few things, and the feeling wasn't so much the pride and excitement of a new pen, it was the feeling that I had improved my lot by a tiny increment, which felt good. I, like Marty before me, was no longer bound to things I'd been allotted at home. But while stealing was about taking control, it would always be about minuscule amounts of control; I'd never be able to steal a suit, for example. I'd never change the color of my own spots, spots I'd first recognized while walking down Plandome Road.

Eventually, I began coming into my own spending money. I started shoveling driveways for a dollar, walks included. I'd shovel all day and come home for supper and go out again for a while, and have eight or ten dollars at night. I'd lie on my back and drop the bills on my chest; I'd count them while returning the top bills to the bottom of the stack, imagining huge sums. I had no idea what to do with it, so I gave it to my mother to put in the bank for me. I was too young yet to have to pay my way. I remember the day Mom came home with passbook savings materials for us. That's when I first understood that the money I was giving her was going somewhere safe. If we got a five from Aunt Helen or Uncle Charlie, Mom took it and put it away. When I turned eighteen and discovered I had a net worth of four hundred dollars, I almost fell down.

A second, very minor source of funds came from Marty, who would steal things from his store for me to sell at school. I'd bring in trinkets like cigarette lighters, ballpoint pens, and flashlights to sell to my classmates, and Marty and I would split the loot. I think Tony was in on this too, but not Paul.

Earning my own money didn't stop me from stealing. I wanted stuff, but I also wanted to retain the dollar bills themselves (another lesson learned from Marty: I left home immediately after quitting school and never once flew twenties over the table). Money was too important to use for making purchases: The bills themselves had a separate value as symbols. Where stealing represented material gratification and a level of self-determination, money represented potential. I remember walking around with a dollar in my pocket many times, not having the will to break it; it was too important to actually *use*. Dollars were power; you could *show* them to people. This was a first step in separating myself from my siblings, in becoming bigger than, other than, those few classmates I might be able to leave behind. Stealing was for the present. You stole some candy and ate it, you lifted some cigarettes and smoked them. Folding money was about the future.

All the Zanichkowsky boys shoplifted, as did a few of the girls. Mostly we took candy from the five-and-ten-cent stores near school. Paul's big thing was model boats. He'd stuff them down the leg of his pants and assemble them at home. He created an entire flotilla of battleships and destroyers in our bedroom, including a *Bismarck* and a fully rigged *Constitution*. He described it as his period of stolen affluence. "They were absolutely meaningless possessions," he says. But they weren't totally meaningless; their meaning was just obscured. "The sensation was that I had stuff," he continues, "something outside of what had been given to me at home." Therapists refer to such things as transition objects, things kids hold on to when shifting between mental or physical states; they provide an anchor of familiarity. Paul was funny about money; he'd convert all his funds into quarters, which he'd then glue to pieces of cardboard and stash under his mattress. This made it just a little harder to steal from him, because you'd either have to steal the whole sheet or leave a scar on the paper.

I stole snacks, or money to buy snacks. There is something very satisfying about sugar, that instantaneous neurological fix, the infinite variety of colored candies. And there's the warm memory of the small control I exercised over my allowance. The idea of stealing or buying a book or a model airplane never occurred to me. Later on I stole cigarettes because, while they were necessary for a public image, I couldn't bring myself around to spending money on them.

Tony didn't care as much about material things; like Paul, he collected quarters. He describes jingling bottle caps around in his pockets, imagining he had money. His first job was helping one of the nuns run the school bookstore at Saint Mary's, where we went to school in Manhasset. "I was pocketing money from there at the rate of a couple of bucks a day, always in quarters. I started buying my lunch in the cafeteria, going back for second desserts, always paying with quarters."

Stolen objects provided the three of us with a sense of achievement, of pride in a risk successfully taken, a beating narrowly averted. Maybe that doesn't sound like much to build on, but we'd get a kick out of the stuff one of the other boys had "copped," and the admiration given by my brothers was more than I could earn from my father.

Although I was a second-rater in terms of execution, my brothers' feelings about stealing were the same as mine: Stealing was the answer to what to do about having nothing, feelings that had become magnified in Manhasset. For all of us, it seemed, it was just too difficult to see those differences every day and not do something about them. Not to rectify those differences, but at least do something so as not to feel them so strongly. My brothers' attachment to money was the same as well: steal what you wanted, but save those quarters. Money, like fire, was a form of power; a single dollar, like a single match, could make all the difference.

Another element in my expanding universe was music. I spent more and more time listening for new songs on the radio. Vocal groups were still popular, but a new kind of music had been coming over the airwaves, music that, now that I think about it, helped me see my alienation as something *about* me, rather than as something wrong with me. I was getting to the age where my passions and fears and interests began to coalesce into my own identity, and some of the new music seemed to speak directly to who this emerging person was.

This was exemplified by the Rolling Stones, who'd first gotten my attention on the *Ed Sullivan Show*. There were tons of bands around from the British Invasion, and most of my school chums were hooked on the Beatles. And I liked them also, but they were too cute and neatly dressed and identical looking; even when they first appeared, they looked packaged. The Stones wore sweatshirts rather than suits; their sound was raw, and they sang about anger and not fitting in. One day, when I was around twelve, I was riding around the beach on my bike, the little transistor radio still strapped to the bars, when the new Stones release came on: "Hey, you, get off of my cloud. . . . " Right there on the radio, they got to me; they were singing about me, for me, to me. Because of me. The music was fast and thorough, the lyrics were pissy and violent and spoke of the isolation I'd been feeling for years. There was somebody out there as angry as I was. I began singing the lyrics out loud, while doing my chores. It didn't feel like an act of defiance, for which I wouldn't have had the nerve anyway, but the undercurrent was there, and my parents could not have missed it: "Leave me alone." I just sang because the words felt right. Dad resisted this completely, and even long after I began earning my first few dollars, he forbade me to buy records. My mother, on the other hand, at least understood that I might be going through a phase, and she was decent about it. She asked me not to sing the lyrics, using the same tone of voice with which she'd asked me not to read the James Bond books. A voice that suggested, very nicely, that there was little sense in looking for things to get beaten over. I didn't quite understand their resistance. But it didn't matter anyway, because radio was everywhere, the songs coming out of storefronts and car windows like there was no tomorrow. Those songs were like batteries for me, they seemed to violate the laws of thermodynamics; every time I sang along with them, I came away with more energy than I'd brought into the room in the first place.

Incredibly, even with the radio, I was still alone. All the kids at school talked about were the Beatles, and I couldn't find anybody who got what I was getting from the Stones, a situation that wouldn't change until I got to New Hampshire, of all places. When the Stones got bleeped on *Ed Sullivan* for singing about getting the girl pregnant in "Satisfaction," most of the people I knew just said it was a disgusting thing to sing about. Everything else about the song, and the band, went right over their heads. Maybe that's what helped me feel the Stones had come into existence just for me, and just in time.

It wasn't sex itself that took me by surprise, but bodies: my own, those of my sisters, the neighborhood girls, classmates. I started having dreams about Liz and Grace, and I don't mean dry. I was surrounded by sisters in every conceivable stage of development, and all of them either had or were working on the full, voluptuous breasts common to our Lithuanian heritage. Our house was a dangerous place for a boy to turn twelve and thirteen, with underwear hanging all over the place. There were girls in T-shirts long after our mother should have gotten them bras; girls emerging from the shallow end of the pool, dripping and glistening and silky; girls' bathing suits turned inside-out and left hanging out to dry on the clothesline.

I discovered that training the shower head on my nether regions produced a range of new sensations. Then I unscrewed the shower head and let the stream play on me like a garden hose, like a strong, wet finger. I'd tear a little hole in the crotch of my pajamas, then go watch television; I could feel the girl-rays emanating from my sisters' strange chests and entering through the little tear, feathering my still hairless toy. The toy would become a hard little machine. I became conscious of my cock for the first time, a body part that, up until this time, had hardly required a name. Peering between the buttons of a sister's shirt, those same sensations would grip me, and I would wet my pants whether I touched myself or not. It felt as if I'd discovered some entirely new aspect of being alive; the sensations were so strong and dark and pleasurable I became convinced they'd come into existence just at that moment, and just for my own benefit. I'd leave poolside, run up to my room and masturbate, then go back down and start all over. The sight of the girls' bathing suits inside-out on the line drove me to fits of blind, pagan ecstasy. I'd sneak out the picture window at night and make for the shore, my cock bolting from my pants like a young colt, and I'd ejaculate onto the still-warm sand while imagining one of my sisters urinating in her bathing suit.

With Martha and Louise gone most of the time, Annie and Catherine were the oldest girls at home now. Spying on them became my primary occupation, but those younger than me did not escape my notice. I'd stake out a position on the upper porch; Annie and Catherine's bedroom was on one side, Liz and Grace's on the other. Thus I could observe a number of my sisters from under the cover of darkness. I remember taking Catherine's bathing suit off her bed and hauling it off to my room, like the skin of a dead animal. I put it on; the hunter dons the animal's pelt during fertility rituals, to assume the magical powers of its owner. The fact that she could fill the cups inflamed me.

On the middle area of the second floor, there was one bathroom done up entirely with mirrors: walls, nooks, closet doors. This was called the yellow bathroom, because of the paint job. The yellow bathroom belonged to the three girls, Liz, Grace, and Rita. They were all younger than me, with Liz just coming into bud, a tall eleven-year-old with stiff little breasts that stood off her

chest like rubber. I soon discovered that, with careful rearrange-
ment, the mirrors on the doors could be aligned to provide me the
convenience of watching the girls change for the pool from the
privacy of my own bedroom; an image would come right into my
window from the yellow bathroom, as if televised.

I had no idea what those bodies meant to their owners. I was
crazy about breasts and felt my sisters had gotten the better end of
the deal, bodywise. I took so much pride and pleasure in my cock
that it seemed almost independent of me, because the rewards it
brought were so intense. I assumed my sisters felt even more enamored of their breasts. In at least one case, I was wrong.

"I dreaded seeing myself naked, or feeling any sensations,"
Elizabeth says. "I rarely showered, and I didn't look down, I didn't
want to know. I had a huge amount of sexual shame, a crippling
amount. I clearly needed a bra. . . . I was still wearing undershirts.
I had seen bras drying on the line and I knew what they were for,
but I was determined not to face my body's changes."

This I found totally surprising. It never would have occurred
to me that something I saw as beautiful, its owner might have
found a shameful burden. I had no shame that I know of. In fact,
my mother came into my bedroom unannounced one evening
and found me standing at the window, in the dark, in my underwear. Luckily, she didn't think to look out the window. "Have you
no shame?" she asked. I didn't know what she was talking about. I
had no negative associations whatsoever with my bodily sensations, and though I had no words to describe all those new phe-
nomena, their accumulated impact I found beautiful and miraculous. Elizabeth's body was so astonishing, so factual, it never
would have occurred to me she would not find it thus as well.

As a teen, I never told anybody about the wet dreams. Dreaming about my sisters and waking up in a puddle seemed like just

the kind of thing the stick had been invented for. With no sex information available at home or school, I had no way of knowing my brothers were probably changing their underwear as often as I was. Later in life, discussing these things with friends, I learned that they'd experienced maybe ten or fifteen such dreams before the phenomenon wore off. They were surprised to hear I'd had thirty or more, continuing well into adulthood. I'd learned not to interrupt my pleasure by waking up from dreams, and felt sorry for my friends' curtailed adolescences. They found it disturbing that the subjects (you could really say objects) were always my sisters. But dreams are constructed of the nearest material at hand, and there was a lot of material in my house. I dreamed mostly with Grace, Catherine, and Elizabeth, even long after I'd had actual sex as an adult. Many of the dreams were so vivid I can still recall unusual details, such as wondering, within the dream, what I should talk with Grace about while making love to her. The dreams would take on a continuous character, so that in one dream about Elizabeth and me I might "remember" that we'd slept together in last night's dream, so there was no need for her to be shy about me.

One day I made a disturbing discovery. I'd tweaked the mirrors in the yellow bathroom and gone back to my room to await developments. Catherine went in. She sat on the bowl, worked on herself down there for a while, stood up. She went to one of the closets, took something out, returned to the seat, worked some more. I was maybe fourteen. After she left, I felt an urge to make a careful examination of the room. In one of the upper closets, I discovered several cartons of large, individually wrapped, cottony wads; for some reason, they reminded me of shoulder pads. I couldn't even begin to imagine what they were for. There were no illustrations on the boxes, and I was in too much of a hurry to read; Mom would have flayed me if she'd found me in there. Then I found some used ones in the wastebasket, wrapped in their original papers. The dried blood made me queasy and disgusted inside. The evidence of my sisters' bloody ritual shocked me. I realized instantly that my sisters were far more complex beings than I'd imagined, a much bigger force than I had ever dreamed about, a unified and maybe sinister species entirely other than males. Suddenly, I felt surrounded by these exotic creatures I would never understand. I'm not sure my discovery caused me to hate or fear them, and it certainly did not curtail my spying, but something had changed: Girls weren't simply visual anymore.

"Those were the tutty garters," Grace explains. "These were the pads, the sanitary napkins. In the yellow bathroom, the one with the mirrors, that was where the tutty garters were kept. It was still the dark ages, you didn't even have the adhesive strips on the back. You had the belt that you wore around your waist, and a little thing with a hook and a buckle contraption on it that dangled down in the front and the back. It was torture, these goddamned things, because the pads themselves had these big, long gauzy strips at the ends, and it took, at least in the early days, at least ten minutes per buckle. The back one hung down in the crack of your ass. You had to take the end of this pad, weave it in and out of this buckle, and then—great—how do you reach the one in the back? Finally I learned to do the back one first. I used those for years. Mom would never let us use tampons . . . they impaired *virginity*."

But where could she *put* the tampon? It wasn't Marty, but Paul who first clued me in that girls had a hole down there. "We were in the pool," he tells me now, "and we three boys had face masks and the girls wanted to use them, and I said to Liz she could use mine for a little while if she let me see her thing. So I'd go under water and hold my breath with my mask on and she'd pull her leg band aside for a second." When he told me this, I felt as if one of the profound mysteries of the universe had been revealed to me and withdrawn in a single instant, while I'd had my back turned. I'd had no idea what the hole could be *for*. Even as I masturbated every day, I never made that connection. I was still ignorant of anatomy, intercourse, and birth; girls' breasts and general shapes interested me, physiology did not. Still, even after I learned more of the facts, there was something threatening about the vagina: Why did they have to *bleed* from there?

Within that same week, Paul pulled me aside and described how, when he rubbed his cock in a certain way, this white fluid came out, and that it was quite a pleasurable experiment and why didn't I try it? I was so distressed that he'd discovered my discovery that I quit talking to him. I became completely depressed that nothing, not even secret pleasures, belonged to me. The three of us shared the bathroom that adjoined our bedroom; now I had to wonder, every time I abused the shower, if they knew what I was doing in there. I had to watch my back when I went about my rounds of spying out on the porch (Tony now explains with a laugh, "I was the guy right behind you"). My sisters, even my cock, were no longer mine.

The truth is, Paul was bringing to me feelings that would hound me for the next thirty years: the idea that, for someone else to have something, it had to be taken from me first; that I could feel another's gain as my loss. Even if I didn't possess the thing, my entitlement to it was denied if someone else had what I wanted. This sense eventually invaded every aspect of my life. If my co-worker got a raise, it meant all the money for my raise was used up on him; I never thought about whether I could *earn* my own raise. If my buddy had a girlfriend, I wondered why she wasn't

interested in me instead; their own qualities, in my mind, had
nothing to do with their choosing each other. I had yet to come to
terms with the idea of *deserving* something, being worthy of it. I
was "worth-less." More and more, I found myself wishing I were
someone else, someone luckier or more interesting, someone getting the breaks.

I was living at the whim of my hormones. I spent entire days
dreaming about girls from school, golden-haired Christine and
another dark-haired Italian beauty named Deborah. But what
could I have been dreaming about? I'd never even kissed a girl,
and these girls hardly had breasts or rear ends yet. It's amazing to
think a boy could get all heated up over girls with no actual experience to draw upon to fuel the fantasies. I must have spent all that
time just imagining what that first kiss would be like. And that's
probably the grace of the whole thing, a boy's innocent attraction
to a girl's pure and simple untouched physical beauty, an attraction uncorrupted by thoughts of sexual conquest. The fad among
the tougher boys was to cut the girl's name into your forearm with
a razor. I didn't have that much courage, so I just cut "Chris"
there, or maybe her initials, and not even deep enough to leave a
good scar. But she had a crush on another boy who was so tough I
wouldn't even dream of confronting him, even for Christine's
adoration. I wonder whatever became of that guy; even at thirteen
I could sense he was heading for no good end.

I found out as an adult that Deborah had been killed in a car
crash in her early twenties. This really dismayed me, even though
I'd not seen her in at least thirty years. I always figured Christine
to spend ten or fifteen years in the fast lane and then end up living
in a trailer somewhere, all used up and discarded. But over the
decades, I'd think about Deborah every now and then, wondering
how she was and taking comfort in the idea that she was probably

okay, just living out a different life on another corner of the planet, maybe sometimes remembering me.

Considering the number of kids they had, it's a bit surprising our parents managed to avoid disseminating any and all sexual information. In light of how many pubescent human bodies were bumping into each other in bathrooms and hallways, those topics must have scared the hell out of them. My father never said a thing, not one word. Perhaps it was shame; he must have known that at some predetermined and inexact but inevitable age, we boys would figure out the precise physical mechanism whereby he'd fathered those babies. I wonder if he ever imagined us picturing him atop our mother, an image that might scare anybody off the topic of birds and bees. Marty was no help either. I wouldn't know until years later that he'd lured one of our sisters into our room back in Queens, for an exploration (they both told me the details independently, and both stories were the same). In spite of all his boasting and bullshitting, Marty had never shared this tale with us boys when we were kids and barely mentioned the mechanics of sex; perhaps he didn't want us to start learning on our little sisters. I can't say exactly when I learned that an erect penis entering a ripe vagina and depositing a seed there would produce a human being, but it was very, very late in the game. It might not have been until I lost my virginity, at twenty.

But it's my mother who surprises me, because she wasn't any help to the girls at all. I still adhered to the notion that women all understood and trusted one another, and I had hoped to find signs of tenderness and trust in her relationships with her daughters. I wanted to believe those qualities, which I saw as peculiar to women, would prevail over the shame and fear that inhibits and limits men from intimate talk. But the fact is, our mother never initiated her daughters into the mysteries of womanhood, and this aligns her more solidly with our father. There was no special bond between Mom and her daughters, not even on the most fundamental feminine level. There was only my sisters' fear. Each of them stumbled upon their first periods in ignorance, and our mother wasn't the only negligent party. My sisters were so afraid of mentioning anything being wrong *down there* that they never even helped each other. "I started my period around ten," Liz says. "I didn't tell a soul. I was just throwing away bloody Kleenex, trying to get through it with tissues. I was never going to voluntarily tell Mom. I already knew: Here's something you don't tell Mom."

Catherine wouldn't go to Mom either. She says now, "I woke up one morning and my bed was covered with blood. I had no clue. . . . I thought I was leaking to death. I was too scared to ask Mom. . . . I thought she'd kill me." One might think that Steffie, as the youngest, would have been the recipient of years of distilled girl-wisdom, of a few tidbits of intelligent information, but no. "When I started having my period, Grace was my only source of education at all," Stephanie says, "and she had me thinking a period was something you sat on the toilet for twenty minutes and it was over. Mom didn't do anything, never said a word about sex. Rita gave me the pads and told me how to use them."

I wonder if my mother also felt shame, and if it was similar to my father's. Rita tells of sitting on Mom's bed one time with a bunch of the other girls. They were just telling stories, "and at one point Mom laughed so hard she just fell over and leaned completely into me. She squished me into her breast and I laughed and she asked me why and I pointed to her breast and said, 'I touched that.' All the laughter was gone. She slammed me off the bed with the back of her hand. I had no idea what I had done wrong but she smacked the shit out of me so hard I fell off the bed. I left the room crying, ashamed, and confused." Rita was four years old at the time, and it's difficult for me to imagine what might have driven Mom to strike Rita under such circumstances if not the revulsion of having to explain her own body. What could a four-year-old girl think after being smacked, but that this part of the body is shameful?

There's a whole book waiting to be written about sexuality, shame, and the discovery of the body, in the context of a large number of adolescent siblings living under one roof. How might our parents have managed to convey all the necessary information to us without starting a stampede? Was the way we learned, on the street and through friends at school, any less useful than home learning might have been? What had my sisters, at twelve and thirteen, thought about my body, how it was built and how it worked? Not much, it turns out. "I read in a book," one says, "that through some process this thing becomes rigid and hard and long, and goes in the same place where the tampon goes. I almost puked. I was aware of male pubic hair . . . and I thought it covered everything, because on me it *does*, and that the penis was totally hairy. So I was left thinking that this thing, this big fat hairy *thing*, goes in the same place where a tampon goes, and I was really ill. It was too disgusting for words. I was thirteen."

The learning curve at home was that steep. When I was thirteen and discovered more or less the same information on the playground, I was left with the impression that the man urinated inside the woman. Like my sisters, I didn't dare ask.

I never touched any of my sisters (they might remember differently, but I don't think so, and I apologize if my memory seems selective). I was never one of the boys to try bribing them into giving me a peek. I was envious and jealous of Paul's nerve, of the reward he got for taking the risk that day in the pool. My own inaction was not due to any sense of morality or honor, but to simple fear: I had no desire to experience whatever it was my father was going to do to me if ever I got caught with my hands down my sister's pants. Barring that, I would have tried in a second. Not intercourse, and nothing at all by force; but if by some perverse and mutual consent the chance for detailed exploration had presented itself, my desire and curiosity and fever would have been difficult for me to resist.

My sisters entered my consciousness during a period of frustration, confusion, and anger, and while they couldn't wipe away those things, they awakened me to the idea of physical beauty. In thinking about them and dreaming about them, they added an entirely new dimension to my little universe and helped dilute the intensity of my father and brothers. Yet, either in spite of my sisters or because of them, I've never figured women out. I've never been married, and to this day I am hopelessly obsessed with the entire female gender while misunderstanding them completely. I say this not with pride but with consternation and dismay for all the grief I've caused them.

8

Our Father

I was eleven years old, fifth grade, when my father occurred to me. There's no other way to express the suddenness and finality of his appearance in my life. It just hit me, like a blast of freezing air coming in a newly broken window. He walked into my life, and I became aware almost in an instant of his presence, his importance, his power. I felt the all-pervasive nature of his being: Not only would he be a factor in my existence from now on, he always *had* been a factor. I'd just never felt it as fully as the gods had intended. Now they were bringing him to my full attention. They used a radio to do this.

I was a boy, in fifth grade. I had few chores, was a mediocre student, didn't care about the sports that consumed the other boys. People interested me less and less, but *things* intrigued me. The physical world took hold of me, and I developed a fascination with its workings. I began borrowing my father's tools. I'd take something apart, glean a bit of its workings, and put it back together again: radios, bicycles, fans, batteries. Tools allowed me to understand and control objects in a world where people remained a mystery. I took tin cans and hollow metal curtain rods and tried to make a water clock; water proved immensely hard to control. I examined batteries for clues as to why they should make bulbs light up, and made my first discovery: A nine-volt radio battery contained six lozenges. I deduced (correctly, as it turned out) that each lozenge had the same value as a standard flashlight D-cell, one and one-half volts, and that battery juice came in one-and-one-half-volt increments. I set things on fire with a magnifying glass and wondered, since it seemed to be an amplifier of some type, why it didn't make my watch tick louder. I started making small science projects for extra credit, to boost my grades.

The transformer powering my electric trains (*our* trains; they belonged to the three boys) proved especially mysterious; a butter knife laid across the tracks stalled the engine and caused the transformer to heat up and buzz ominously. I took it apart and found nothing but iron and wire, nothing that would stop or start a train. Motors intrigued me, because no matter how far my dissection went, there were still only wire and iron, nothing that could possibly account for *turning*. Our brother Marty got us three boys slot cars one year. Those motors were so tiny they didn't even have screws you could take them apart by. How could these things put themselves in motion? What was it about iron and wire and electricity? I read about electricity and magnetism; I electrified a nail with some wire and a battery, and it became a magnet. I read that it worked in reverse: If you moved a magnet inside a wire coil, you'd get electricity. I had stumbled upon the *field*. I was flabbergasted; there existed in empty space a complete and perfectly tuned system of invisible forces that (I would learn this part much later but with the same astonishment) accounted for every single motion in the entire universe. It seemed impossible, miraculous, and beautiful all at once. And gravity, another invisible field, entirely unrelated to the others—how could they possibly know that Halley's comet was going to return when I was thirty-four? And if gravity really worked, why *didn't* the moon fall

down? Why did gravity and light both weaken over distance according to the same inverse-square law?

Looking down a storm drain one day, a habit I'd developed in
Queens, I spied a tiny radio. I went home, got my pole, and fished
it out; cracked white plastic case, folding wire handle. I popped
the back off, but saw immediately this was even more complicated
than a regular radio. Not even any tubes you could yank out of the
sockets; they'd been rendered obsolete by transistors. Pure intuition told me not to start messing with it, but to get a battery and
see if it worked. It did, and although the paper on the speaker was
worthless, I strapped the radio to the handlebars of my bike. I
never took it apart, I don't even know what ever became of it. But
I did take the back off many times, to confront its internals; I remained confounded by the very fact of its working. Further reading showed that the transistor had been invented in New Jersey at
Bell Labs, that this was what now did the work of the tube. There
had been a Nobel Prize for it, whatever that meant. I daydreamed
about Bell Labs as a place to work when I got bigger.

I had to start somewhere. I would make a radio. Not that I ever
expected to fully understand how it functioned, but I needed to see
that it could be done, that actual sound could be captured from the
air by an assembly of copper and plastic and carbon parts, with nothing at all in motion except the paper on the speaker cone. A motor I
could never make, but a radio was possible. Not a transistor one, but
a tube one. It wouldn't be a ham radio and I wouldn't be able to talk
to people with it, but so what? There was a science fair coming up,
and I asked Dad if he'd help me build a radio as my project.

I knew by now that there were invisible waves in the air and that
they could reach Mars, that they were landing on me as I scanned
the night sky for *Sputnik* with my paper towel tube. I knew that
ohms and amps and hertz were named after people who'd figured

out electricity, that Maxwell had explained electricity and magnetism as different forms of the same energy. I vaguely understood that
radio waves were related to sunlight. But mostly I knew that after
the radio had been demonstrated at the science fair, I'd still have it,
and I'd be able to listen to the rocket launches with it, keep up with
the Stones on it. In the basement, Dad had resistors and condensers
and spools of copper wire covered with shellac, for wrapping coils.
The so-called channel knob was a variable resistor, a set of fine
metal plates that gradually merged like a folding Japanese fan; as
you turned the dial, you tuned in a station by allowing longer or
shorter waves to pass between those plates. I made a drawing from a
radio magazine, with little rectangles and squares and circles repre-
senting all the parts. That's when my father gave me my first science
lesson, and my last one. "That's a drawing," he said. "You need a
schematic diagram." I'd never asked him for anything much I could
remember, and his clipped manner confused me. But I went back
to the book and learned the symbols for tubes, condensers, ground.
With my friend Eddie I read American Radio Relay League magazines at the library. I learned the color code for ohms, so I knew
how much resistance I needed, and where. My mother contributed
money for a battery and a tube.

The tube thrilled me, another example of intricate machinery
with no moving parts. Walking back from the store with my brand
new SR5, I traced the base pins through the glass out to their desti-
nations in the tube, while practicing my explanation to the class:
The battery will heat up this little metal fin, which will glow red; the
red light will race down the tube and strike this little metal plate;
electrons will boil off the plate. . . . I couldn't wait to say "photoelec-
tric effect." I didn't really know that much about it, but just the idea
of making a radio kept me awake at night. I was going to tap into one
of the mysteries of the universe with a battery and a tube.

But it didn't work out that way at all. My father did everything except let me plug in the soldering iron. He never even talked. I stood at hand as he sat on the little metal stool and worked his way from the battery anchor over to the tube socket, took some wires from there over to the channel knob, took others through the resistors. I followed the path of the electricity, still not understanding where in the process it turned into sound. I struggled to keep my hands down, eager to do something, afraid to interrupt him. He was coming to the end now, absorbed in his work, leading the electrons like tiny sheep towards the volume knob, out from there to the headphone terminal. I waited anxiously for him to show me where to apply the finishing touches, but he didn't seem to need my help, and then it was too late. He snapped the battery home.

I knew he was done because he said "There," and there it was, sitting right in front of me, and me waiting for him to give me permission to take it. He went upstairs to watch the news. I stared stupidly at the thing, very bomb-looking with its battery and metal coils, the tube sticking out of the landscape like an early and desperate skyscraper. I stood there trying to imagine I'd built it, already trying to live with the lie I was going to have to tell my classmates about how much fun the project had been. Already ashamed of lying. The radio didn't belong to me, and never had; it'd been my father's radio all along, had become his as soon as I'd asked him about helping me with it. I felt torn between wanting to cry and wanting to smash it. But I did neither; there was no fixing what was wrong now.

It would be many years before I understood that the most painful part of the whole episode was knowing ahead of time I'd never be able to share with my father the experience of building my own radio.

He raised the stakes a little while after that, at Christmas. I was watching Marty string lights on the tree. He was by far the tallest boy, and he brought tons of decorating stuff home from his department store job (was I the only kid who found silent comfort under the covers with a glow-in-the-dark icicle?), so fitting out the tree fell to him. The lights were the kind where the front end of one string plugged into the back of the previous one. I started plugging them in while they were still in the boxes, just to see how many would light up. Suddenly, some tiny metallic sparks appeared, and a puff of blue smoke, and the lights went out. There'd been a short in one of the strings, and I'd blown a fuse, although I hardly understood even that much at the time. My father came in and yelled at me, "Just because you built a radio it doesn't mean you're an engineer."

And there he was.

I became aware that my father was now present in my life in a new way: He was noticing me. I began to feel his eyes upon me, and realized I would never be free of him again. He quickly emerged as the central controlling force in my life. This I just felt as a true thing; an alien invader had occupied my recently expanded universe. His position of power and authority was well known by us kids, because he *was* powerful, even if only in the most vulgar physical sense; with earning all the money and keeping the house going and beating kids with the stick, there was no mistaking his authority. But I hadn't been beaten during the radio and Christmas lights episodes, and my new awareness of his power wasn't about the usual physical violence. I'd been *diminished*, nullified in ways I could feel but not understand. I had no idea yet how, or even *that*, one human being could be downgraded, reset to zero, by another. This was a whole new category of power; it invoked feelings unrelated to those induced by the stick.

It took a while for me to feel the fear and impotence and rage, and a while longer for those things to morph into image and action. Then I got pretty good at it. I imagined grinding his face along the street, his head disappearing like a melting crayon on the hot pavement, until all was lost except a smear of red against the blacktop. I'd replay the scene, slow it down, substitute chalk for the crayon. Or I'd imagine cutting his flesh and filling the wound with sand. Such scenarios felt unspeakably satisfying, and my urge towards violence became more and more familiar, the images more and more graphic. In each case there was a constant: I needed to hear my father cry out. My imagination was the only thing I had control of; it was the only place I could try out having power of my own, and I became comfortable with hate as an emotion. I didn't know, back then, what a poison it was.

All of a sudden, my father seemed to be everywhere at once. He began to loom larger in my consciousness, so large I no longer had any way to think about him, to imagine or describe him. He was just a feeling now, a chemical presence coating my nervous system. He was like food: I never even thought about life with him or without him. He just *was*.

But why? Where had his temper and his volatility come from? What was so pressing on his mind that he had to make such a strong negative investment in his kids? My guess is that he resented the fourteen of us for making his life both chaotic and predictable at the same time, and for destroying his wife and their dreams. Maybe he just woke up one day with eight or ten kids and suddenly and slowly (again at the same time) realized that everything yet to occur in his lifetime was already known, accounted for; that there was to be no future for him, only the eternal present; that he was doomed to immobility. But instead of being overwhelmed like my mother, he fought back by trying as hard as possible to control and manipulate his environment. Paul suggests that, robbed of both his beautiful young wife and the promise of glamour after two smoky episodes at the Waldorf-Astoria (because they'd gone back for their first anniversary, to create Louise), he began to resent us as thieves who'd stolen his future. I would add this: When he awoke that day to the eight or ten kids, he snapped not only at the kids but at the gods. And why not? If any of us were made privy to the sum of events remaining in our lives, we would lament and rebel against not only the knowing, but against what we would perceive to be the limits of what the gods were going to allow us to experience. And maybe he snapped at himself as well, because he must have understood on some level that he'd done it to himself.

Well into my thirties, I wondered that I was alone in this thinking. It feels to me I wear my nervous system on the outside of my skin (one therapist said I had no filters), and perhaps I just felt my father's abuses more keenly, allowing me to overstate his influence and power. But I no longer think so. After the funerals, once I started in with the tape recorder, I collected sad and depressing stories from almost all the kids. My father's power, it seemed, fed on the humiliation and diminishment of others. Martha brought home straight A's on her first-ever report card, making the honor roll in first grade, yet Dad dismissed her because they weren't the highest marks in the class; one girl had managed an A+ average. Catherine had already performed as Miss New Hampshire in the Miss America pageant in Atlantic City, yet Dad would not allow her to use her award money to attend music school. She tells of singing at Rita's wedding: "I sang the Ave Maria; that was Daddy's favorite. I was right in front, and Mom and Dad were right there and I sucked in my cheeks and I sang it and it was great. I really felt good about it. Afterwards people were coming up to Mom and Dad and congratulating them on their daughter's singing. And Daddy stood in front of all these people with Mom right next to him and he turned right to me and he said, 'You know, it's a real shame you never did anything with the gift God gave you.'"

// At the younger end, Jane tells how Dad would shut the door against her piano practice, saying that no one would ever want to hear her play anyway. When she later graduated college after four years of music study, our father secured her a position as a secretary for one of his colleagues at Sander's Associates, a defense contractor.

While Tony offers that towards the end of Dad's life they put together a decent, friendly relationship, only Stephanie among the fourteen kids says she'd had a loving, caring, understanding, devoted relationship with him all her life. "And the things I've learned about him since after he died," she says, "the not-so-nice things, the negative things, some of them are really dirty rotten awful nasty things, they don't change the fact that, every single day of his life that coincided with my life, I adored my father. And he wasn't my father, he was my Dad."

Though I can't deny the validity of her experience and opinion, nor speculate on Stephanie's present emotional composition, I have my doubts about her version of life with our father and suspect my sister is in serious denial. In any event, she's heavily outnumbered among the fourteen. Simply put, my father played to poor reviews.

I'm not relating these tales to beat up on my father. I've tried to understand his actions in the context of his troubled past with his own father, and the burden we fourteen placed upon him. I relate them more to show I was not singled out by him; the interviews were so depressing and overwhelming I actually felt *saved*; I no longer had to wonder that the universe had sent Dad down specifically to work me over. Others had experienced the man, witnessed his handiwork. Sometimes I think we became a family of housewives and secretaries and blue-collar workers because, knowing in advance no amount of effort or even actual achievement would win his words of praise, we simply gave up trying to become anything bigger.

With my poor grades and sloppy penmanship, my father re-signed himself early on to the fact that I'd never be a great student, never follow in his footsteps as an electrical engineer. Maybe it frustrated him, knowing I wouldn't be able to back up my curiosity about radio with useful academic work. Or maybe he was disappointed none of his boys went in for the priesthood, a path not one of us considered even though it might have cinched his approval. I remember *wishing* I could get better math grades, so he'd like me more, but Dad was never able to help me. He was too smart to bring his knowledge down to sixth-grade level. I remember for a while Sister was having me get my homework signed, either to make sure Dad knew of my difficulties, or in the hopes he'd start helping me. One particular night, there were questions about baseball and runs batted in, which I got wrong. Baseball never interested me, and I knew nothing about the rules. My father looked the work over and asked me, "If there's two men on and the batter gets a triple, how many runs are batted in?" I asked, "What's a triple?" It's the only time he ever looked at homework of mine with a D on it and said, "Good grief." His bemused response somehow relieved me of the charge of incompetence; an ignorance of baseball was un-American, but at least it wasn't laziness, and he allowed me to wiggle off the hook. But he didn't take the time to explain the game to me, either. "If you didn't make it on the first try," Marty says, "you were out. He gave up on you real easy, rather than explore what you were doing. You either started out 'good' or he stopped." Instead of working on the arithmetic, I drew a grid of lightbulbs and tried to figure out how the lights on the scoreboard were instructed to display a message. I had a waffle iron and punched-card system in mind. Dad looked over my shoulder at the drawing and told me to quit dreaming. I had no idea back then that he'd patented electronic switching devices of his own design.

My therapist once asked me if I'd ever done anything together with my father, with just the two of us, and I told him about the radio and the Christmas lights. I'd never told it to anybody; I'd completely forgotten about it. My ego must have swept it all under the carpet, because of the danger to me in carrying it around. Now it poured out of me in a second, thirty years later, as if I'd been waiting for the right moment to let it escape. I kicked the shrink's desk so hard I scattered his pens and pencils to the floor. Then I broke down completely. When I got home, my girlfriend took one look at me and asked what was wrong, and I broke down again. I was amazed that I'd held on to something for so long without knowing it, and even more amazed that my feelings could become stronger with time, even while buried, as if I'd stuck them in brine and left them to cure. It seemed miraculous that we have built-in mechanisms to protect ourselves from the memories of our own experiences. It also amazed me to realized that, well into my thirties, I still didn't understand how thoroughly my father had taken over me as a kid.

Since I was always afraid of him, never felt love from him, it's difficult to write about my father in an evenhanded manner. Sometimes I doubt the origins of my fear of him. My mother beat me with the stick as viciously as Dad did, yet I didn't fear her nearly as much. There was something pathetic in her beating me; I felt her frustration with her inability to control me. There was a sense that she hated punishing me with violence, as if she were doing so against her will, to save me from something worse: Dad's giving me the stick. And she almost never humiliated or ridiculed me. But when my father beat me, it didn't feel like punishment or justice, it felt more like contempt or disgust or even hatred. Sometimes I think it was about the resentment and despair he felt just for my having come into existence, into his life. As if he were beating me for his own resentment of his own choices and mistakes.

My father, from my viewpoint, never changed. The ingredients of anger, bitterness, and annoyance were his constants, and he fluctuated only between those ingredients and indifference. Not that my mother's moods were anything to write home about; she dwelled in a dark land of despair, sorrow, and an exhausted resignation that, even as a kid, I found painful to watch. Yet there were times she seemed happy, like when she was preparing for company, and you could tell that, even if she was difficult to approach, she at least possessed a complex emotional response to the outside world. She was not the same all the time, and to me, those shifting moods made her more human. My father, by comparison, seemed immune to the possibility of emotional growth; I couldn't find any way to embrace him because the only response he generated in me was apprehension. I think the only way he could function was to remain detached from his children and apply himself to his job. For Mom, because she had birthed us, there was no emotional separating to be found; the children *were* her job.

My mother once told me God never gave her a problem without also pointing the way towards an answer. Thankfully, the universe provided me with support, discoveries that showed me there were forces greater than my father. First, there was the electromagnetic field, that strange and wonderful miracle I'd discovered through the radio magazines, something so mystical that even my father could not control it, maybe couldn't even explain it (because even after he finished building my radio, I still clung to the idea, the hope, the wish that I knew more about the field than he did). What was light made of? Were there magnets with only one pole? How did the sun's heat get to earth through the vacuum? The field was responsible for all these marvels; it was the first thing I ever encountered that seemed to be more important than my father.

The second was Hitler, the ultimate manifestation of earthly power. Like the field, here was a force against which my father paled into insignificance. Newsreels brought me images of the goose-step, the endless ranks and files, the blitzkrieg knocking countries down like bowling pins. I clicked my heels together violently and fashioned iron crosses from black cardboard, edging them with tin foil. Of course, I was too young to know about the Jews; they didn't mention the Holocaust in Catholic school history books back then. But I was not too young to understand force, and in Hitler and his henchmen I'd found the guys to teach Dad a thing or two. I clung to the idea that, even though the war was long past, some of these guys still lurked behind the scenes. It was their detached manner that attracted me. If I sent my father to the gas myself, I'd have to cry for all the pain and resentment and fear he'd caused me, and because his death wouldn't make all that stuff go away. Hitler's guys would just send him; there'd be no need to dignify my father's death with remorse or tears. His screaming wouldn't bother them.

As an adult, I discovered William Faulkner, a talent so profoundly beautiful as to be inarguable, even to my father. I'd read the same lines over and over not because I couldn't understand them, but because I couldn't believe them. I wondered why the ink didn't disappear off the page as I read, because I seemed to be getting so much for nothing. After finishing a few novels, I remember feeling there was now an alternative to destroying my father: I could study those who outshined him, those who created beauty. It pained me a little, as I read those books, to know I'd never be able to share them with my father.

Later still, my interest in the electromagnetic field led to a fascination with radiation, and to my discovery of the atomic bomb and its creators. The fission bomb is a terrible weapon, but it's also an object of great technical beauty. It revealed to me a universe vastly more complex than the one offered by my father. The intellectual reach of the men behind it, their creativity and intuition, helped me see my father for the simple engineer he was. And the hydrogen bomb, a miniature and handmade sun, the inordinately complex reactions it sustains, bringing forth a power previously reserved for gods, a power both beautiful and elegant compared to my father's crude violence.

There were other contributors. Newton's calculus and Kepler's planetary laws revealed to me a world ruled by harmony and order and reason. Galileo's discovery of Jupiter's moons challenged the influence of the pope, something my father would never consider. It was greatness I found reassuring now, not power. Bohr, Hendrix, Curie, Giacometti. These people and their ideas, taken as a whole, created for me a broad new environment I'd never imagined. I had discovered discovery itself, the joy of discovery. The universe, Einstein said, was *knowable*. When he came to America, he'd described Princeton as a quaint village of puny demigods on stilts. Reading that, I couldn't help visualizing my father, towering pathetically over his children.

I began to see that, in time, my father's place in the universe could be diminished. It might take a while, but his position at the center of Creation could be put into perspective.

9
The Fear

*B*ut who was really in control of Things? We'd been taught at
school and at home that it was God; he looked after everything, he was the one you went to for help. He ran the show, had
built the whole thing up from scratch. Faith meant believing this
to be so, believing you were being looked after by God personally.
The Roman Catholic Church was the official link between God
and man; the pope knew what God intended, and the bishops and
priests would fill you in. But none of this had ever made sense to
me. Even my earliest efforts at prayer made me feel stupid, as if I
were talking out loud to myself, and the few things I prayed for
never came to pass. It never occurred to me there might be other
ideas of God than the ones we'd learned, that prayer could be
more than a stream of memorized words aimed at a personified
deity. What I did know was that God never seemed present to me,
except as a source of fear.

Still, I could not dismiss God entirely. If he *did* exist, denying
him would doom me to hell; talking to my parents about my un-
certainties would mean the stick. I held to the middle ground:
Assume he exists, don't piss him off, don't try to understand his
methods. I left him in a corner, reclusive and inscrutable and

useless, and hoped he'd mind his own business. And then, one afternoon, in fifth grade, God fell away from me in one instantaneous and final realization. He just walked quietly off the set and
was heard from no more. Once again, a radio played a significant
part, the trusty white transistor I'd fished out of the storm drain.

It happened out of the blue, during the games of October,
when the nuns would report updated play-off or World Series
scores to the class. The smartest kid in the class (a.k.a. the brown),
had the privilege of monitoring the games and filling Sister in if
anything big happened. That kid wasn't me, of course, but I'd
bring my transistor to school if there was any rocket news to be
had. One day I was listening in, the tiny twisted earphone wire
snaked through my jacket sleeve. Sister had been talking about
miracles, everyday miracles, and had asked for examples. Some
kid mentioned an acorn becoming an oak tree by the addition of
sunlight and water. Pretty good, I thought, not an overnight thing,
and probably a miracle although obviously derived from the mus-
tard seed parable. There were other suggestions. Then I chipped
in with *transubstantiation*, which happened every morning at the
Eight, when bread and wine became the Body and Blood of
Christ. It was the longest and most impressive word I knew, and it
concerned one of the fundamental tenets of Catholicism. I'd only
spoken up because I wanted Sister to like me. She beamed; how
could she know I was hedging my position not even with God, but
with her, because she was the one who graded my homework?

Suddenly, between my own thoughts and the voices at Mission
Control, the word *transubstantiation* floated before me, as if on a
screen, disconnected from anything I felt as real. I said it a few
times to myself; it meant nothing. My entire religious structure collapsed on me in the following second, a house of cards destroyed
with a single puff. I thought to myself, "That's the stupidest thing

I've ever heard of." The electromagnetic field was a miracle; maybe radiation was. But not anything going on at the Eight. It was that fast: There was no God. My theology had existed as a series of memorized answers to unanswerable catechism questions. I knew in that one second that I didn't believe a single sentence I'd memorized over the years from my dog-eared blue Baltimore Catechism. But the whole system of prayers and commandments and sacraments had carried so much weight for so long, I found it a bit unnerving to imagine that none of it might be true.

I should have doubted even earlier, when I began making up sins for confession. I could never tell the priest I was beating off, smoking cigarettes, shoplifting. This had nothing to do with his ability to grant forgiveness. I just couldn't trust that the priest would keep silent; I assumed he knew who I was, knew who my father was, and that it was a few short steps from confession to the stick. I had no faith in the sanctity of the confessional booth.

It took a while for the loss of faith to sink in. I said my night prayers for years afterwards, driven by fear. I went to confession, took Communion at mass; too many people who knew me would notice if I skipped those things. I continued to hedge my sins by playing the game of plenary indulgences. What a racket that was. Prayer values in years were listed in a table at the back of the catechism, as if Rome had somehow determined exactly how many years off purgatory God was willing to cut the sinner for each category of prayer. Only the sinner could be sap enough to fall for that, but I kept it up anyway, rattling off the prayers with the largest numbers, tallying the whole thing on paper.

Eventually, I accepted my day of reckoning with Mission Control as confirmation of a longstanding nonbelief, like a preexisting medical condition revealed with an MRI. I decided that even if God did exist, he shouldn't punish me, because I hadn't *chosen* to reject him. I mean, if the very concept of God didn't make sense to me, some of that had to be his fault, for making the idea of God too incomprehensible. I soon quit worrying that my doubts had doomed me to hell.

Still, I couldn't escape the feeling that without God, something was missing. This was yet another topic I never discussed with anyone. Had I done so, I might not have felt so alone. Paul had already become comfortable with a godless world. I remember a specific Easter Sunday when we were walking to mass. I was still exploring my own doubts and I asked him, quite casually, what he thought about Christ rising from the dead. I think I was looking for oblique confirmation of my own doubts. "I don't care who rose from the dead," Paul said, "I want chocolate." I was actually afraid of the firmness and certainty of his declaration; I fully expected a lightning bolt to hit him in the chest and stick there like a steak knife.

God's disappearance left a power vacuum, and my father took up residence there. Marty used to refer to the four Booming Voices: God, the pope, Father Kruzas, and our father. For him, chief among the four was Dad. "I figured there was no other authority higher than Dad, because he could beat the shit out of me," he says. "So the rest of you guys, get in the back of the line." When God left the scene, at least my scene, he took the pope and Father Kruzas with him, and I found myself in the same boat as Marty. But it was just too absurd that my father was the highest authority; powerful as he seemed, I still suspected he was mortal. I began to get jittery. Who was *really* in charge, and what were they in charge of?

I started freaking out. Looking back, that time feels so compressed now; sometimes it seems to me as if I discovered my father, my sisters, and my alienation all on the same afternoon. I was being mowed down, and that's when the panic came.

It was maybe towards the end of sixth grade. I was sitting in the bathtub; there was no self-sex involved, no directed thinking of any kind. A mild sort of anxiousness came upon me; I didn't dwell on it, but I couldn't figure it out. Within minutes, it became a fear. I looked around: It was my own tub, the same old room from which I'd receive those stimulating images from the yellow bathroom. I became a bit lightheaded and found myself suddenly trying to reassure myself: *There's nothing out there.* Then began the odd tic that would become a signature in the years to come: My glance began darting from wall to wall, seeking different views, different objects, trying, I suppose, to change my visual input and therefore, hopefully, my mental channel. My head moved like that of a sparrow, desperately seeking any little crumb of salvation, but nothing changed. The fear became a wave; it had no subject. I felt hot and cold at the same time. I tried to think of something, anything, because my eyes had failed me. But my mind had a scheme of its own; an infinite series of questions and answers like coupled train cars, one following the other with no gaps, in no time. In an instant, the train cars derailed, dragged each other off the tracks and into the ravine. Then a dreadful conclusion: There *was* nothing out there — no God, no reason, no purpose or explanation at all for what I was doing here on earth. Nothing mattered. The wave of fear became a tide. I was really scared now, but there wasn't time. The tide washed over me, and I went blank with terror. I don't know how long the blackout lasted, maybe a few seconds. I woke up crying.

I never told anybody. For the first time in my life I became afraid in a durable way, more afraid than I'd been about hell or my father or anything else. I became aware that I could actually lose my mind and turn into a babbling idiot playing handball, in Philip Roth's words, with my own shit. Something was wrong with me. I was twelve years old; it was the beginning and the end of something. It occurred to me on that afternoon that I might not live very long.

The attacks came every few months, out of nowhere, and left just as mysteriously. They were always the same, and if I'd known for even one second they'd continue well into my thirties, I might have pulled the pin on myself. As soon as I got to the sparrow-head phase, flitting my head around to change the signal, I'd start crying, because experience had shown me there was no escaping the rest of the attack. I still never told a soul. I thought nobody had ever had this experience before, so they wouldn't know what I was talking about, and I feared that talking about it might bring on another attack. The few times I did try to explain my fears, even as an adult, I was misunderstood; words like *panic* and *anxiety* have become devalued through overuse, to the point of meaninglessness. "Oh," people say now, "I had a panic attack the other day, when my computer crashed."

Everything was flying by way too fast now and there was nobody steering. For all I knew, there really was a God after all, and this panic was coming straight from the Source. Was I being punished for not believing? Discovering the brutal reality of a godless world? Or just losing my mind? More and more, fear became a central element in my daily experience. I began living by the minute; I ate candy, played with my cock, dreamed about my sisters. I would go up the hill across the street and smoke cigarettes to kill time, only to find out that the time went by instantly and my mental state was exactly as I'd left it before going up the hill. Nothing had changed. I never thought about anything that looked forward more than a week. I became permanently anxious, and almost anything could pitch me into a crying jag.

The episodes always ended with that horrible blank emptiness, the feeling that there was no tomorrow in my cards, and I took this to mean I was going to die young. It was impossible for me to imagine being twenty years old, not because I couldn't picture what I'd want to be doing at that age, but because I couldn't imagine myself *being* that age. When I later dropped out of college, it was partially because I couldn't see squandering what little time I had left gaining an education I wasn't going to be around to use.

Had my sudden loss of God created an insurmountable uncertainty about the nature of the world and my place in it? Was this what theologians meant by a crisis of faith? Or was it closer to the angst described by the existentialists? I couldn't believe in my father, like a normal boy should; I didn't believe in God, and I didn't believe in myself. But in a world without God at the center, who else could occupy that position but me? I was adrift in a directionless, windless universe, becoming more fearful every day.

Later, when I discovered LSD, something both scary and reassuring happened: The terror came back, exactly the same feelings of anxiousness and fear I'd discovered at twelve. This happened on several trips, and I slowly realized there was a definite chemical component to my panic, that the anxiety attacks were at least related to my physical being. I quit taking acid. It was a minor relief to know that, while my father might have short-circuited me, and my own emotions and chemicals might be wreaking havoc on me as well, I could at least discount the gods.

Today, I can understand another possible cause: the fear of my own annihilation. I'd been too young when I first heard the beatings of my siblings, and had gone into a type of shock. I heard and saw those older than me getting the stick long before it was my time, and probably knew the sound of their screaming before the sound of television. That would be difficult material for a five-year-old to assimilate, and it's not out of the question I sealed that knowledge in a safe mental compartment until I became old enough to figure out what it meant. Then, with the chemical onslaught of adolescence, that door reopened, exposing me not only to the buried fear of my siblings' beatings, but to the remembrance of my own original terror. If Tony had got the stick at six years old for pissing in that drinking cup, perhaps I'd got it at that age as well, and it's no mystery that a kid would have to bury that experience: You just couldn't *survive* if you had to keep remembering and reliving what would seem like, to a six-year-old, a conscious attempt by your father to beat you to death. But what does "survive" mean? As damaging as the first experience must have been, I was still alive afterwards, and a few molecules in my brain recorded the fact that a beating would not cause death.

The worst part of a beating was the psychological and emotional part. It began when Dad sent you for the stick. When he did that, you knew you were fucked. There was a tremendous amount of fear and panic before you actually felt the lumber on your ass, and while you could tighten up your ass-bones against the stick itself, there was little you could do to alleviate the fear. It's the memory of that fear, and not the memory of the beating itself, that ends up in the vault.

I got one of my harshest beatings for something I didn't even do; my only crime was covering up for Tony. He'd burned a bunch of Palm Sunday palm, to make ashes for Ash Wednesday. He'd done it on the plastic toilet seat, melting a hole in it the size of a silver dollar. I was well aware, we all were, that beyond a certain level of wrongdoing, a beating with the stick was inevitable, and a type of nausea sets in once you know you're going to get it. This was one of those times. We both knew he was fucked. But I was fucked twice; once for not squealing on Tony, and again for trying to repair the damage with plaster. It was some weeks before our mother found out. It's almost funny, the games my mind played in the interim. Sometimes I'd convince myself that they couldn't get too pissed, because too much time had gone by. Statute of limitations and all. Then the nausea would set in, the awareness that the sword was hanging over my head. But I'd sweep it away blindly; the thought of the beating I was waiting for was too terrifying to take seriously. Then one day, she walked into the room; bathroom door was open, toilet seat down. There was no hiding it. She hissed through her rotten, clenched teeth that we'd get it when Dad got home. Maybe she no longer had it in her to beat us as severely as she figured we deserved. Or worse, she wanted us to spend the rest of the afternoon thinking about Dad coming home.

Tony and I got it on our beds, bent over the mattress, pants down. Maybe the worst part was the waiting, running to the bathroom all afternoon with loose bowels, having hot flashes and cold spells, not being able to look at Mom because she'd sentenced us already and was not going to step in to save us now. Or maybe it's knowing the other kids know you're going to get it but can't do anything to help you. Maybe the worst part was watching Tony get it first, watching my father push his wristwatch up over the elbow so it wouldn't fly off during the action, propelling Tony towards the bed, stick in one hand and holding Tony to the bed by the shoulder with the other. Twenty strokes, because matches had been involved. My father almost calm in his rage, Tony screaming and helpless. Me wondering, believe it or not, how my screams would compare with his. Because your mind literally has to do something, and it's not going to be comprehending and accepting what the eyes and ears are picking up. It's going to be counting the strokes and taking comfort that it's a finite number; noticing that there's no blood, no broken bones. In this sense, survival means entering a state of denial beyond belief, perhaps beyond definition.

There was no room in my mind, during the beating, for hatred and rage of my own; it's the guy with the stick who has the monopoly on those things. I tried to take the beating with my ass, because that would endure. Once the beating began, the worst was actually over, and my consciousness of the event was reduced to counting and waiting and bracing. I hoped to get no more strikes than Tony got. The interval between strikes became an eternity, my mind trying to relax my body in that tiny infinity before the next shock. I realized my father wasn't working very hard to beat me; he'd beaten two or three kids in one sitting before, and it probably takes some of the steam off. In the end, the body survives; our father never broke a bone that I know of, never even caused a need for stitches. And because you're still alive afterwards, your body heals.

But the soul comes away with a hole in it; the heart comes away filled with hatred and revenge; the brain cannot align what has just happened with any other life experience; and in the end, the beating just refuses to make sense. You are diminished by the many aspects of violence. It began at one year old, when I recognized the other kids' screaming as nothing like my own. My screams were about food, about shit in my diapers, about fever and teething and rash. I didn't even know this much at the time, of course. But I did sense, whether I consciously knew it or not, that the screaming I was hearing from others was not the same as mine; even a one-year-old knows when something is *that* wrong.

The stick was about my father's anger and frustration and lack of control. I remember a therapist asking me if I'd ever experienced a sense of sexual arousal while getting beaten with the stick. She'd learned about violence in books; it became instantly

apparent to me that she would never begin to understand my experience, that with all her schooling, she'd never be able to wrap
her brain around the image of a kid bent over a chair, being held
down by the hair, with his pants down at the knees.

If I plotted our beatings against time on a graph, I'd get a bell
curve. It would begin to climb around 1955 and would start to fall
off about 1965. It took our parents a while to get so frustrated that
they began beating kids with the stick, and Martha doesn't remember getting the stick at all. Neither do Jane and Steffie; our
parents had either given up on the idea that the stick worked as
punishment or deterrent, or they just got tired, physically and
emotionally, of beating their kids. But not before the rest of us had
collected scars. It's the beating of the girls that bothers me, the
fact that a girl would get beaten like that. I remember a beating
Catherine and I got for "stealing" a handful of Cheerios from the
pantry (Marty had seen us and squealed—another cheap abuse of
power, like what I'd exercised with Jimmy). Dad said to her, "This
hurts me more than it hurts you." When she started crying from
dread and fear, he said to her, "Quit crying, I haven't even started
yet." It was some years before I calculated that what was really
happening was this: A forty-five-year-old man was beating a four-
teen-year-old girl with a bed slat.

Rita remembers driving around Gull's Cove on the hood of a
friend's car and passing by our house to find Mom standing in the
driveway. "All my blood drained to my shoes, and I thought, 'This
is it, the stick, the belt, the buckle, the knife, the chains, the wheel,
the sponge.'" (We both cracked up at mention of the sponge, but
for entirely different reasons. I thought she meant the vinegar-
soaked sponge they'd offered Christ at stick's length, but with Rita
on the cross. She meant being forced to suck on the kitchen dish
sponge, which was seldom replaced and whose filth and smell

were unspeakable.) "But one of the boys had hidden the stick and she couldn't find it, and the more she couldn't find it and the harder she looked, the more pissed she got. So in direct proportion to how long she couldn't find it, her anger grew and my beating got worse. She beat the living fucking shit out of me with the bed slat, chasing me around the dining room table. I could not believe the beating I was getting." By the dates of Rita's birth and when we left that house, she could not have been more than nine years old. Louise says that Dad would give her a choice between the stick and the strap; she'd take the strap, "because I always feared that he would break my legs or backside with that bed slat."

These are the stories that fill me with hatred. Because my mother would do it, too, and because either one of them would do it to girls. And even when they were beating boys, they were still hurting the girls. Rita tells about watching Paul get it from Dad with the buckle end of a belt; she remembers Paul stumbling around with his pants down at his ankles, trying to get away, tripping over himself in his fear. "I couldn't have been more than six. . . . I was so full of rage that I wished to God I was older and could have a knife in my hand and go and kill Dad just so he would quit hurting Paul. He wouldn't stop, he would not fucking stop long after the beating should have been over, and here's a little Catholic girl who still said the rosary, praying to God to let me kill him, that I wish I had a knife, draw blood, feel the serrations grate against his tendons . . . a girl having those thoughts at that age."

I spent too many years in a state of shock to understand what the stick had been doing to me over the long run. I learned not to contest anything. I learned that all conflict and argument should be avoided; if I smell an argument coming now, I walk away. I learned that might really did make right, and by eleven or twelve years old, I'd become a complete and lifelong physical coward. I spent years in karate schools, trying to toughen myself up. I remember visiting Dad to tell him about my getting a brown belt. He asked me why I was paying good money to have people beat me up, and even though I now knew I could kill him with my bare hands, I said nothing. When I tried to imagine hitting him, the image that came up was him hitting me first.

Today I still flinch at unexpected physical gestures, even gestures of love.

10

Liftoff

*B*y 1966, my father's business venture, Long Island Electronics Company, had collapsed. He'd never taken me out
there or talked about his work, and I had no way of assessing what
closing LIECO's doors meant for him emotionally or financially.
He was forty-four years old, responsible for a mansion, two cars, a
wife, and their ten youngest kids. But he knew his microwaves, the
defense industry was booming, and he was available, and a number of companies tracked him down. One of those was Sander's
Associates, a huge military defense contractor in New Hampshire,
and we moved up to Nashua that June.

On moving day, a garbage truck backed in the driveway. I recall the temperature breaking a hundred. The men were loading
some stuff from the garage when a gallon of bright red paint ex-
ploded in the jaws inside the truck. I ran inside screaming, "Mom,
Janie fell in the truck." She didn't even belt me, but I'd scared the
hell out of her, and that helped me sense her unhappiness. I hadn't
thought about how much she was saying good-bye to, because
there was no trauma in it for me. Manhasset had been a miraculous
improvement over Queens, so in my experience moving meant
"better." I was graduating from eighth grade and starting high

school, so the idea of change had already taken hold of me. I wasn't attached to my classmates; I wrote a few letters over the summer, but as soon as school began up north, I forgot all about them. But my mother had never left New York City that I know of, except for day trips, in her forty-six years. Now she was leaving behind everything she knew for a small town of French Canadians. In her old age, she never tired of stating how much she hated that move north.

Of the kids, Catherine probably had the worst of it. She'd done three years of high school in Manhasset, and two of her friends' families offered to take her in for senior year. She had a singing career in mind, and the decent thing would have been to let her stay in New York and take a whack at the casting calls. But my father insisted on dragging her with us, offering to pay her way through secretary training at a local women's college. Even winning Miss New Hampshire in 1970 didn't advance Catherine's career, because she had to give the money back when she didn't use it for college. She got married, took a job, and settled down. She didn't learn until much later that Mom had fought valiantly but in vain for her to remain in New York.

Grace defined the change most of us felt only long after we'd said good-bye to our old place. "I hated New Hampshire," she remembers. "Apart from hating that house, there was a sense of having been ripped out of what frankly made life bearable, the larger social context of those Annunciation traditions, having all those aunts and uncles nearby. In Nashua there wasn't anything of significant weightiness, history or ritual or emotional attraction to substitute for the structure we'd left behind in New York. That whole existence felt like nothing but bare-bones survival. It was unrelievedly grim."

Our step down from the giant Manhasset house was so steep as to feel like punishment. Again we were on a private, closed street, but there any similarities to Gull's Cove ended. Our single-story ranch house, clad with dented gray aluminum siding, was easily the shabbiest house on the block. We three boys spent the next six years in the basement, starting in a cement room we shared with the oil tank. It had one or two casement windows too far off the floor for us to see out of, and it was damp and bleak in there day and night. Where in Manhasset we'd had two rooms and two baths in an atelier, now we shared a cave. The three girls occupied the next bunker over, with the same conditions except for the tank; the six of us shared one bathroom, with no window. Our rooms were eventually finished off with flakeboard walls and acoustic tile ceilings; the floors were covered in maroon indoor-outdoor patio carpeting. There was no pool, and the seashore was now fifty miles away. The only redeeming feature in the entire place was an intercom system that allowed room-to-room communication, the novelty of which wore off after a few weeks.

Although I'd always had difficulties understanding my place in the family, the family itself now felt exiled, splintered, and unimportant. I hadn't fully appreciated the value of having the four oldest as a barrier between the rest of us and our parents. I especially hadn't realized that I'd miss Marty. Without him around, there was nobody to look up to for swear words, cigarettes, encouragement, and advice. It just seemed ridiculous that my brother Paul, an inconsequential kid less than a year older than me, was the oldest boy at home now. I didn't know then that birth order would lose its significance, that the kids were now going to grow up in parallel.

That summer, I took my first job, caddying at the Nashua Country Club. I hated golf itself; it was too slow and idiotic, too full of pudgy rich guys. I couldn't imagine taking up a game with so much potential for pissing myself off. But bicycling those three miles to liberty and income, this was not to be sneezed at. If I took doubles for eighteen holes, I'd make twelve or fifteen dollars for the afternoon and feel like a wealthy man. On other days, there were more caddies than golfers; I'd go down to the club and sign in, but not work a game. This possibility came with the job. I'd noodle around on my bike and come home empty; I spent a lot of that time daydreaming about breasts and bands and violence. By the time my mother caught on to how little money I had to show for all my days at the country club, high school was starting.

My father had done pretty well by public schools, but we kids went to private Catholic schools; I think he felt they were safer with the advent of drug use and open sexuality, but it turned out not to make much difference in the end. The girls were sent to Mount Saint Mary's, and we boys went to a small Catholic boys' school, Bishop Guertin. It was a college prep place, with no wood shop or art classes, no automotive stuff. It was run by cassocked brothers perfectly willing to slug a guy for clowning in the hallway. B.G. prepared kids to be doctors and lawyers, although to my knowledge, the kid from our class who makes the most money is Mike Lupica, the New York sportswriter. I hooked up with the wrong crowd immediately, not bad boys, but kids who weren't going to amount to much. A few were already smoking cigarettes, listening for new music on the radio, watching girls; they asked discreetly about my sisters. An ultra-cool radio station, WBCN, had just started broadcasting out of Boston, and we spent a lot of time hunkering around different radios, trying to pick up the best signal.

I didn't take to school very well. I knew B.G. was a boys' school, but I figured this meant boys and girls were seated in different sections. The all-boy atmosphere presented me with a challenge, since there were no girls to distract me and only boys to impress. I clung with some desperation to my New York image and tried to project a rough street savvy by smoking cigarettes, using city slang, and trash-talking my brothers. I worked on the whole look: dragging my heels, shirttail untucked, the loping walk, swearing as much as possible.

By second semester I was flunking French, algebra, and English. French was required because of our proximity to Canada, but it sounded so pretentious and faggy I could barely endure it. Algebra was another story, because I wanted to do well, but couldn't grasp the mechanics of it at all; how was it possible that all the information contained in an equation of letters and numbers could be represented by a curve on a graph? It seemed critical for me to manage mathematics, because of its applications to radio and rockets. More than that, math possessed a sophistication beyond mere words; numbers were the first things I'd come across that promised order and reason and logic, and I wanted the key. I needed to know that those things really operated in the universe. I was still too anxious around my father to ask for help, and rather than offering me any, he accused me of laziness. But it wasn't that; if not for biology and French, I might have had more energy to put into algebra, and done okay. My mathematical ineptitude did not help my relationship with my father, and I felt his opprobrium accordingly. My first real chance at impressing him was fading behind a fog of X's and zeros.

At home, our system of putting the oldest kid present in charge began to crumble. We had a playroom in the basement (more casement windows), with Mom and Dad's old radio, but no television. Because of school, chores, and after-school activities, the senior kid changed many times in an afternoon, and control over the radio was heavily contested. A rough democracy slowly evolved: If two or three kids wanted to listen to a certain station, the oldest kid on the scene no longer had veto power. It might have happened because of WBCN; it was a solid station playing what most of us wanted to hear, so fighting over the channel gave way to listening. Four kids would rock in the sofa, arguing about staying out of sync so as not to rattle the sofa against the wall. There was an overstuffed chair as well, a single, which was taken on a first-come-first-served basis, with no reserving. We must have looked absurd down there, rocking away like Harry Harlow's rhesus monkeys, deprived of nurturing to the point of cuddling themselves.

Tony and I began playing basketball and hockey with neighborhood boys down at Atherton Field. We played hockey constantly, and I became a pretty good skater. Skating was fast and silent and graceful, and you got a lot of motion for little effort. I picked up my first-ever stitches when I took a puck in the eye; they made me feel I'd taken a step into manhood. During baseball games, I'd shoot baskets by myself on the side, unless they needed me to round out a team. I had no feeling of being left out; I preferred shooting baskets with nobody talking to me. I daydreamed constantly and created violent fantasies. But I'd come to see my father as so powerful, I couldn't fantasize well about killing him. I substituted the bullies at school, at Atherton. But I never picked fights; I was afraid of getting hurt myself, and my fantasies left me the same type of person I'd always been, a powerless dreamer.

My mother let up on her rule that we had to play in our sibling groups, and for the first time I could make friends who were mine simply by right of discovery. This bit of freedom soon led to a splintering of the kids' groups. I now seldom associated with Paul, and very little with Tony except down at Atherton. Finally, the three boys and the three girls were becoming independent people, discovering friends from our own grades. I hung around with the McCarthy twins and with Anderson and Dirubbo (last names were fashionable), because they all lived within walking distance. Sometimes we'd go down to the Merrimack River, which flowed south behind Anderson's house, and hang out smoking butts; the river itself was too filthy to offer recreation. My entire social investment seemed to lie in trying to figure out who was cool and how to be liked by them. But alliances shifted, a shifty look at a girl could create an enemy, and there were teen-boy fist fights, sometimes pretty good ones. The first time I saw another kid get punched full in the face I realized two things: The violence I'd known at home operated in the rest of the world as well, and it was much more bloody and violent in the real world. In addition, those rough kids were never going to like or respect me. Because I was fearful and easily intimidated, I became invisible to that segment of my peers. I realized again what a chicken I was: There wasn't anything I could think of that I'd defend or protect by fighting, if it meant risking getting hurt like that.

There were well-defined cliques at Guertin: the hot-rod gang, the serious students, those interested in girls, the browns, the jocks. All our gang did was talk about bands and records. Every day we'd stop in the record store to check out new titles and read liner notes. Or we'd drool at the guitars in Progress Music's windows, stuff we wouldn't be able to buy in a million years. Ours was the first gang to discover smoking pot. Four of us chipped in a buck and a quarter apiece, to split a nickel bag, and I drew the short straw: I had to take the stuff home and roll it into joints. There was so little pot I used the nose of a Mister Potato Head toy as my measuring scoop. We got two joints apiece. I was scared shit, doling that stuff out on the back of the toilet at three in the morning, imagining my father walking in on me. I kept it stashed behind the intercom in our bedroom wall.

The summer after freshman year I found work as an electrician's helper, at a dollar twenty an hour. I'm surprised my parents let me work at all, since my grades were so poor, but there was no summer school. I fell in love with the work immediately; I was working outdoors in rough clothes, learning how to use tools, building muscles, learning how to smoke and swear properly. The smells were intoxicating: the damp, freshly milled lumber; the newly dug cellar holes; the small fires we'd start with a few lumber scraps even in the summer heat. When second year started at B.G., we all talked about our summer jobs, and I felt sorry for those kids who'd spent the summer in gas stations or greasing cucumbers in grocery stores. The next summer, I brought Anderson into the trade with me. That job reassured me somewhat about the future. It was something I liked to do and could do well, and would pay well if I stuck with it and got a license. It was my first taste of the possibility of self-reliance.

In my second year I had to repeat algebra, and I started flunking that again, along with geometry. French too, but that didn't bother me. I had some shame about being in Tony's freshman class, mixed with worry about taking math classes for the rest of my life. I still liked algebra, though; the world was more complex than the simple counting numbers would lead you to believe. There were irrational numbers, imaginary numbers, primes, nonrepeating decimals. There were infinitely small numbers, the "infinitesimals" of Newton's calculus; this was the language of the field, of planetary motions, of physics itself. Why couldn't I get this stuff? And geometry looked really clever, more creative than algebra, and my failure to comprehend the elegant beauty hidden there filled me with despair. Mathematics was an occult world calling to me, but I could do nothing about it. What was math trying to say to me, and why was the hatch so securely locked against me?

I could already pick out the kids who were going to flunk out, and didn't want to be one of them. Some of those boys were going to be married or unmarried fathers before they were twenty, or working in a garage somewhere, or in the army. Although I had no idea what I wanted to do with myself, I was sure I didn't want any of that. I *had* to master math; to me it represented an escape route of some kind, and when the stuff wouldn't come, I didn't feel failure so much as a sense of incompetence and despair, the recognition of opportunity slipping through my fingers. I *gave* a shit, but was going to end up with the kids who did not.

I was grounded constantly because of my grades and felt that the smarter kids were more confident and self-assured. There was something they had that I desperately wanted, but I had no idea what it was. Some kind of security or reassurance perhaps; proof that I was more interesting than my report cards indicated. And acceptance, but by whom? I hid in a world of records, girl fantasies, skating. I spent my high school years wanting to be liked, dreaming of being someone else.

My father returned to the scene one day and became the focus of my violence. I'm surprised it took me so long to recognize something I must have been carrying around inside me for years. Maybe I'd just kept the knowledge hidden from myself, since there was nothing I could do about him anyway. Or maybe it was my turn to surface, and in doing so, conflict with him was inevitable. I wasn't a delinquent or troublemaker; I just didn't care anymore. When my mother asked me to quit singing certain rebellious Stones' lyrics, I decided to buy the album. My brother Paul had some money—I forget what his job was—and we stopped by the record store one day. We were forbidden to buy records, but the day had come when it was time to push my father. I didn't want to be the only one to come home with a record, however, so I talked Paul into buying one; I figured if we both walked in with them, Dad might figure we couldn't *both* be wrong, that there must have been a misunderstanding about what he'd forbidden us to buy. Paul knew otherwise, but went against his instincts. He bought the new Byrds record, and I got the new Stones.

It was an ugly scene. It was all Paul could do to explain that I'd cajoled him into buying his record, so Dad let him off the hook with a severe warning. My father took my record and tried to snap it one-handed against his knee, but it wouldn't break. Then he tried bending it, pushing so hard he turned purple. I started to dissociate, wondering what was going to happen to me if he couldn't break the thing. Then it snapped. I was so overcome with hatred, rage, and impotence that I started crying. Elizabeth was in the room, and she still recalls the episode. She describes my reaction as "so strong but so quiet that I felt like someone had sent an electric shock through my body."

I became aware in that instant of the relation between violence and empowerment, between powerlessness and self-hatred. I loathed myself, because I was powerless. It was perhaps the first time I ever thought of killing myself, because I was so sick of being at his mercy, so sick of knowing I'd never be able to do anything about him. I would kill myself because I couldn't kill him. We were not equal and honorable enemies like Hitler and Stalin, because I had no weapons. My father could beat me, ground me, deny me funds, forbid me use of the telephone; he could force food down my throat or starve me. I could do nothing. I realized at that moment I'd need to get out of the house as quickly as possible, that escape, not force, was my only hope. I also understood that, until that day arrived, I'd have to get expert at operating behind his back. One of my first steps was leaving new album purchases with Dirubbo. Years later I learned that my sisters were doing the same thing, leaving their tampons with trusted girlfriends.

I don't remember much about my mother from those high school years. Perhaps she'd pulled away some, or maybe boys my age did the pulling away. She mostly left me alone, left the disciplining to Dad. Her arthritis was terrible, her knuckles growing into the golf balls they'd eventually become. She was driving a huge station wagon and could barely pull the door closed. A friend of hers with the same woes had started smuggling non-FDA-approved drugs from Mexico, but even these could not help my mother. She became more listless and despondent, sitting at their little table in the dining area (they still ate separately from the kids) reading murder mysteries and eating coffee cakes; reading was her only known activity. Once in a while she'd get together with Anderson's mother, but she really didn't have much of a social life during the day, and not much of one at night, either. She never took up bridge or stamps or anything else. She had a lot more free time in Nashua, more disposable income, and fewer kids, but as far as I recall, she didn't take advantage of any of it. She didn't even listen to opera so much anymore. I happened to get a peek in her medicine cabinet one day and saw at least a dozen prescription bottles. While I didn't know what any of the pills were for, I began to feel sorry for my mother because I knew that anybody who needed that much medicine was in trouble.

All the model boats and ships Paul had stolen and built over the years now caught up with him, and he started talking about the navy. I wasn't quite sure what was happening at first, and then I caught on: He was making a *plan* for getting out of the house. He probably saw beyond that, but I couldn't think that far ahead. First, put in two years at the vocational-technical college, because the navy wouldn't take him with just a high school diploma. His game was to study drafting, mechanics, maybe engineering, whatever it would take to land him on a ship. I realized something immediately: That ship was going to take him around the world, as far away from our parents as you could possibly get. The whole thing, college, boat, navy, even the existence of a plan, overwhelmed me with its potential.

Still, I thought it was a stupid idea. It was going to take too long. And once he reached the navy, my brother was going to start at the bottom of the pile, with people telling him when to get up and when to go to bed, and what to do all day. It would be a nice boat ride, but it wasn't going to be free. Worse than that, it was 1968 and Vietnam was everywhere; had Paul remembered to factor the war into his plans? He talked about the navy in glowing terms, but not about the war itself, and I wondered if there was some inside information I was missing, about how to save oneself from front-line combat through special preparation before signing up. But my inability to talk to him, my fear that he knew more about the world than I did, prevented me from asking him about it.

Even we sophomores were talking about college deferments. I wasn't foolish enough to think the army wouldn't be as bad as living at home. It was still too early for me to wonder what I was going to do about the war, but I knew the military itself would kill me even if the war didn't, and that my plan couldn't involve enlisting. On the other hand, my grades weren't going to get me into college. I'd read about people escaping to Canada, but I wasn't sure if you'd ever be allowed back home once you bolted across the border. Exile held no appeal for me. Plus, I'd have to speak French.

Halfway through sophomore year the gods stepped in and gave me a break. The whole math problem dissolved, all by itself. I don't know what happened; I can't even remember the teacher's name. There was a kid named Skidmore who took time to show me a few things. Maybe my brain finally resonated with the timeless and universal beauty of Euclidean geometry. The work just slipped into a perfectly machined slot, a well-oiled slot, and stayed there. It seemed miraculous that you could prove so many things about the physical world with geometry's three permissible tools: pencil, straight edge, and compass. The relationships tying equations to graphs suddenly seemed obvious and self-evident. The elliptical orbit of Saturn, the curve of a suspension bridge cable, or the path of a home run could be exactly described by a few numbers. Any of those curves could be revealed by slicing through a cone with a bread knife: they were conic sections. The universe had been built thoughtfully; had men discovered the language, or merely created a language to describe their observations? My math grades started hitting the nineties, and I began looking forward to junior year, when we'd tackle the dreaded *quadratic equation* in advanced algebra. That summer I went back to the electrical racket and contemplated, almost realistically, a career in mathematics.

The quadratic equation: $ax^2 + bx + c = 0$; solve for x. It was quite a piece of work, not without its challenges, but not without beauty, either. I felt like I'd gotten a special license once I'd figured it out, a permit to go further into the world of numbers. I began entertaining ideas of college, and my father lightened up somewhat. We weren't exactly pals, but I no longer felt the evil eye upon me, and I wasn't grounded as much. I went to the Guertin dances, for which they shipped in Mount girls. I remember paying a dollar to see a battle of the bands at Nashua High; Aerosmith took the prize. Although they seemed to be copying the Stones a little too much, I was amazed at how good a local band could be, and this intensified my interest in records. I started a "one-a-week" habit with

Dirubbo; we'd try to buy a new LP every week whether we'd heard of it or not, to keep ahead of the scene. My world was expanding rapidly. A couple of boys reported their first sexual encounters, a few had taken LSD, some had purchased cars. Keenan said fucking his girl was more intense than dropping acid.

I met girls at the dances, but the rules of the game were alien to me, and I had no idea how to actualize my desires. I'd gone steady for a while with Caron, a girl from Nashua High who sported the nicest rack of any girl we knew, easily. I'd bike over to her place near Guertin and make out in her basement until my testicles felt ready to split open, but I never went further than feeling her up. There was another girl who had a butterfly patch sewn to the crotch of her jeans. We were kissing for an hour when she asked me if I wanted to pet her butterfly. I had no idea what she meant. I remember talking to Paul about his early sexual experiences; he described himself as a "frozen hake" at the time. I wasn't too far behind him. My sexual activity took place in the shower, and during REM sleep.

I returned once more to the electrical business for the summer of 1969, and prepared to attack trig and precalculus in senior year. It didn't quite sink in that it would be my final year, that college was next, that I was going to be the elder student the freshmen would look up to. I had a recurring dream, that I'd started actual adult life without graduating yet, that I still owed Guertin a year somewhere. The end was in sight. All I'd have to do was keep up my grades, at least in math, and stay out of the old man's line of fire.

Hendrix ruined it for me. I'd been buying his records on the sly, keeping them at Dirubbo's. I didn't know what to make of his music, but certainly something new was being done with the guitar; while everyone else was playing in black and white, Hendrix was playing in color. You could hardly imagine how he was doing it, and we spent a lot of time at the guitar store, reading up on tape loops and fuzztones and Marshall amps, trying to figure out how Hendrix might be doing by himself what the next three guys couldn't do combined. He played before a solid wall of Marshalls; some said he wore an LSD-soaked headband.

I don't know what ever made me think I'd be able to disappear for three days, go to Woodstock, and return home as if nothing had happened, but that was my plan. Part of that was about seeing Hendrix, and part was simply about going to a concert. My friends had starting going to shows in Boston, but this experience was closed to me. I knew from their tales how much I was missing, and saw Woodstock as my initiation into taking music more seriously, and being taken more seriously by my cronies. None of them could wrangle permission for Woodstock; it was just too big, too far away, too dangerous. In light of my situation at home, my plans took on a historic quality, a legend in the making. The gang plied me with questions; we reviewed the playing schedule for each day; I had to swear to remember every detail and report back faithfully. I'd become the self-elected emissary for our gang, reporter-at-large for those who couldn't go. I got a second batch of glory for the nerve it was going to take me to pull off the great escape against my old man. Once we'd got as far as such talk, however, the plan became something of a juggernaut, and I had to follow through in spite of my fear of death under the wheels of my father's fury. I refined the patches on my jeans, and hand-stitched red stars into my sneakers, à la Joe Cocker. I fashioned a giant peace-sign belt buckle from half-inch-thick aluminum wire at work.

I was making exactly $54.74 a week as an electrician, handing most of it over to my mother to put in the bank for me. That particular payday, I kept the money and took a bus down to New

York. I'd never had so much money on me in my life, and riding down to the city, my future seemed filled with possibilities. At the same time, I was scared shit. I didn't have the slightest idea what to do once we landed at Port Authority. I had no ticket for Woodstock, no food or spare clothing, no bus ticket to Bethel. I walked around the station smoking cigarettes, trying not to look conspicuous or pathetic. I worried about calling my parents. I bought a cheap pocket watch, I think now because of a need to feel serious and responsible, in control somehow. I checked the time every ten minutes, as if I had something important to attend to shortly. I already knew I wasn't going to Woodstock, and felt terribly alone and sad at the station. I didn't even worry about what they were going to do to me when I got back home.

Wandering aimlessly around the boarding gates, I never guessed that the festival wasn't the issue, that simply getting on the bus had been the key. The most valuable part of the whole plan turned out to be my unconscious recognition that the time had come to take charge of myself, take an independent action, piss my father off heavily, and try not to figure the consequences against the benefits. I could worry about the fallout later.

Maybe that's why I called them, because I already knew it didn't matter anymore if I bought a ticket to Bethel or to Nashua; since I'd skipped out and got on that bus to New York, my world back home wasn't going to be the same whether I went to the festival or not. It was just like it'd been with Jimmy taking that swing at Mom with the stick: Connecting with her was completely beside the point.

I approached a pay phone, rehearsing a few lines I thought might demonstrate responsibility on my part. *"It's okay, I'm fine. I'll be careful and I'll come straight home when it's over. Don't worry about me."* Oh yes, *that's* what I was going to say. And once they understood I had it all under control, they'd wish me well. To this day I don't understand why I couldn't *not* call them. A slightly more violent beating for leaving them in the dark over the weekend? The thought of them taking thumbscrews to Paul and Tony for information? My father got on the phone, threatened me with the state police, and my adventure was finished.

Afterwards, once I'd seen the film, I realized what a disaster it would have been for me. I would've been way out of my element. I was still a virgin; I'd never done acid; I'd never even been drunk before, or gone swimming in the nude. I hated to admit it to myself, but the film made me feel better about having missed the whole thing. I hadn't the slightest bit of life preparation for the mud, the naked public sex, the crowds, or anything else that might have happened to me there. I never would have lasted until the end, when Hendrix came on. I would have freaked. I suppose that was the whole point for lots of people, but I wasn't convinced of the hold I had on my own psyche to begin with.

But that film was a year away. I took the bus back to Nashua because I was still a coward, and even the idea of Hendrix couldn't erase the idea of the stick. I don't remember being scared on the bus. I'm not sure I feared a beating, or was just detached from the idea. Perhaps I sensed that whatever changes had occurred in me already weighed more than any beating he'd be able to give me, that nothing could return me to the place I'd started from two days before.

My gang members were dismayed, but since they knew about my father and me, they let me off the hook without much ribbing. My sister Liz said coming home was the stupidest choice I could have made, that I could have changed things in my favor ten times over, had I gone all the way and been missing for a week. For one thing, Woodstock had overwhelmed the system, and it might have done my father some good to learn that even the state police can't fix some things, such as picking Marty's kid out of half a million faces and sending him home because he's pissed off his father.

The fallout back home was that I had to quit my job, my assets were frozen, I was forbidden to use the telephone, and I was grounded for the rest of my life. My father seemed careful about disciplining me, almost cautious. When I walked in the door, he asked me quietly to sit down; for a second, it felt like we were buddies, and I almost took out my butts. I could tell by his restraint he was pissed, perhaps trying to figure out the appropriate punishment, yet afraid of going too far. He didn't beat me. He never even yelled at me, and in fact, he never beat me again. I think the whole thing spooked him, made him realize the day was coming when he could no longer stop me. I'd made my first dry run across the Rubicon; any given Tuesday I could leave for B.G. in the morning and never come back. I didn't really believe this back then, but my father couldn't know that. An element of mutual wariness and mistrust crept into our relationship; for perhaps the first time, he had to worry about *me* instead of it always being the other way around.

In spite of the restrictions placed upon me, or maybe because of them, my math grades picked up where they'd left off the year before. I began applying to colleges, which relieved my concerns about the draft and calmed my father down somewhat. Yet the idea didn't excite me; I couldn't think of a good reason to go to college like all the other boys. It still amazes me that most of them knew what they wanted to study, what they wanted to *be*, at seventeen. It also amazes me how much they knew about college and studying, what kind of an effort would be needed to make the enterprise pay off. I had no idea what I was in for when the engineering school in Lowell accepted me. I spent the last three months at Guertin wearing the same unwashed jeans; my pals cut them off me with scissors the day before graduation. At the ceremony, the principal mentioned the college each kid was heading for. Those not going to school were dismissed with a single word: "Industry." You'd think getting a job was a bad thing. I was happy to have a decent engineering school named with me, but being an electrician didn't feel like a shameful second choice.

I hadn't learned enough about studying at Guertin, and the work load at Lowell was tremendous: chemistry, physics, calculus, engineering, English. I was swamped immediately, although I still say if it had been just calculus I might have done okay. The whole thing was fifty times harder than I'd ever imagined; I didn't even know where to begin asking for help. These were still the days of the slide rule (another beautiful piece of mathematics: multiplying numbers by adding their logarithms on fifty cents' worth of scaled plastic). Only a few rich kids had calculators, and they couldn't use them during exams, because it was too much of an advantage over the rest of us. Once again, I'd befriended the lower tier, the nonachievers, the hockey boys, the record buyers. It seemed important to be casual, to try to fit in not as a college student, but as a kid with a car (I'd purchased my mother's blue station wagon), away from home all day. But I felt divorced from the serious students and made no enduring friends, as if my presence at Lowell involved no academic or social responsibilities. I was liberated from life in Nashua, but felt unable to capitalize on my liberty, unable to point myself in any useful direction. I wandered around campus in a fog of "adult" behavior: reading the *New York Times* in the canteen, eating at local diners, smoking like there was no tomorrow.

But I did study. I studied night and day, and for the first time, my books looked employed: underlined and highlighted and dog-eared. After one semester of sleeping with the books, I pulled a 1.7 and knew I was fucked. The school admitted 1,200 freshmen and graduated 400 seniors; I was far from alone, but that knowledge wasn't going to do me any good. I was finished as a student. I didn't quite give up, but second semester I started playing more hockey, smoking more pot, buying more records. Since my father wasn't helping me with school, my funds were limited and I had to go in halvesies with Dirubbo on records. We'd alternate taking them home week by week, and if one of us got sick of a record, the other guy would buy him out. Kids were dropping out of Lowell like flies. The worst students would enter the exam hall, sign their tests, and walk out; they knew they were failing and didn't need to waste three hours pretending otherwise. They were smarter than me; I spent the three hours securing a 1.8 my second semester. One kid had written physics formulas all over his slide rule; they kicked him out to general groans of "You're *cooked*." I began wishing I'd gone to a liberal arts place, but I know now I wouldn't have been any better off. I wasn't ready for school; what I needed was room to explore and expand.

My writing career began with that 1.7 at Lowell. The plane to 'Nam was waiting on the tarmac for boys like me who'd got into college by the skin of our teeth; we were doomed to evaporate out of the school system and condense in the draft pool. I wrote a series of essays to the local draft board, explaining why I wanted to be classified as a conscientious objector. I was working nights in a department store, and I'd bring my homework to the job. But every time a new thought about the war came to me, I put the calculus aside and wrote. Without realizing it then, I was writing about autonomy. After a lifetime of being powerless, I was on the verge of cutting free, and it infuriated me to think other powerful figures were going to take over just where my father had to leave off. It seemed absurd that total strangers would determine my duty and my fate, simply because my parents had had me in New York rather than in London. The father of one of the kids at school was on the draft board, and I addressed some of my work directly to him. In one letter I asked him if he'd kill his own son if it would stop the war immediately, and if he wouldn't, why should he ask me to kill someone else's son for a much less certain outcome. I suppose those essays are on file somewhere, but I'd never want to read them over. I can't imagine how righteously pedantic and embarrassing they must have been, since I'd never studied morality or politics, ethics or philosophy.

My father went through the roof; he was beside himself when he discovered he had to *sign* the C.O. clause (it was part of the draft registration form). I defended myself as best I could during the screaming matches. He asked me absurd questions, like what I was going to do when the Chinese came marching up the sidewalk lobbing hand grenades through the windows. I gave absurd answers, telling him I'd take out a bottle of Jack Daniels, and they could either drink with me or shoot me, but I wasn't going to war. I was applying for C.O. and that was that. I don't know where my courage to defy Dad came from. Maybe he should have beat me to a jelly after that aborted trip to Woodstock, but he had not, and it was too late now. He was in decline; all he had now was a voice. I didn't even thank him when he signed it; I didn't recognize it then as his first act of surrender.

To my utter astonishment, my mother took his side. She went so far as to say it didn't matter that I couldn't vote yet, that anybody could pull a trigger. This demoralized me so badly I couldn't even answer her. It just plain wasn't possible for me to believe she herself wanted me to fight that war. Having spent her whole life reading suspense mysteries and listening to opera, she knew even less than I did about communism and politics and the history that had placed Vietnam on Americans' shoulders. I became convinced, finally, of her truth: She did not do her own thinking and would never cross her husband's path, ever. No, it's worse than that: My father's path, her husband's path, *was* her truth. My mother, in my mind, had betrayed me and disgraced herself. It hurt me to think they now admired Paul for following Dad into the navy. Even today I wonder about my parents' thinking. My father had made his own choices against his father's wishes, so he had some idea of both the value and the price of self-determination. But as a devout Commie-hater, he could never abide my passivity against Red expansion in Asia. Worse than that, he could interpret my decision not as a refusal to obey Nixon, but as an affront to *him*. But my mother had had very few choices, and no opportunities; she'd lost her freedom the day Martha was born. Did she resent my intention to enter adulthood without paying the toll-keeper? Did my decision to deny my father make her wish she'd done so, maybe ten kids back?

But my parents' thinking no longer mattered to me. I was quitting school, I was getting an apartment, and I wasn't going to the war. All those things were clear to me now, in spite of my uncertainty and fear. I took some comfort in the signed C.O. documents and some in the knowledge that hard work in a respectable trade didn't scare me. I'd get my electrician's license and take care of myself.

❖   ❖   ❖

Our time in New Hampshire was marked, in my mind, by one event that defined the family as a whole, that gives a clear picture of the dynamics of our family in its decline. It was my parents' decision not to attend Catherine's wedding. After she won the Miss

Nashua pageant, she began dating Greg, the guy who'd covered the pageant for the *Nashua Telegraph*. When she won Miss New Hampshire in 1969, he asked the paper to assign him to follow her to Atlantic City. Even though he was a Lithuanian and a Catholic, our parents weren't crazy about him. Neither was I; he was a pudgy, hard-drinking sportswriter who turned out to be an abusive lout as well. Greg had given my sister a copy of *The Prophet*, by Kahlil Gibran, the edition with those mildly suggestive "nude" ink drawings, and this had not helped him in the standings. My mother had unearthed the book while searching through Catherine's things and had shown it to Dad, who sternly disapproved (although they later admitted to Catherine they'd not read any of the text). Catherine didn't know anything was wrong until Martha and Louise gave her a bridal shower in New York and Mom wouldn't go. She called Mom and got the addresses of all the kids and sent out wedding invitations; it never occurred to Catherine she'd have to mail her parents one, and she assumed Dad would be giving her away. But that job fell to Paul; our parents decided not to attend the wedding on the technicality that the invitations for us kids had not mentioned Mom and Dad by name. This was November 1970. I'm not sure why they let the rest of us go, but we did.

It was a huge wedding, four hundred people. Yet I remember feeling that the wedding lacked authenticity, because neither my parents nor Father Kruzas was there, because Dad hadn't walked the bride down the aisle, and because we weren't at Annunciation. The ceremony had no context; there was nothing connecting Catherine's wedding to our collective past. For the first time, one of us kids had married somebody who had nothing to do with New York. It was my first experience of a post-historical feeling of New Hampshire, that we were now living after the fact, that events in New Hampshire didn't matter. This is perhaps what Grace means when she complains that our life in New Hampshire lacked tradition and weightiness. Even the presence of a huge Brooklyn contingent couldn't erase my sense, and perhaps it was only my sense, that the event (not the ceremony itself, but the actual physical gathering) didn't mean anything.

Skipping an event of such magnitude was unheard of in our family. Even though I disliked and mistrusted my parents, their deliberate absence seemed so huge a thing that I found myself wondering if they were actually right about something Catherine had messed up on. I was an unworldly eighteen at the time, and my parents were still the ultimate authorities. While I wasn't convinced their absence invalidated the proceedings, the fabric of our historical continuity seemed to have a hole in it, and I remember wondering what their absence meant. I see it now as similar to their response to Jimmy: a concrete act of withdrawing support from their children. In both cases, when something about their child became too difficult to manage or understand, their solution was to pull away. Whatever they considered love to mean, theirs was not unconditional.

Oddly, very oddly, the next morning, Mom and Dad had a huge breakfast for all the relatives who'd come up from Brooklyn for the wedding. Almost as if they had to atone for their sin. A lot of people had driven up without knowing, until they arrived at the church, that Mom and Dad weren't going to be there. It's hard to imagine my parents not feeling humiliated entertaining all their peers, after standing up their own daughter. How did they imagine they were going to field the looks and the questions? What shabby principle could they adhere to in defending their decision? Even Mom's brother, Leon, had come up with his wife for the wedding. This was unusual because he had never once closed his Brooklyn pharmacy on a Saturday, for any relative, for any reason. But Leon and his wife would not go to the breakfast. He phoned my mother from his hotel and told her, "Joanie, I don't know what you did, but you did the wrong thing." Mom hadn't even known Leon was in town, and Catherine reports that our mother's reaction was, "Leon closed his *store*? Leon closed his *store*?"

Had my mother brought misery upon herself, created it out of nothing, by violating Catherine's privacy? By sharing the fruits of her search with a husband whose response she knew would be predictable, excessive, and final? I wonder if she coerced my father into having the breakfast party in exchange for his insistence that they weren't going to attend the wedding. Because if our mother had been dead set against the wedding, why would she set herself up for the backlash by inviting everybody to that breakfast? It's inconceivable to me she would have skipped her daughter's wedding over that stupid book, but not at all impossible that Dad had once again "patriarched" his will upon his wife, while tossing her the bone of a party for her loss.

Mom and Dad's behavior during Catherine's wedding demonstrated to us just how far our parents were willing to go in undermining our choices, in sticking to their moral or theological high ground at whatever cost, and it became easier for them after they'd set a precedent. They went on to skip both of Stephanie's weddings, both of Paul's, one each for Liz and Rita, and two of Grace's. They skipped the wedding of Louise's elder daughter, Larisa. In a perverse way, I can understand them. Mom explained that it would be a sin for her to attend the marriage of one of her children to a divorced spouse because, for her, it would be condoning adultery by bearing witness to the ceremony. Jews and atheists were likewise out of the question. But her adherence to principle does not explain why they couldn't manage to visit Paul in the hospital after his aorta ruptured in 1987. When Mom called me to ask how Paul was doing, I told her as coolly as possible that he was her son, and why didn't she find out for herself. But Paul had married a divorcee and was therefore living in sin, and my mother never called him. Our parents had drifted to the point where they almost never called any of us, perhaps for fear of getting one of the spouses on the phone. It was as if they were too old and tired to fight anymore, so they'd find a loophole and ignore you. The only event that was guaranteed to get their attendance was a Roman Catholic baptism.

What little sense of family we'd retained after leaving New York now began to decay right before our eyes. Catherine's wedding was the watershed event for another defining process: Kids began flying out the doors and windows of our little aluminum dump as quickly as possible. Although it would be a while yet before our parents got around to skipping those other weddings, the groundwork had been accomplished with Catherine. The kids saw they were on their own, that any notion of the Zanichkowskys as a cohesive family unit was finished. As quickly and thoroughly as we'd inhabited the big Manhasset house, we left the New Hampshire one.

Catherine was the first of the kids to admit to marrying primarily to get out of the house (she and Greg had problems immediately, and their marriage ended in divorce). She was what I call the transitional kid, still so bound to the rules and disciplines at home that there were no creative avenues of escape open to her: If you were a girl, you either lived at home until you were twenty-one, or you got married when it was legal, at eighteen. After her, in accordance with the liberal, self-actualizing thinking of the late sixties, the kids' paths became more self-determined. But also, the rest of us recognized that things were never going to get better, that the real choice was between making your own decisions or having Mom and Dad make them for you.

Paul finished his second year at the voc-tech in 1971 and joined the navy that same summer. That's when I dropped out of school in Lowell and got an apartment in Nashua, with Tony. He'd graduated from Guertin in 1971; his prayer for avoiding the draft (it was answered favorably) was to skip registering in the first place. Elizabeth moved to Wisconsin in the summer of 1972, so she could establish residency there and go to school at Madison the following year. Grace moved to Vermont in 1973, to study Italian and history at Middlebury College. Annie was renting a room in downtown Nashua. Where it had been one kid leaving each year or so, seven kids fled in three years. Rita, still too young for actual planning, descended into near panic, describing this exodus as a wall of protection crumbling before her eyes, bringing Mom and Dad that much nearer.

11

West

*I*t was clear when I dropped out of Lowell Tech that I wouldn't last long at home. Confronting my father with a plan to strike out on my own didn't excite me, but the thought of actually paying to live with him made me ill. Giving my father anything— especially time or money—was out of the question; one way or another I'd have to be out of the house before September. I had the summer to figure things out. My parents were funny that way: If you weren't going to school, they granted you that first summer off before making you pay for your keep. I had a job with all the overtime I wanted; my only worry and regret was that I'd pissed away my savings on books and tuition at Lowell and hardly had any money for a security deposit.

One of my buddies had a two-bedroom apartment at 237 Main Street, not far from our old school bus stop; he was the first of us to have his own pad. I could see it for what it was: his space, with his things lying about, and only his things. Sometimes his girlfriend spent the night, and though I hardly knew what this meant yet, it seemed like the highest manifestation of adult liberty. The allure of private space did not escape me, and when my friend said he was vacating the place (to join the army), I fixed myself on the idea of taking it over. I even became fearful of losing it, as if it were the last apartment in the known universe. My imagination ran wild, not with orgies and excess, but with the idea of quiet, of coming home to an empty place, with the idea of staying out until the wee hours with no accountability. I imagined driving to work, putting in a solid day wiring houses, coming home like any other blue-collar guy to a cold beer in the comfort of my own chair. Listening to records by myself, having friends over. Going to concerts in Boston and returning to the sanctuary of my own place.

These dreams won out over my fear of Dad, and Tony and I took the apartment when my friend moved out. It came available very suddenly, and our move took on the feeling of a jailbreak. Our father was furious; his first assumption was that I'd dragged Tony into it by talking him out of college, and he browbeat my brother for ruining his life by passing up school. But Tony wasn't planning on school anyway, and although this would come back to haunt him twenty years later, in 1971 he knew as well as I did that the good life began on the street side of our father's front door. Dad asked me in extremely heated tones why I needed to have an apartment, and I couldn't help detect a note of desperation and fear in his voice. It was the recognition, as it had been with the draft forms, that he didn't control me anymore. I was going to be the first kid (Tony was the second) to move out of the house without any pretense towards marriage or college or the armed services; I was just moving out. I even gave him a reason, one being as good as another: so I could see R-rated movies. He turned away in disgust. My mother was curiously silent during these proceedings. She eyed me and Dad with almost the same look, as if she wished she could ask her husband to give it up because she knew I would not. But whatever actual feelings she had were kept to herself; again, unless some debate took place behind their closed bedroom door in the middle of the night, it was all my father's agenda. I don't think reason or logic or my frustration with Dad had anything to do with my mother's detachment; she was just watching kids *leave*, and she had to recognize that at least part of the reason for our urgency was that there wasn't any love holding us at home.

My own sense those days was of being in a fog or a film. For the first time in my life, I didn't have any idea what tomorrow might be like; the whole world was right in front of me. I was too young to know that a lack of schooling would hold me down, that the really good stuff wouldn't be available to me, because I hadn't prepared myself properly. But still, there was a lot out there you could attain without a college degree as long as you were willing to work hard.

Tony and I had separate bedrooms for the first time ever; we had cars; we could smoke in our own living room. It wasn't exactly as I imagined, because I shared the place with Tony, but the transition from living with ten kids to living with my brother translated to essentially the same thing as living alone. We got along fine, sharing the same sense of relief and empowerment. Our friends would come over every now and then to get high and listen to records. Radio Shack made a gizmo that would shut your amp off after the last album had played, and we installed one of those so we could smoke ourselves silly and pass out. There were some great records coming out: David Bowie, the Stones with *Exile*, The Who with *Who's Next*. I was in the electrical game full-time now and loved it; no matter how high I got the night before, I was at the job at seven-thirty sharp the next morning. I worked as much as possible. Money felt great. The rent ate up only a quarter of my income; the rest went towards entertainment, records, alcohol, gasoline. I spent a solid year decompressing from the confinement and order and rigidity at home. Getting used to answering only to myself. I ate out of cans, or ate dinner straight out of the pot. Sometimes I didn't eat at all. I felt so free and enriched I didn't even give thought to travel, to losing my virginity; why ask for anything more? It took a while for me to realize every decision was up to me: when to do laundry, what food to buy, should I get this or that car. I remember a story Louise told me about the first day she was married, living in her own place. Ernie came home and saw her staring out the window, and said she must be thinking about what she should make for dinner. Louise said, "No, I'm not thinking about *what* to have for dinner, I'm thinking about *if* we should have dinner." It's that nascent sense of self-determination I was beginning to feel now.

My favorite activity was simply driving around at night, absurdly happy with the realization I didn't have to *be* anywhere. The lack of traffic, the dampness of the night condensing on buildings and pavement. Just being on the road at four or five in the morning made me feel as if I were in another country. In those days, you didn't call friends and make plans. You'd just drive over to the guy's house to see if he wanted to go for a ride. We called them space cruises. Although a lot of us had cars now, I still had my mother's old station wagon, so it frequently fell to me to haul a bunch of us around. We'd drive to the beach or go to the Nashua High football games. We staked out an abandoned cornfield for drinking at night, and sported fedoras for those occasions; if you showed up at someone's door with your drinking hat on, they knew what was on tap for the evening. I drank and drove for twenty years without a mishap. We'd drive to Boston for a Red Sox game, climbing the billboard sign across the street because we didn't want to pay for seats. The view was excellent; a sharp eye could call a ball or a strike before the umpire's call lit up on the scoreboard. There was a lot of stage planking behind the signs, and you'd see guys up there with charcoal grills, radios, and beer coolers.

Someone invented mailbox duty, whereby a carful of us would tour the rural roads with a baseball bat, liberating mailboxes from their moorings. One guy would hang out the passenger side window while somebody else held him firmly by the waist; the idea was to take a huge swing at the mailbox on a drive-by and knock it off the post. That was the extent of our vandalism. One night on mailbox duty we drove by the house of a family named Stone. They had a beautiful wooden sign, very old, that said "The Stones." I never touched their mailbox; I just took my electrical pliers and clipped the chains.

A kid named Burns brought over mescaline; he said it was for those who couldn't handle acid. This was the stuff for me. LSD brought me too close to panic for my own good and comfort, and I'd sworn off the stuff. Mescaline was such a clean high, putting me solidly in touch with every nerve in my body. I drove around one day, ate some mescaline, and climbed Mount Monadnock. I baked on the rocks like a lizard in the sun for a while, listening in on a conversation some couple were having. I could hear every word; it was very hushed and personal, as if I knew them. When I opened my eyes I was astonished to find the people in question were a hundred yards distant. My senses were so highly tuned, I could see their speech taking place, as if they were speaking in color. Mescaline became my drug of choice until the following year, when I discovered mushrooms in the desert out west.

When I was twenty, I lost my virginity to a fifteen-year-old girl from Pittsburgh. It was her idea, and it wasn't her first time. In Bowie's words, it took me minutes and took her nowhere. In spite of the intensity of my sexual dreams and desires, I had no idea what I was doing and had a lousy time. I knew it was supposed to be a key lifetime experience, and I was disappointed not to feel much; I savored the idea of the experience rather than the experience itself. I don't think I had sex again for at least a year. I much preferred to spend my time seeing bands and listening to records, and in those days, girls weren't listening to the bands that interested me. I wouldn't dream of taking a girl to a concert. Sex didn't interest me enough to start changing my life around for it. Although the idea of further sexual discovery interested me, the idea of love and friendship and compromise prevented me from following through. Celibacy didn't yet feel like too high a price for selfishness.

I didn't see much of my parents that year. Not at all, in fact. They had some inkling of what the scene was like at our apartment (Tony was busted for pot after a while), and our sisters were not allowed to visit us there. They'd tell Mom they were going to the library and then sneak over to 237 for a visit. If memory serves me accurately, that was the year Dad had his first heart attack and told me not to bother coming to see him at the hospital, because he'd be out in a few days. I took his advice, even though the hospital was directly across Main Street from our apartment.

The only time I did see my parents that year was by pure co-incidence, when they happened upon an accident scene right after a guy rear-ended me. I'd got rid of the wagon by then and bought a Fiat sports car from Joey Applegate, who was in the electrical game with me (his father worked with us as well, and I spent years envious of their father/son relationship). A week later, Applegate creamed into me at a red light with his new Galaxy 500, knocking the gas tank clear out of my car. My father, on his way to a restaurant with Mom, chanced to be in the same intersection. He gave me a ride to the gas station but all he said was, "You must have been horsing around." Yeah, Pop, I backed into him doing fifty.

I put the gas tank in the trunk of the Fiat, re-piped it, and drove her around for months like that, popping the trunk lid to fill her up.

All the while, as I experimented with my liberty, two thoughts stayed in mind, one barely understood and one right up front. Deeply buried, I carried a nagging sense of unhappiness. I was drinking to try to fit in and be liked by my friends, not because I especially liked being drunk. I felt as if there were something more important I should be doing, but could never get a handle on just what it was. There had to be more to life than being an electrician in Nashua. I was missing a sense of purpose. I was very angry, and it was easy to piss me off; I could launch myself into a rage over nothing at all. I couldn't tolerate advice or suggestions; they felt like criticisms, indicators that I didn't know what I was doing. I felt that nobody understood me except one of the boys from the drinking fields, a kid named Sinky. He didn't fit in either, drinking with the same reluctant bravado that I did, and we approached each other with a wary desire to connect, to trust somehow. It would take a while before I came to see that Sinky and I were much the same, displaced persons looking for the acceptance we'd never found at home. I felt we shared the same sense of alienation, of events going too fast without meaning or direction. Sinky seemed unhappy in the same ways I was. Only with him did I start to understand what *best friend* meant. It meant nobody else understood it all but the two of you.

The more immediate concern was that, by dropping out of school, I'd put myself in the available draft pool. I remember the pity of some of those boys still in college, pity that I'd be setting myself up for a trip to Vietnam by dropping out. But the situation at home left me no choice, and I'd swept their warnings aside, figuring I'd worry about the draft if my number came up. Sinky had already quit school, and I felt that whatever happened to me, I might not be in it alone. I was relying on him more and more, but not for guidance or direction, since he was drifting as much as I. It was more of a need for reassurance that I wasn't the only one feeling lost, that one could operate within the framework of being lost. Sinky didn't have to know stuff ahead of time (funny that that's how my mother defined religious faith), and this was something I wanted to figure out how to do. We climbed Monadnock late one afternoon; we'd brought some LSD with us but decided to talk about it rather than eat it. We talked for fifteen hours that day, with Sinky hitting some dark and edgy tangents. He said if life was only about the journey, and not about attaining a completed state and cruising for the finish line, then he was more interested in what came next, what an afterlife might be about. I found it difficult to listen to him, and shut him out because I didn't want to think about what he meant.

We'd started up the mountain too late in the day to climb back down safely, and once up top we discovered that the park service had torn down the little emergency shelter we'd counted on using. We ended up spending the night on bare rock. We had no gear at all, no food or water. A lightning storm came sweeping in from the west, and we were thankful we hadn't eaten the acid. But the storm brought no rain. We were above the entire world, watching the bolts landing in all the little faraway towns around us. We talked about the war. Sinky was definitely not going, this I just knew, and I took a lot of comfort in the idea of following his lead. All I felt capable of in terms of preparing for the war was praying my number wouldn't come up, and having him as my friend.

237 Main Street. Six of us were sitting around our apartment, smoking pot and drinking a little beer and watching the draft lottery on television. They were drafting up to number 120 that year, so my chances of being called were roughly one in three. Then, the strangest thing happened: The guy on the news pulled four of our birthdays out of the cage right in a row: 67, 68, 69, and 70, just like

that. Sinky and I got the middle two numbers; the other two boys were still in school. The coincidence of our numbers being pulled serially like that struck me as strange and beautiful; it was almost a statistical impossibility, but there it was. Then I felt a slight twang of relief, remembering that I'd hedged my position by being granted C.O. status by the board. But that twang passed in a sudden burst of even greater relief: the realization that it didn't matter anymore, that I wasn't going. It wasn't about the war, nor about alternative service. My time at 237 Main had changed everything. I was in charge of me now; there was no room left for authority and regimentation. I was all done giving myself over to others on demand. Anything anybody else wanted to take from me, they were going to have to take by force. My body felt the excitement almost before my brain could assemble those thoughts. I made a promise with Sinky to avoid the war at all costs. I chose the starvation route and lost almost thirty pounds in two months; I was so sick I had to quit working.

The night before the physicals, we went to see the Stones at Boston Garden. It was my first time. There were about ten of us; we'd kept our tickets in the freezer for months, wrapped in aluminum foil, just in case the apartment burned down before the show. We had center stage seats, maybe thirty rows back. I didn't even get loaded, because I knew ahead of time I'd want to remember as many details as possible. It was unbelievable; the Stones looked like gods. The lighting, the equipment, everything perfect and professional; no tuning up between songs, not even a broken string. Towards the end of the show, they did something I'd never seen done before or since: They turned the house lights up full, as if for a hockey game. My dream that the Stones had been playing in front of me for the past hour faded away in the glare, my trance broken; in reality now were five live humans, on stage, life-sized, broad daylight, playing Stones hits.

The next morning, we drove to the armory for our physicals. Sinky had done nothing to prepare, and I watched with dismay as they tested and passed his weak eyesight. As they tested his hearing he stared off into space and gave random hand signals to the technicians, all the while carefully tapping his feet. Afterwards he told me he'd been counting time, allowing a certain amount of the tone to pass him by before indicating he could hear anything. In this manner he failed the hearing test by identical margins three times in succession and was declared unfit for military service. He told them he played in a band and couldn't hear a thing, and the truth wasn't far off; the Stones hadn't come on until after midnight, and our ears were still ringing.

I was measured to be an inch and a half under my actual height, and the weight I'd lost no longer mattered; I was deemed skinny but serviceable. We left the armory and headed down to the Garden, where we had tickets for the second Stones show. I was so pissed I couldn't even think about the Stones. I didn't say a word to Sinky, not even to congratulate him. I was pissed at the army, because now I'd have to change my life around just when things seemed to be going my way. I was pissed at Sinky for having saved his hide in five minutes with a clever trick, while I'd starved for months and been cheated out of my escape. I was doubly pissed because I had to admire him in spite of being pissed, because I could see how, with a little nerve, he had made his own luck. I hadn't been smart enough to fool them, nor brave enough to try something extra risky; I'd relied on the oldest trick in the book, and they'd picked me off in one second. I felt ashamed that they'd seen me coming.

I had to do something. Giving myself over to the army was out of the question; alternatives like hospital work or teaching poor kids in Appalachia seemed intolerable. It had nothing to do with the things

I'd written about in those C.O. essays, about morality and war. It was purely about self-determination: I couldn't swallow the idea of surrendering a couple of years of life just because someone had extracted from a birdcage a ball with 7/21/52 scribbled on it.

Anderson was still in the electrical trade with me and had replaced my brother at 237 Main. I'd forced Tony out to make room for my friend and felt pretty awful about it; it'd be twenty years before I learned much about compassion. Anderson had graduated near the top of our class at Guertin and been nominated for West Point, but he'd turned it down. I took a lot of flack from his parents over that one, for exerting undue influence, but the reality was that the Point wasn't a path he seriously considered; he just wanted to see if he could qualify. His mother came up to me one night around that time and said, "I don't like it that my son smokes." I snuffed my cigarette and said to her, "Cigarettes?" She looked at me, horrified, and asked, "What else *is* there?"

Anderson's number was in the two hundreds, and he had a full social life. He felt no pressure to run from the war, and maybe that's what drove him to leave town with me. There wasn't much of a plan; it was as if our action constructed itself out of sheer possibility. Our neighbor Chris came over one Friday night with some mescaline and his Gibson electric guitar; we got pretty high and cut up the lampshades at the apartment with our electrical knives while Chris played for us in the background. That Saturday morning, Anderson and I sat around trying to decide whether we were too hung over to work some time-and-a-half. I said to him, almost in jest, "Let's bolt." I still don't know why he decided to go with me; perhaps he felt the same as I did, that draft or no draft, Nashua wasn't the kind of place where you'd want to wake up at sixty or so, wondering where you'd gone wrong. The move happened very quickly, within a few days. We gave a lot of our stuff away, and I left my vinyl collection with friends. Chris threw his Gibson in my car, and we drove across town to see the only lawyer I knew. There, we traded my Fiat for his guitar, all perfectly legal.

The lawyer lived next door to my parents; I used to baby-sit his kids. It was a Saturday morning and both my parents' cars were sitting in their driveway. It felt strange pulling in one driveway over, as if I'd made a mistake. I worried about my parents spotting my orange sports car, because I had no intentions of visiting them. I hadn't been in their house in almost a year, and my first thought was that I didn't even live at home anymore and I was still sneaking behind their backs to get what I wanted. For a few seconds I felt like going in just to tell them I was leaving, but I squelched the impulse. I realized I wanted them to miss me and thought maybe my mother could. But I had no doubt my father would have been happy to inform the proper authorities that I was fleeing the draft. I drove away, wondering for perhaps the first time in my life how she had managed to stay with him for thirty years.

Anderson was driving a beautiful car at the time, a 1966 Thunderbird he'd bought from our boss. White, solid leather interior, black landau roof, total luxuries inside, and a 429 Thunderjet under the hood. A real pimp-mobile. We crammed whatever we could into the trunk, scouted around town for some weed to take on the road, and drove west into the sunset, just like it says in the book. I remember leaving in daylight, conscious that each building, then each mile, then each state, was being left behind for good; the feeling itself was reminiscent of nightfall. We hadn't said good-bye to very many people, and there'd been no farewell party. I didn't even bring my tools, that's how little expectation I had that my new life would resemble my old one. I sat in the back seat for long periods, figuring out guitar licks coming from the tape deck. The beauty of high-speed driving across the open west at five in the morning was something. I felt a little sad about Anderson coming with me, it being his car and all, and doubted I would have managed to leave by myself. It had all happened too fast, and I couldn't figure out how I'd managed to get that far along without Sinky as my guide.

Fearful of being unearthed as a draft dodger, I cast around for a new name for myself, to employ wherever we landed. The names I made up all sounded predictable and uncreative, like guys in fiction. I chose Bill Wyman, bass player for the Stones, figuring Keith Richards would have been too obvious. I lifted a famous person's name because I needed to feel cool, because I was twenty years old and driving into oblivion and wanted to start out with an edge. Bill Wyman, not an impossible name, a slick coincidence that wouldn't go unnoticed among Stones fans. It slowly came to me that nobody would know me, that I could leave my entire past behind. I could pretend I had no brothers or sisters, that my parents had been killed in a car crash, or that my brothers had been killed in Vietnam and they never send the last surviving son into combat. This last one, that's what Sinky would tell perfect strangers if he were in my shoes. Make them feel sorry for you right off.

Low on money and out of gas, we rolled to a stop in Longmont, Colorado, and took a motel room. Neither Anderson nor I could have predicted we'd spend the next year living out of that single room. I never wrote to my parents, I never called my friends back east. Once again, like when I'd roller skated out of my old neighborhood in Queens for the first time, nobody who knew me knew where I was, and nobody where I was knew me. But I was more lost now than I'd been back then, and it showed. I was paranoid, completely lacking in self-confidence. I couldn't save money, I wallowed in uncertainty, picked boring friends. I argued with Anderson constantly, not wanting him to call back east either, for fear of giving me away.

I was carrying my lucky charm, the pocket watch I'd got on my aborted Woodstock adventure, but it wasn't doing me any good. That Thanksgiving I had a cup of coffee and ate peanut butter out of a jar.

In that motel room, I had my first and only dream about the death of my father. In the dream, a giant shell descended from the heavens, fitting tightly over the earth and destroying everything on it. The sensations were so vivid I remember my chest being crushed against the ground, and turning my head to snatch a last breath before my ribs caved in. Then I awoke, and found my sister Grace with me. We strolled silently over the desolate plain. The world was destroyed; there was nothing bigger than a shoe box as far as the eye could see. We came across the intact body of our father. He was face down; I nudged him with the tip of my boot, as if to roll him over for a look. Grace said, "He's dead."

He had lived until the end of the world.

12

In the New World

I wasn't in control of anything. I had what I wanted most, the
freedom to choose any path, but my choosing apparatus was
completely inadequate; I didn't have any idea what to do with
myself.

A year or so after I'd hit the road with Anderson, the war
started winding down and there was talk of a general amnesty, to
heal the country's wounds. After all that time in Colorado, I had
no money, no car, no girlfriend, and I headed back east to see if I
could pick up where I'd left off in the electrical racket. I figured it
couldn't be as bad as it'd been out west. I got back in the late fall,
picked up a job, and made plans with Sinky to hitch to Tennessee
for Christmas, to visit some friends I'd made out west. A few weeks
later, his brother dropped us off at a Mass Pike on-ramp.

It was not like the old days. Sinky was more edgy, more distant,
disgusted that the citizenry (he now referred to the populace as
"sheeple") had given Nixon another term in office, and by a wide
margin. But there was more to it than that. I couldn't help feeling
something was really eating him, and rather than facing it, he was
choosing to channel his tension elsewhere. It didn't help that we
were cold and under-financed and ill equipped for the road. I was

the one who'd hitched across the country, and it seemed important for me to be leading just then, as if I'd *matured* somehow just by dint of being away. But the hitching was going poorly, and I felt Sinky judging me as a poser. It'd taken us a whole day just to get across the pike to Syracuse, with Sinky sniping all the way; he was probably as pissed as I was that even between us we didn't have the gas money to take his own car. He'd just quit a depressing job in a bread factory, and it bothered him that there was so much antlike work in the world, that some people spent their entire lives making house paint and snow tires. In Syracuse, everything was locked down for the holidays, so we broke into the laundry room of a dorm and slept on the machines. I had a dream: I was in an abandoned farmhouse back in New Hampshire, in the hayloft with some old man and an atomic bomb. The man was setting the bomb to detonate at ground impact, twenty feet below. The trigger was primitive, a wing nut that moved a lever along a threaded rod. It could not possibly be accurate in the range of mere feet, and I began sweating as I awaited the first nanosecond of iridescence.

At five in the morning a security guard kicked us out to face a gray dawn with a cold, flat sky. There wasn't any place open to get breakfast. We were cold and hungry, and it took us until sundown to reach Pennsylvania and the outskirts of Harrisburg. Now it was dark, and we trudged along the roadway in search of a motel and some food. The shoulders were piled high with old snow, so we hugged the thin margin of the road, cars just whizzing by. The last thing I said to him was, "Plow coming, Sink," and then he flew past me upside down and landed with a muffled thud in the snow up ahead. I entered a strange zone of unreality and silence, which I later learned was called shock. As he lay next to me in the snow, all I could think about were the onion sandwiches he used to eat, frying up slices and putting them on buttered Wonder bread. He'd stare intently into the frying pan, as if expecting the onion to give him back talk while he sealed its fate; I could still see the grease splattered on the thick plastic of his eyeglasses.

Back at his house, they found a note stuck with a diaper pin to the back of his bedroom door, so that if you came into his room, you wouldn't see it unless you closed the door behind you, and you wouldn't do that except to look for something that was none of your business. Then you'd see it: "Merry Christmas to all and to all a Good Night." Had it been an accident, or had Sinky really taken charge of his despair? I spent years wondering if he'd heard my warning about the plow or not. I feared the strength of his decision; suppose he *had* thought about leaving me alone there, and acted anyway? We'd talked a few times about suicide, but had he really made the biggest decision of his life without telling me? His death, seen as an accident, made me realize you could die at any time, for no reason, and that in order to live with such knowledge, you had to live in a way that promised few regrets. But seen as suicide, it meant one could be so alone in the world that no one could help you, that your only choice was to quit, and you couldn't even discuss that with friends because the idea was so big it would fry their senses. How had Sinky taken control of such huge thoughts? Did he comprehend death? I felt left behind; in the second before he died he probably understood everything, and while I didn't want to follow him, I couldn't help feeling I was missing something.

When I think about it today, his death caused me more fear than everything my father had done to me in the twenty previous years. It helped convince me, or perhaps just reaffirmed, that the world was not a safe place; not that it contained intentional meanness, but that, if there were indeed a God, he was indifferent towards his creations. It was a world in which plenty of us were not going to be allowed to dream. Maybe Einstein was wrong, and the universe was not knowable after all.

After Sinky died I went back to Colorado; my returning to electrical work and living in Nashua with the same old crowd seemed pointless. Out west I fell in with two women from Chicago. We drank an awful lot, changed jobs frequently, went dancing, discovered magic mushrooms. We slept together in various combinations, discovering sexuality and its traps. I felt I was living in a new world, but a general feeling of insecurity and anxiousness pervaded all that I did. Those women seemed so much more courageous than I, more willing to take risks for the fullness of the moment at hand. One day, as we finished up lunch, they packed their outsized handbags and announced they were hitching to Mexico. Another night, the three of us went out dancing; Mary and Barbara came home with partners and I did not. I stayed up quite a while trying to understand our relationship, how we three had each other and relied upon that, but did not belong to one another. We inhabited a world with no rules, where sexual intimacy did not bind you to your loved one, and I found this world very threatening. I didn't know whether I loved those women or was just attached to the beauty and physical kindness they offered. I believe now I did love them in spite of my fear of them, but that the world they lived in was too hard for me. I slowly fell in love with Mary, but felt paralyzed to act upon it; even the promise of love felt shifty and confining at the same time. Hers was a completely sensual path. She loved colors, soft fabrics, makeup, scents, desire itself. Her full embracing of the here and now made me jittery; if something more interesting came along tomorrow, she might abandon me. I walked away from her promise; she moved to South Africa, where she fell in love and married. I saw her again a few years later, in a Chicago hospital, as she lay dying of leukemia.

I hitched around the country imagining my true path lay just over the next hill, in another place. I was now a licensed electrician in three states, but the work bored me. I remember a guy telling me once that you can't run away from yourself, that you always carry who you are with you. I'd thought he was just another babbling acidhead at the time. He was, but I was beginning to understand what he'd meant. I went to Maine, back out west, to Tennessee, back to New Hampshire; I drove through Texas and California. It was all the same.

For years, I paid little attention to my family. Like my parents, but for different reasons, I skipped my siblings' weddings and birthdays; I found I did not miss my brothers and sisters. One could say I made a conscious decision to turn my back on them, but at the time, that's not what it felt like. I didn't intend to snub them, but once I was away from them, after that first year on the lam in Colorado, I realized it felt good to be away from the noise, the obligations, my parents. What I needed most was to be a separate thing from them, to become whatever it was the universe had in store for me besides being a Zanichkowsky. When I did occasionally attend a family gathering, the feelings of claustrophobia returned. There was the same clamoring of loud voices, the desperate need to be heard, endless stories from our collective past. I'd return to my apartment in a state of turmoil, thinking it hadn't done me much good to be with my family that day. Now I look upon those years away not as a period of abandonment, but of recovery.

I lived with Barbara for a while, but the attachment I felt was not satisfying or fulfilling. It was more like a desperate neediness for affection and attention. I could not decide whether the love I saw others share was an illusion, an act of lonely desperation, or something beautiful and magical but totally beyond my understanding. My friends, and my siblings, began having children, but

I could not rejoice for them, and the thought of having children of my own horrified me; all I could picture was loving them and having them die on me. My whole existence was constricted by a fear of loss so great as to deny me positive action. I was not deciding anything, merely following paths of least resistance as they opened before me, like leads cracking open in polar ice.

More than anything, I wanted to live alone. I craved human physical contact, yet had no idea how to align this need with the burdens of companionship. Often, I found myself wishing I were a different person, someone well liked, more interesting, someone in action. Yet . . . I'd burned my draft card, hitched across the country, worked for myself; why could I not believe in the value of my own experience? Why was it taking me so long to figure out how to be in charge of myself?

I went in and out of therapy, but came to places so dark and fearful I could no longer trust the doctors to lead me through the dangers; I had too much fear that my mind would just snap into insanity. One day, talking about my father, I became so filled with disgust and rage and hatred, I had a meltdown. The doctor had to call one of my friends to come get me. I began keeping a journal. Almost the first thing I wrote was "I come from a planet without any love on it." After a while the writing shamed me; I found reading the stuff unendurable, and I started a ritual: Every vernal equinox I fed the books into the fireplace, keeping only the pages with dreams on them.

But something changed during those sessions, even though it would take me a while to see it: *I* was the only thing I had to be afraid of anymore. I began to see my father as a pathetic little cockroach like me, and that there was no need to fear him anymore. I still hated him, but the feeling of having to do something about it slowly began to fade.

In 1987, doctors detected the heart disease I'd inherited from my mother, the stuff that had helped kill her parents that October afternoon back in 1946: the faulty aortic valve, dilated aorta, atrial fibrillation. Paul had inherited these as well; his aorta eventually ruptured, necessitating the hospital stay when my parents couldn't find time to visit him. My discovery of my own cardiac inheritance had the effect of slowing me down and allowing me to take stock. I cut down on drinking and quit smoking weed; I had to curtail the basketball and kick-boxing I'd come to rely upon to keep me sane. In my newfound leisure time I took to writing and serious reading; I expanded my record buying into classical and jazz. I began going to museums to look at paintings, and learned to watch films for camera work and direction rather than plot. In spite of all the medications and testing and worrying about the inevitable aorta replacement and valve job, I became thankful for my disease. This new world was much larger than my old one, and I might not have discovered it without that bit of bad genetic luck.

A second influence was a small boy I met in Maine, on a huge lake up in the sticks. He looked to be about four years old. He'd play at the dock all day long, always by himself, in an orange life vest. He never seemed bored, or even busy, just present. He had black hair and gray eyes and soft skin the color of candle wax. I thought he was the most beautiful child I'd ever seen, the most quiet, the most serene, at play in the world. I'd watch him from my porch as he discovered things in the world for the first time: a sudden wave, crayfish, the calls of the loons, kingfishers zeroing in. When I tried befriending him, he wouldn't say a word to me. At first it bothered me, because I wanted to find out about him, wanted him to like me. He reminded me so much of myself. I had an urge to hold him, as if this would bring me to a safe place of my own. This boy was still innocent, and I wanted to recapture that for myself, to imagine that I'd once been like him.

But then I understood it: He wasn't spoiled or tainted or influenced in any way yet, he was on that cusp of engaging and negotiating with the rest of the world. He'd have to do it soon, and once he started, there'd be no going back. I began to hope he wouldn't talk, would forget I'd asked him his name, would never answer me. If he once talked, we'd both be destroyed. Like crawling; once the child gets up on two feet he'll be there for the rest of his life, so why rush it? We were safe as long as we didn't talk. It remained so for the rest of the summer.

I felt a little perverted for thinking about him so much, as if confronting an innate and buried pedophilia. One night I couldn't sleep because of this, and in the middle of the night, with my attraction to the boy bugging me, I began writing about him. I suppose I hoped to write my way into some understanding of my fascination. I started with describing him physically, then trying to create his past, imagining his thoughts, his feelings at the discovery of a new thing; I imagined his parents only vaguely capable of entering his sanctuary. I must have written ten pages; I'd never written anything before, except for those essays for the draft board.

It turns out the boy was hearing impaired; he couldn't speak because he couldn't get a handle on how the words sounded. Did his innocence and serenity come from not needing to do anything about the noises others were making? His parents had become frustrated, then worried, about the boy's apparently total lack of interest in speech. But I didn't know any of this when I sent them the story, the description of the boy. I'd just wanted them to know how stirring their boy was, how beautiful, how special. I sent it in the mail; it got to their house the same day they brought the boy home from the hearing specialist. They saved it for him for six years and read it to him when he was ten.

Soon after I got those three licenses, I quit the electrical trade and took up woodworking. The shift was partially because electrical work wasn't creative, and I'd begun feeling a need to do something more satisfying. It was also that the trades seemed to be filled with morons who cared nothing about anything except the Red Sox and the Bruins. It was getting harder each day to face eight hours with plumbers and masons and cement guys. I began an apprenticeship with a couple of men who built replicas of Shaker houses. This was the real thing; they made their own doors, stenciled the plasterwork with milk paints, made all the stairs and peg rails with old hand tools. Working with them was more like school than a job. In winding up each project, there were just two of us, the old-time craftsman and myself as the student. It wasn't even a work site; it was more like the two of us just hanging around, shooting the shit and adding fine wooden touches to an already fine, old-looking home. Chuck took me to flea markets to buy old planes and saws, showed me how to cut dovetails by hand, how to sharpen chisels. I learned that you could date a piece of furniture, sometimes even pinpoint where it'd come from, just by certain tool marks, or the shape of the foot. We sat admiring an old window sash at one market, and I asked him what tool they'd used to make the joints in the old days. "Time," he said. "That's all anything takes."

13

The Unconsoled

After Jimmy was sent to Creedmore, I didn't see him for any length of time until we had lunch one day right before our parents died. This would be around 1990; he'd been out of the hospital for twenty-five years. I hadn't seen him more than a couple of times in between, even though we spent some of that time living only a few miles apart, when he was on Staten Island and I was in Manhattan. Our getting together was a fluke after so many years off. I'd written to all the kids about the heart condition Paul and I were carrying, suggesting they get tested since it was hereditary, and Jimmy responded to that by calling me in SoHo. He never mentioned the heart disease, but was all excited about getting together.

The lunch was in midtown, at a little place outside Grand Central Station. He was working for a paper company near there, designing software. If you called him at work, he'd answer the phone with "Systems," so I began calling him that. He never mentioned the institutions at that lunch. He described how he'd dropped out of high school at Thomas Edison, how he couldn't get along with the teachers, that they didn't understand him and he wasn't getting anywhere. But you didn't drop out of school in our house. That was not a decision you'd have had the autonomy to make, and you wouldn't be coming home on Sundays if you had. He was giving me a yarn. But even back then, at that lunch, I'd let him give it. The look in his eye was not a good look. It was a brittle, sad, hard look that said something about the fragility and fear and regret of the storyteller; it was the look of a man who expected you to have the decency and courage to accept a bullshit story not even because he wanted you to think it was true, but because it was all he had to offer. I couldn't even look him in the eye; I just stared at the tiny gold crucifix stuck to his lapel. He seemed so defenseless, I quit my roundabout digging into his past. But he was not at all weak, and I came away from that table thinking that, for the first time in my life, I'd eaten lunch with a guy who had it in him to kill a man. What bothered me most about knowing this was, I would never know whether he was like that before they sent him, or if he'd become like that in Creedmore, once he was locked inside for five years with the seven thousand others who were living there in his day.

It was seven years after that lunch, and after our parents were dead, when he told me about the rubber band beating. He'd never told anybody about the beating before, nor about the institution. At least that's what he said. It occurred to me back then that he might be making the whole rubber band thing up; today, it doesn't matter. I went out to Creedmore and interviewed a director who described what the place had been like in the late 1950s and early 1960s. If you spent five years in there back in those days, she said, you'd learn a completely different set of social skills than you'd need on the outside, including lying, stealing, threatening, and manipulating others. There was no other way you'd survive inside. She described a mixed population including the criminally insane, manic depressives, schizophrenics, people whom judges threw in because there was no other place to put them. There were no education or athletic programs whatsoever; Creedmore was a warehouse. I imagined a small town with no school or library and where every citizen is emotionally unstable. I imagined the story Jimmy might have told the inmates on his way in the door, and the ones he might have told five years later on the way out, not to mention those he told me twenty-five years later. I imagined none of them overlapping very well.

I never told Jimmy I'd been out to the hospital; it would have been too hurtful for him to learn I'd done something like that behind his back. I'd gone with the intent of finding out why Mom had sent him there, if there was a single reason; I was motivated by what Annie had told me about the molestations. But because Jimmy was still alive at the time, they wouldn't tell me why he'd been admitted. Nor could they tell me about the dozens of insulin shock treatments and the comas they caused, nor about the Miltown and the Thorazine, nor about the electroconvulsive shock sessions; I only found out those things after he died. Our brother had experienced the darkest period of American psychiatric care, and again I found myself wondering how much of that care he'd actually needed, and how much they'd just "done" to him as routine. The record from Creedmore, some of it dictated by my mother and some gleaned from doctors' interviews, revealed little of Jimmy's pre-Creedmore behavior. He'd been on probation for molesting a little girl at the time of admission in 1961, and had admitted to raping a six-year-old girl. But, as the doctors quickly discovered while talking with him, "it is difficult to state whether he is lying deliberately, is stating delusional material, or is being factual." When asked to make drawings of human figures, my brother drew only heads, and said, "I can't draw the bottoms of any people."

Jimmy was living out of a single room in a boardinghouse in White Plains during my last visits with him. A used-up white station wagon was parked outside; you started it with a toggle switch on the column. Inside, I saw that his life took place entirely within that room. There was a lot of computer stuff on the desk, because he built and programmed machines. There were no books, a few CDs still in the cellophane, some clothes hanging on a little rack. Some music books, because he sang in the local church. A television and a few adventure videos, a valet with a few more clothes hanging on it. A carton of the mini-cigars that he'd smoked for as long as anyone can remember and which finally had put him in the hospital. A Bible, well worn. An easy chair and some convenience food and a little bed on a metal frame, the same size bed that the five of us had had back in the old days in that front room in Queens. There were no pictures of his family; looking around the room, you wouldn't figure he had any family.

He described Creedmore in some detail, in particular, how people watched television in the day hall and fought over the channel. He worked in the kitchens and did small favors for the staff, such as waxing their cars, for pocket change. "I had to do something," he said, "or I'd go crazy."

He told me that after he got out of the institution, he'd gone to the police academy and become a cop, that he had quit after his partner got killed. He told Tony he was a pilot and had flown his boss around in the company plane. You didn't know what to believe anymore, from him. It hurt me because he was still, at fifty, trying to invent a life somebody could be impressed by. I believed him about the police department stuff for a while, even though alarm bells were going off: How could they possibly make a cop out of a guy with no high school diploma, give a gun to a guy who'd spent his teens in Creedmore? But I really wanted to believe him. I needed to believe something exciting and interesting had happened to him, because I could start guessing, sitting there in his single room, what his life must really be like. But I didn't call him on it. It hurt me, afterwards, to think he might have been wondering whether I'd believed him or not.

After he got out, he married Mary, a former patient who'd got out before him. I'd known about her, but not that they'd met in Creedmore. I don't remember going to the wedding. That marriage was pretty rocky. Jimmy felt she was cheating on him, and it ended in divorce. There were three children, and when I asked him about their paternity, he said he wasn't certain about any of them, but that he'd brought them all up as good Christians and given them an education and a last name. Louise says she and Ernie visited them in an apartment Father Kruzas had got them in Brooklyn. They saw a huge dog cage in the middle of the living room floor. The kids were locked inside. When she asked Jimmy and Mary about this, they just shrugged and said the kids got out of control sometimes.

Jimmy told me lots of stories as we sat in his room. I became increasingly uncomfortable with how poorly all the pieces of his life fit together, because they wouldn't fit together at all; he was making it up as we went along, just filling in blank pages for a new audience. The only thing that seemed undeniably true was that he was a born-again Christian and spent an awful lot of time reading the Bible. He asked me several times if I were happy, did I pray, if I'd ever considered God; he could quote long passages from memory. It seemed urgent to him to share with me the teachings that had come to make his life tolerable. He was just like my mother in this regard; they'd both arrived at that station in life where it seemed better to put your faith in the world to come.

In the end, Jim even lied about how sick he was. Just two little tumors in his brain, for which he was going to start treatment next week. Why didn't he tell us about the ones in his throat, which made him sound like Mickey Mouse? Was he afraid—as he'd probably been most of his life—that we wouldn't care? Was he afraid I'd yell at him for still smoking after the lung cancer operation two years earlier? (I did.) It was the lung cancer that had spread to his brain and throat, finally finishing him off.

At Jimmy's funeral service, there were a bunch of pictures of him on a side table, pictures I'd never seen before. One was from Manhasset; he's standing inside a little wooden shed down by the yacht club, which I didn't remember existed until I saw that photo. Another was an Easter picture of him that had only surfaced after our parents were dead; it was from a series, each of us individual kids in our Sunday best, taken outside on the slate terrace. Another, taken very recently, with somebody's kids in it; he was their godfather. In this picture he's smiling, he's quit coloring his hair. It looks very much like he's come to some semblance of peace within himself, as if he's surrendered.

Only when I'd been seated in the pew for a while did I notice that right next to those pictures, nestled among them, was the urn containing his ashes. Just before the ceremony began, Marty leaned over to me and said, "Do we all move up a number now?"

For some reason, when he said that, I began to understand why my brother had been such a storyteller. His was a complicated and foundationless life, a pathetic and painful visit to earth; not empty of experience, but empty of things like joy and pride and hope, empty of love and trust. When you asked him about himself, he took license to create scenes of his own choosing and design. He had to, because there was little in his past he could tell somebody and have the listener like him for it. Jimmy was just that much more desperate than the rest of us to be loved: If he couldn't be loved for what he actively was, he'd settle for being admired for what he was not.

But because of a lifetime of fabrications, he probably never knew how he felt about himself, and could never know how we felt about him. And although we could never know how he felt about us, I imagine he did not like us very much; we had lived at home, remained a family without him. I sat there looking at that urn, wondering why his head had not melted long ago, from all the heat contained there.

I wasn't going to miss Jimmy. None of us were, since he'd never been around us long enough to form the attachments that could cause missing. Annie and Stephanie hadn't come to the funeral, and I didn't know whether it mattered or not. But I cried for Jimmy, because the universe had never given him a break; with everything that had happened to him, the gods still saw fit to kill him first. It seemed unfair that only at fifty, once he'd got scared about the lung cancer and reached out to us (and, for the most part, been accepted), had he begun to become a member of our family, and he never got to finish the job.

I thought about that tiny gold crucifix in his lapel. I was furious at Jimmy's God, for having brought him here just to toy with him and see how much he could take. And maybe I was angry then with Jimmy, for having had faith. It seemed to me he'd been bamboozled; we'd all been told we are God's creatures, that he loves us and has put us on earth for a reason. Yet when it all goes desperately wrong and you're left hiding in a corner somewhere trying to figure out God's plan for you, and you can't, you're told not to bother, that God works in mysterious ways, and it's not your business to question his intentions.

But I was relieved that he'd died first out of all us kids, and this made me feel sad; as if even God felt Jimmy was the least important of us. And I felt empty, because my father's death hadn't done very much to me, and because my mother's death hadn't done much either. I was relieved that, with three deaths in my family, I hadn't been demolished yet. I cried for myself at my brother's funeral because I couldn't understand what was so wrong with me that I was almost *waiting* for someone closer to me to die so I would feel something, as if such feelings would prove to me I was capable of love, after all.

❖   ❖   ❖

Annie graduated from the public high school in Great Neck in 1966, the year I graduated from eighth grade. That summer, our parents and the youngest ten kids moved north to New Hampshire; this made Annie the oldest child living at home. In her own words, she doesn't know how she managed to graduate. She figures they slipped her past ninth grade entirely, because there are no school records of her being in ninth grade at all. She graduated from high school with the same diploma as the rest of the kids, with no indication of having been in special classes. For all the outside world knew, Annie was just another mediocre high school graduate from the New York public school system.

"About three months after we moved up there," she says, "I started working full time, but I got fired. I don't recall the reason, but it was my first job and I didn't really have any skills. I went from high school right into working, and there were a couple of problems, okay?"

Those problems took her through jobs pretty quickly. She had poor social skills, and routine office jobs, which might require talking to people on the phone or scheduling appointments for others, were out of the question. And since we'd just arrived, my parents hadn't enough connections yet to know what type of resources might be available to help Annie. Eventually, they located a school in Montpelier, Vermont, that ran sheltered workshops.

The idea was to take troubled kids and teach them basic social and working skills in a closed environment. And so, soon after we moved north, Annie was sent across the Connecticut River. Like Jimmy seven years earlier, she was taken out of the house without much being said to the rest of us.

"I lived at that special school for a year and a half," she recalls. "It was a group home, we went to school all day long. I dated up there, and somebody told Mom and Dad that there was something with the relationship. The result of it was that the boy I was dating committed suicide right on the premises, and I got blamed for it. He left a note. He had a fixation with me, he wanted things to be serious, and if we were not permitted to continue our relationship, there was no reason for him to live. That was the note. Boom, down he went. A couple of days later Mom and Dad pulled me out. I came back home and found just whatever jobs I could do."

Catherine explains how Mom and Dad made one last-ditch effort to help Annie, now approaching twenty-one. They went to court to try to be declared her legal guardians after she reached majority. New Hampshire is a conservative state, however, very strong on individual rights and seriously uninterested in interfering with the affairs of its citizens. They required three doctors to sign statements declaring Annie incompetent before they'd allow our parents to take charge of her. Mom and Dad could only find two.

"Annie was going to enough doctors," Catherine says, "and maybe she figured, 'Are they going to put me behind a wall somewhere, like Jimmy?' So she caught on and put her best foot forward, because they could never get three doctors to sign her in."

It was the diploma that saved her. The doctors were unwilling to strip a perfectly legitimate high school graduate of her independence simply because she was a bit slow.

So she was out on her own, twenty-one, renting a bedroom in a private home in Nashua. Paul remembers helping her move some stuff to and from the YWCA, where she had rented a room for a while. I was still living at home then and remember her coming and going from her jobs. Back then, if a kid had a job, the big thing was to buy a dozen donuts for the family on payday. Buying payday treats for our siblings was our first adult step; we all did it, and Annie did too.

"The first job I had," she pauses, "was at the Pancake House. When that fizzled out, I went to work at Zayre's. And it was one job after another after that, because I had no skills." When the jobs didn't work out, she'd go on unemployment. This cycled until she'd had so many jobs, she couldn't keep track of whether she was on unemployment or not. Inevitably, she crossed her own path going in one door and out the other. "I was helping her with her taxes," Catherine says. "One year, she had fifteen W-2 forms, that's not even a month at a job." Annie was arrested for welfare fraud, and Mom and Dad went to bail her out. They explained her background to the judge; my father was particularly pissed about the diploma, which was identical to Marty's and did not mention special classes. The judge let my sister off the hook.

Probably the only miracle that ever happened to Annie occurred in 1980, when she got married to a marine she met through the correspondence column in a Marine Corps magazine called *The Leatherneck*. Mike had been in the service for years. He and Annie were together for about ten years, and they had a daughter, Meaghan. The marriage disintegrated, but it's generally agreed among the kids that Mike's going to heaven eventually, for having looked after our sister during that time. With the exception of Catherine, it's more than any of us had done for her.

Except on a superficial level, we were and still are incapable of helping her. We saw Annie as just another Zanichkowsky with a bunch of problems. Most of us have been divorced; some of us have changed jobs frequently, moved around, suffered economically for lack of education. A few of us still live marginally, are on antidepressants, are in therapy. We don't have the patience or understanding, much less the training and knowledge, to help someone like Annie. Although our kindness and attention could make her day-to-day life more tolerable, make her feel more loved, there isn't much we can do to help her feel fulfilled, less bitter about her childhood, or more understanding of all our mother had gone through trying to help her.

The last few times I visited her, Annie was living with her boyfriend, Wayne, and her daughter, Meaghan, now a teenager; the three shared a medium-sized apartment in Hooksett, New Hampshire, just up-river from Manchester, the former textile capital of the world. Annie was working as parking attendant at the Manchester airport. I'd rented a car so we could drive around. I took her on errands she usually accomplished on foot or by bus, then we went over to the Manchester Historical Society. We visited the Amoskeag Mills, where they had a few looms and carding machines left over from Manchester's glory days.

Annie is entirely without ego; she is unaware of the Annie others see. At the same time, when you talk to her, she is all that exists, harmlessly self-centered, completely needing, yet perfectly selfless in her lack of awareness of those needs. Because of this, she shares her experiences as if she were recounting them for and to herself, as in a reverie, thus avoiding the intermediate step of reconfiguring them for a listener. She would never try to impress you and is incapable of guile or deception, of consciously portraying herself in favorable light. She seems unaware of these things

about herself, and it's difficult for her to assess her own limitations. "I don't really know whether to believe it or not," she says,
"but I've mentioned it to a couple of people, even my own therapist that I see periodically now, and he seems to think that it is possible that the problems are still happening today."

Annie's life has been a struggle, the same struggle, for forty
years. She has little hope of improving her lot through hard work or
education, through self-discipline or self-knowledge. Spending time
with her (or Jimmy, for that matter, when he was around) makes
me uncomfortable because she stands as a reminder that sometimes the universe will not even allow us to help ourselves. Annie
walks the surface of a sphere, a surface finite but unbounded, with
no beginning and no end. The surface of a sphere looks the same
from every vantage point; the smallest bit of its surface can stand in
for the whole thing. A sphere is, in this sense, one-dimensional, and
even traveling in a straight line can feel circular. She is doomed to
encounter the same few surface markings again and again: They
are the scars we kids, and our parents, left upon Annie with our lack
of understanding and acceptance of her.

But why would any God bring her here and abandon her to
such sad geometry? So that I, coming into contact with her, might
learn compassion and patience and understanding? Maybe that's
what bothers me: My sister is a symbol for all in the world that I
cannot understand, that I refuse to accept, a metaphor for all that
cannot be fixed. She reminds me of how easy it is to exist without
purpose. But what in life gives us purpose? And who am I to wonder if her life has any?

When the questions are too big for answers, the idea of God
becomes inescapable. Is Annie's purpose to bring me closer to
God? I search Annie's life for purpose, not for her, but for me. In
my search I find nothing; again, not for her, but for me. My

search draws a blank, but in looking, I find that even I, who can't convince myself of the existence of God, find myself contemplating the possibility of God.

If you define nostalgia as wishing the past had been better than it actually was, then Annie's words have a nostalgic quality. If it's true that she suffered a lack of oxygen to the brain at birth, then the real tragedy isn't that Annie became mildly retarded; it's that she was left with just enough brain power to know her own misery. She has never fit in, she has never belonged, and she has never not known those things. Annie has been hurting for so long, and the only people who know the details are a bunch of Zanichkowskys who haven't got the slightest idea how to help her.

We are in her apartment as we talk. She gets up and walks towards the wall (but not directly: a bishop attacking a rook), looks at a small group of pictures. Wedding pictures; some from our parents' funerals; pictures of our parents when they were younger; some of us fourteen kids; a few of her kid with our kids. She drifts towards a particular pair of photos. I ask her what she thinks about when she looks at them.

"To me, that's happy times with my siblings, okay? Those are times that I want to remember, those are times that I want to look back on."

The pictures in question were taken in a restaurant the day of our father's funeral.

14

Death of the Patriarch

I remember a game I used to play with my sister Rita, after we'd both been living alone for long stretches of time. In our darker moments, we'd wager on which Zanichkowsky would be the first to die. This seems millions of years ago now, when there were still sixteen of us running around and even our parents still seemed young, when the time for anybody's dying seemed a long way off.

Sometimes I bet on myself, because I was pretty depressed back then and was awfully tired of the struggle. We favored Annie, because her life appeared so lacking in love and joy and accomplishment, and it didn't seem you could hold on to life for very long under those conditions. Jimmy was always a front-runner because he'd been smoking his thin little brown cigars for so long he'd begun to take on their characteristics, looking more and more like a cinnamon stick stood on end, reedy and brown, ready to fall over at any moment. Then Paul's aorta ruptured one day while he was raking his lawn. He really threw a rod, tearing out the aortic valve and flooding his chest cavity with blood, so I started betting on him. But they installed a shiny new titanium valve (Bjork-Shiley, Paul says proudly) and a new Dacron aorta, and three operations later he's still fiercely among the living. We never considered our parents, in spite of how we felt about them. It's not so easy for kids to imagine that the day will come when they no longer have parents; it reminds them they're next in line for the reaper. Rita said that after they were both dead, she felt like an orphan even though she was thirty-five at the time.

It was our father. He died in two seconds. He'd had two heart attacks and a quadruple bypass during a lifetime of hard work, cigarettes, stress, and fatty foods, so although he must have seen it coming, he never saw it arrive. My mother had dozed off on the couch, and when she awoke she found him folded in half over the edge of the bathtub. "He left me so quickly," she said to me afterwards, "that it felt like he'd walked out on me for another woman."

I was alone when Rita telephoned from Portland, Maine. It was night; I was living in Manhattan at the time. "Has anybody called you yet?" Reet said. I knew all about those words. They were the same words she'd used four years earlier, when my brother's aorta had burst, and four years earlier than that, when our mother had had a lump of cancer removed from her lung. Rita's words triggered a sense that I was about to be drawn into something against my will, that something so big had happened that naming it would seem incidental. When she told me the news we fell silent for a while and then she started crying and I started crying too, because I wanted her to hold me but she was three hundred miles away and all I had right then was a telephone. My immediate reaction to her words was a wash of sensations, emotions and colors so strong I became dizzy. At the same time, I was somehow thankful for the distance, thankful I was alone. Compassion generally makes me uncomfortable; it compels people to say things they can't possibly mean, such as "I know just how you feel." Rita knows this about me; we stayed silent on the phone for a while, said good-bye, and hung up.

I was trying to decide whether I should, or even could, call my mother, when she called me; she asked me right off would I please come to my father's funeral. That's when it struck me, that the distance between my father and me was something she'd probably tried to traverse many times, a distance I'd never figured she'd measured. I told her I was sorry, because for her I *was* sorry. My feelings about Dad weren't her fault, and I was sorry for what she was probably feeling. But she could tell by my voice I wasn't sorry for the loss of my father. That's when I understood that my feelings towards my father had hurt her too, which they weren't intended to. I wondered if I was the only kid she'd asked about coming to the funeral, because I could name the kids I thought might not care about Dad's passing. At the same time, I wondered why it was important for her that I go. Was it for me or for Dad, or for her?

I didn't give my mother an answer. It annoyed me that she had asked for my presence so bluntly. Suddenly, my thoughts and feelings about my father and his death now involved her. My immediate reaction, a reaction unconnected to her asking me, was that I wouldn't go, and now this consideration was distorted, because my going or not going to his funeral wasn't about what I wanted to say about my father, it was about what I'd be saying about him to my mother. My response to my father's death had been rendered impure by my mother's request. Once again, he seemed to be two men: my father, and my mother's husband.

After she hung up I felt the twang of regret that accompanies the realization that something's just gotten finished that you should have had a hand in. Twenty years had elapsed since I'd left home, and I'd wasted most of it refusing to understand either my father or myself. I hadn't wanted to understand him, since understanding seemed only a short step from forgiving him, and I couldn't allow myself to slide into compassion. I didn't want to give him anything, not even forgiveness. I'd expected *him* to fix things, to come to me out of the blue and apologize for not having loved me. I was the one who was bitter about all he had withheld. I was the one who would never forgive my father for making mistakes. I was the one to whom Grace said, "Forgiveness has nothing to do with releasing another person from responsibility. It has only to do with releasing yourself from perpetual torment."

When my father died, the most hoped-for solution to the difficulties separating us, the ideal solution, evaporated, because *reconciliation* became impossible. Anything less than reconciliation wasn't going to help me, and I felt a certain despair in knowing that with his death, all the other options had disappeared as well. I began to awaken from the dream of salvation, the dream that my childhood, our relationship, could have been otherwise. There wasn't going to be any fixing between us. He was gone, and all I had left of him was however much of him I was going to carry around with me.

The most startling sentences I heard when asking the kids about his death came from Rita: "I thought he was too powerful to die. So for him to keel over in the bathtub like that, and die at home with a weak human body like the rest of us, really blew me away." I'd expected people to say they were relieved, saddened, shocked, even happy, and all those things were in fact expressed. But Rita invoked a concept probably none of the rest of us conceived: the possibility that Martin Zanichkowsky could be physically missing from our lives, that he could cease to exist. Although I had fantasized about his death, dreamed about it, and even prayed for it, I had never really believed in it.

I knew my father's death would be complicated, but I also knew it wouldn't crush me. I didn't think about the other kids, at least not right away. Later on, the next day, I felt a weak current of excitement. I knew his death was monumental and, knowing I'd survive it easily, I wondered with a slightly perverse voyeurism what it would do to the others (and now the man became a third person: *their* father). I didn't think it would be tragic, just incredible and shocking. But that first night I didn't do anything right off. I was too shocked to do much except drift along on a tide of sensations. I went out for a few drinks. I knew something profound had just happened, but I wasn't sure what to make of it.

In the bar, I realized I was trying to figure out where my father *was*. If I wasn't going to his funeral, I wanted him to know why, so he'd be hurt. But since I didn't believe in an afterlife, I had to accept that he wasn't going to know whether I went or not, because he wasn't anywhere where he could study my reactions to his death. And this really annoyed me, that I could no longer touch him. No, it was more than that: I'd never touched him in the first place, and I couldn't touch him or hurt him at all now. He'd gotten away with it, and the time for getting to him was past. He was, as he had always been, untouchable. My relationship to him had gone from fear to nothing in those two seconds it took him to die.

Now I was shocked, and perhaps this was the same shock Rita was talking about, the sudden realization that one who had seemed omnipotent and eternal, one who had possessed me so thoroughly, was actually and finally gone, not just absent, but missing in a way that leaves a huge void. Like phantom limb pain. It didn't have to do with my father being physically missing as much as with the idea that he'd stopped, like he'd quit or surrendered or walked off the job; there was nothing more he could do with his family, so he might as well take his leave. My overriding sensation wasn't one of loss, or that my father was dead, or that I was alone, or even that Mom was alone. I was trying to figure out how and why he didn't exist on earth anymore.

And now, I understood why I had to go. I'd skipped Grandfather's funeral, maybe ten years earlier, over the same types of reasons: my anger at Dad, my unwillingness to allow anger to be forgotten in a time of my father's loss. I'd avoided Grandfather's funeral in order to hurt my father, to punish him for his neglect of me. In doing so, I'd robbed myself of the opportunity to experience whatever feelings I was entitled to in seeing my grandfather off. Now, I wanted that experience; I didn't want the memory of my father's funeral to consist of a day at home spent in bitterness and regret. Something profound was going to happen to me from seeing my father in a coffin, and I didn't want to have to accept a newspaper clipping with a captioned photograph of it a year from now. I called my mother back to tell her I'd be there.

They gave us a discount rate at the motel because it was a funeral and because there were so many of us. I drove over to the funeral parlor and stood around outside for a while, watching the others arrive. I hadn't seen Jimmy since that lunch we'd had near Grand Central. When I hugged him and asked how he was handling Dad's death, he summed up his feelings in two words: "There's one." I saw Marty for the first time in twenty-five years; I'd never noticed he had a snaggletooth, like me. When the last few kids pulled in I realized it was the first time we'd all been together since Manhasset, maybe thirty years earlier, when that family picture had been taken. I watched them work, bouncing off each other like bumper cars in blind and pointless collisions, compressing their lives into a few quick sentences; you would never have known by their gestures that these people were at their father's funeral. It was hard for me to remember sharing a house with them all back in Queens, and I remember saying to myself, reminding myself, as if it were a truth about me I couldn't fully understand: These people are my siblings, this man was their father.

Finally I went inside. Tony stood in the anteroom, going through the holy cards like a collector: "Got it, got it, need it, got it . . ." We went back outside for a few cigarettes, with Marty. None of the girls smoked anymore. It was cold as hell.

Inside, my mother was sitting in the front row, six feet from the coffin. She was alone; maybe the other kids knew not to crowd her. I tried to imagine how alone she really was, what it must have been like for her to wake up from that nap and find her husband folded in half over the bathtub like that, suddenly gone after fifty years of inseparability. I took her hand for probably the first time in my life, a knobby and arthritic appendage that had smacked me a hundred times but could no longer open a jar. She thanked me for coming and reiterated her fear that I might have refused. I began to cry because I suddenly realized how alone she was going to be in a few days, once Dad was in the ground and all the kids had gone back home. I'd thought all my life I knew what being alone felt like, and now realized I knew nothing of the sort; my mother was the one you could ask about being alone. I had this feeling she could read through me and was reviewing all I had thought and felt about her husband over the past thirty years. I found myself wondering if she knew about the radio I hadn't built, since it had just come up in therapy. I was lost for words and said nothing; I wondered which it might be, guilt, or some stunted and anemic residual love, which prevented me from telling her I couldn't feel a thing for him. Yet there was a little part of me hoping it was just shock, that in a few days something would open up for me and allow me to feel the experience of my father's death.

Looking at my father I had no feelings whatsoever. He looked heavier than I expected. I wanted him to be diminished not only in psychological stature, but physically as well, for there just to be less of him. But he looked rested and well fed, which confused me; his still-strong belly loomed like a landscape of one great rolling hill in a blue satin sky, framed by the raised pewter lid of the coffin. It was I who felt diminished, who felt that because he looked healthy I had been beaten out of something yet again. I imagined some fierce radiation melting him away until just his shirt buttons were left, balancing on the knobs of his spine. Strange venom rose hot and fast and took me by surprise. I turned and left the room, fearful of any words that might escape my lips. I heard solicitous voices inquiring with impotent compassion as to my well-being, but I felt hopelessly alone. I escaped into the frigid blue air and the smell of winter evergreens. I wept.

I never really knew my father. We'd shared in each other's lives only tentatively, superficially. All my life I plotted and schemed to win him over while pretending I no longer needed his love, as if being older rendered the love I should have had as a kid unnecessary. On a parallel track, I imagined killing him, so his power over me would stop. I dreamed of talking to Dad on equal terms, dreamed of being interesting to him. Sometimes I even dreamed of salvation: the life I might have led had my childhood been other than what it was. But before those dreams could come true, and this I didn't understand at the funeral, I needed him to have loved me as a child. My relationship with him never grew, because I went to him without ever recognizing that adults cannot be helped by being given later in life the things they'd required as children.

The next day they put him in the ground; we were not allowed to the actual grave site. Stephanie, in Marine dress, took possession of the flag.

After the funeral, we went back to the house with Mom. Martha and Catherine had arranged catering, and we all sat around the living room for a while, eating and drinking, especially drinking. Mom's mood was not that bad; I think the fact that all her children were there meant a great deal to her. We looked at old pictures, some of which by now had been organized into albums, and we told stories; almost certainly, we'd never all been in a room like that, where there was a complete absence of tension and expectation.

Looking over their bookshelves, I came across a book, an illustrated history of technology that I'd given to my father years before. Inside the front cover I had penciled: "To my Father, Christmas, 1979." But now I'm uncertain as to the exact words, because as soon as I saw the inscription I erased it. I'd been sitting on their bed when I did so, and there happened to be a pencil on the nightstand. I didn't even think about it; it was a sudden impulse, and the whole thing took only two seconds. It didn't really upset me until I got home later and saw what I'd done. Then, searching for the original words with a lens, I was stung by the thought that I'd needed to blot out even the memory of having made this gift to him.

The book is James Burke's *Connections*, which relates the history of a number of inventions by tying together the many strands of agriculture, coining, plague, and traditional science that brought those inventions into being. What had attracted me to the book in the first place was Burke's suggestion that major inventions resulted from a confluence of circumstance and collaboration, even serendipity, and not from a lone genius locking himself in a room, only to emerge years later with a television or a rocket. There was quite a bit of stuff in there tying the inventions to social and political changes caused by religion and war.

I bought the book for my father because I'd appreciated all the technological and historical subjects it touched upon, and because it shed light on another way of regarding achievement. Only much later did it occur to me that, in scrutinizing engineering landmarks, or at least in putting engineering into perspective with the book, I had begun leveling the playing field for myself by qualifying my father's authority. Perhaps he saw the book as a slight to his knowledge or prestige; I'd handed him a book about people I *really* admired.

I still have both copies of *Connections*, mine and his, and it pains me to see his copy looking brand new, in the original dust jacket twenty years later, while mine is thumbed to death, underlined, dog-eared. I hate to think he'd merely skimmed it, or hadn't read it at all. It would mean that even one of the few times I felt capable of reaching out to my father to give him something I'd actually thought about, I'd failed.

I still wonder why I erased the inscription. My father, in the end, never did encourage me in the sciences or anything else; perhaps I erased my words to punish him for this dereliction. Or perhaps I was embarrassed, because the book and its dedication were not a gift but a plea for his affection. I'd wanted my father to be fascinated, as I was, by all the connections Burke had made, so we would have something in common. I'd wanted him to find me knowledgeable, even if only by association, because he was knowledgeable, and the book seemed like a safe bridge to that possibility. Maybe sitting on his bed, I saw in that dedication the transparency of those needs, which shamed me. Perhaps it just angered me that I'd needed to employ the device of a gift to obtain his love or attention, and it was that anger I was trying to erase. Or maybe I was trying to erase my wanting him to love me, because the wanting was still there but it was too late for him to do anything about it.

Looking where the inscription was, I wonder about shading in the area where I'd written so long ago. I'd pressed hard with that pencil, tearing the fibers in the paper. The compressed letters might stand in relief against the charcoal field. Would I find "Love" there?

15
Saint Joan

O ur mother died eleven months later, in February 1992. Louise called me at work, I was alone; it was only late afternoon but in the dead of winter it seemed like night. "Mom died," she said. I entered a cloud. I don't remember what we talked about after that. I didn't have the slightest idea what to do. I was living alone, so there was no one else for me to talk to. I wandered the streets of SoHo like an automaton, afraid even to stop into a bar for a drink. I bumped into a woman I knew, who asked me what was wrong, and I told her my mother had died. She looked at me and said, "Jesus, you mean right now, this second?" She walked around with me for a while, but she had someplace else to go. The subway entrance scared me; it would require a response. I didn't want to go home, but there was nowhere else to go. I didn't want to be on the subway for as long as it would take to get to Louise's house in Queens. I must have gone home, to the room I'm in right now. I have a small place. I must have sat right here in this same chair, at this same table, that night. They're the only ones I have. But I don't remember.

Mom's death did not take us by surprise, but it caught us up short just the same. We'd expected her to die before Dad, because she was in much worse shape physically, and we understood that if it came out the other way she would find life without her husband too miserable to endure. Still, some of us wanted him to go first, so we could have her to ourselves, at least for a while, because there were so many questions about Dad that only she could answer. It was important that she live long enough to leave her husband behind; not to get over him and the loss of him, which wasn't going to happen, but long enough for her to be able to talk to us about our father, not about her husband. Why was he so distant from us? What had happened between him and his father? Was he happy? Did he, during his last months and years, express regrets?

We'd hoped she would have four or five years left in which we might become friends, but that was selfish of us; it was we, and not Mom, who weren't ready for her death. Mom was in constant pain, lost without her husband, enduring the last few years of a brutal existence. If God himself had come down to offer her a few more years, I doubt she would have taken him up on it. Catherine was with Mom at the end, watching her slip in and out of consciousness; Mom kept asking, "Why doesn't He take me?" But we had questions for her as well, and even if Dad survived her, they weren't questions he'd be able to answer. Had she really wanted all those kids? What did they talk about when they were alone? Had she, in the middle of the night in bed with him, tried to defend us against him? Had her faith made her life any more tolerable?

I only saw her once in those last eleven months, and I might never have mustered the nerve for that visit if she hadn't been so insistent about it. Every month for the first four or five months she was alone, she asked me to see her, but I always put her off. She was still way down there in the sticks of New Jersey, and any visit would have required an overnight, at least. I couldn't imagine what we could talk about that might need so much time. But I knew why she was bugging me; I'd set myself up for it the previous year, when I went down to visit them while Dad was still alive. I think we'd started something on that visit that Mom now wanted to see through. That trip had been at my father's invitation, but only after I'd practically dared him to talk to me.

My mother had called me to let me know some relative had died. Although this had happened several times before, and had pissed me off before, this was the first time I'd done anything about it. I wrote them a letter in which I complained that they never asked about my work or my girlfriend, never asked what I was up to or how I was (although, to be sure, I didn't ask them these things very often either), and that I didn't want to hear from them anymore if it was only to learn about somebody's death. I went a step further. I said that if they wanted to have frank dialogue on any subject at all, such as the beatings, religion, the size of the family or whatever, I'd be happy to come visit them; otherwise, take me off their mailing list. The only condition was that Dad had to listen and not just browbeat me. To my utter astonishment, my father wrote back to me that same week, inviting me for a visit. "Any time," he wrote, "just call ahead and we'll pick you up at the station." It was the only letter I'd ever received from him in my life; I realized as I read it that he'd never once called me on the phone. I remembered back to Nashua, when he'd had that first heart attack and told me not to bother visiting.

It was quite a time. The first thing we started talking about was the size of our family. My mother could not understand why I hadn't seen my siblings as God-given playmates, why I wasn't more thankful I'd never had to spend my days alone while the other kids were in school. "I'd always thought that the nicest thing I could ever give one of my children was a younger brother or sister to play with," she said. I could tell she meant it, and her earnestness made me sad; it meant she was that much further away from ever understanding me, and vice versa. I tried explaining about my appreciation for privacy and quiet, about needing to feel special, about having things and space that were *mine*. It never occurred to me she might not know what I was talking about, since she'd never spent a day by herself in her life. "But why would anybody want to be *alone* so much?" she asked, with so much emphasis on "alone" you'd think it was a four-letter word. She found it sad, for both of us, that I could feel, much less admit, that by the time Jane and Steffie came along, I was completely indifferent to my siblings. And she seemed especially forlorn over my certainty about never having children of my own. I never did manage to convey to her what I liked about living by myself. And I never managed to understand, even for a second, the joy she might have found in her children, since I'd seldom seen her expressing anything joylike around us. I thought about Frankenstein talking with the old blind man: "Alone . . . *bad*, friend . . . *good* . . ." Such was my mother's simplicity.

My father steered towards his favorite subject. "What we really can't understand," he said, "is why you rejected our religious teachings," with "rejected" standing out more than somewhat. Did he feel I'd rejected his religion, or him? For the first time in my life, I could answer my father with confidence instead of fear. "I never rejected it; it just never made sense to me, never took root," I said. "A world with a God, as God was presented to us, never convinced me. It's not even like I believed it for a while, then changed my mind. I don't think I ever had any faith to lose." I told them about that day in fifth grade, when with a single word, *transubstantiation*, even my nebulous God had ceased to exist. It fascinated me to watch him try to understand me, because he'd never tried before. Like my mother, Dad found a world without God tough to imagine. But where he normally would have worked me over with reason and logic (not to mention his favorite trick: quoting the Bible as proof that the Bible was the inspired word of God), this time he said nothing; I could almost see the gears turning in his head, trying to create a picture of a world running itself, that had come into being by itself. I wish I'd known during that visit about Dad leaving his father's church back in Brooklyn, because I could have asked him how he imagined his decision differed from my falling away from God; I might have gotten an answer.

I asked Mom how she knew that everything she believed was actually true; I wanted her opinion as separate from Dad's. She said she wasn't sure, that maybe that's why they called it the gift of faith. "You ask too many questions. You always have. You think too much for your own good; if you have to know ahead of time, it's not faith anymore."

I realized I'd been away for a long time, that it'd been a while since I'd been afraid of them. My father looked plump and doughy now, like somebody from an ad for old-people products on very late night television. His hair was thinning to zero, his teeth sepia-toned from cigarettes and age, skin marked here and there with liver spots. He looked fragile, something I never would have imagined possible. It was sad for me to recognize in my parents, so clearly now, that the handsomeness of their wedding day was long gone, that they were actually decaying slowly into nothing. But Dad's hands, the hands he'd beaten me with, you could tell by those hands he'd been a powerful man. He and Mom sat on one side of the table, and I sat across from them. It was amazing how comfortable they looked together, even knowing they'd been together fifty years already. Every once in a while I'd get the feeling they were the same person, or two of the same thing. I used to wonder what they talked about when they were younger; now I could imagine them not talking at all, not because they were all talked out, but because they didn't need words anymore.

As I talked with my parents, it became clear that, in spite of our efforts, we would never see eye-to-eye on any subject except Glenn Miller. At the same time, none of the three of us had it in mind to convert others to our own views. It didn't even seem urgent that we understand one another. It was okay just to be talking as equals for the first time, to have my mother offer me a Manhattan, a drink she made by the pitcher for relatives and guests, and which felt to me now as if she were acknowledging me as a peer or companion. Still, I couldn't escape the sense of my mother's sorrow, and I came to realize my views were not mere intellectual concerns for her. Several times over the course of those two days, she came to tears over both her fear for the final resting place for my soul and for my lack of love and appreciation for her other children.

On the bus ride back to Manhattan I felt a mixture of gratitude, relief, and satisfaction that at least we'd made some kind of a start. We would never share a close and trusting friendship, but even détente was better than what we'd had for the previous twenty years.

I never saw my father again. But it was that visit with them, the first and last of its kind, that my mother wanted to continue now. Some of my siblings expressed actual envy that I'd had such a "working" visit with Mom and Dad; they were jealous that Mom was pushing me to go further with her. A few of them had gone down to visit Mom after Dad had died, but none in response to continuous invitations bordering on insistence. My mother had chosen me as her last question.

I had a car this time, and on the drive down I kept imagining her waking up from that nap and finding her man passed away. No matter what I felt about the guy, that was a harsh way to end fifty years together. I thought about the time they'd asked me to move back home with them, when I was about thirty, and I made a mental note to ask Mom if any of that had been Pop's idea, though I didn't think so.

It was immediately obvious that life without her husband was killing her. There was no evidence of joy or fulfillment, no signs of hobbies or visits from others. It had not occurred to me she would still be so disconsolate over the loss of her husband. She said she was tired, but her *tired* had that quiet finality of one who has fully contemplated surrender. She made no secret of how much she missed her man, and I felt incredibly sad for her. I was still solving my own problems with my father, but missing him wasn't part of that process. Perhaps I was unconsciously assuming that, since he was now dead, she'd come around to seeing him for what he really was (by which I mean she'd see him the way I saw him), and that she shouldn't be missing the guy as much as she was.

Years earlier, when I was living alone in Manchester, about twenty miles north of where they were, they'd asked me to move back home. That invitation had taken me completely by surprise. I didn't sense it had come from the two of them, since my mother was doing all the talking. She had suggested that living alone must be *costly*, that it wasn't good to spend so much time *alone*. They offered me the entire basement: the three boys' old room, the three girls' old room, my own bath. I was past thirty, with a good job and plenty of friends; why were they now concerned with my well-being? I remembered back to when Tony's first wife was cheating on him, and then his house burned down; Mom and Dad weren't in too much of a hurry to attend to his needs back then, and Tony lasted exactly one day under Dad's roof.

She knew Dad and I would find it difficult to live with one another and that I wouldn't be able to attend to their increasing physical needs. Still, I could look after the place for them, run errands. But our collective welfare, it turned out, was a red herring. "We worry when we don't hear from you," she said; this was in the days before answering machines, but during a time I almost never answered my own telephone. "I worry that your living alone is leading to depression, and we can't think of any other way to help you." When she said that, my dislike for my father became tinted with filaments of tenderness, which rendered the dislike less pure. This idea had never occurred to me, that my parents might want to watch over me. Nor had it occurred to me living alone could lead to depression; I always figured it the other way around.

On the other hand, I didn't believe her. They'd invited me back home only after I'd quit living with Barbara and had been alone for a couple of years. Before that I was Dad's dropout, draft-dodging son, living in sin with a whore, and therefore we hadn't spoken more than incidentally in years. I explained to my mother that Pop had never seemed overly concerned for my happiness.

Not happiness, she said. Salvation; they'd been concerned for my spiritual well-being. And when she'd call on the phone and not get me for weeks, she worried even more. "It is not your life to throw away. It is on loan from God, and we feared the condemnation of your soul not because of sin, for which there is atonement, but because if you take your own life, there is neither purgatory nor penance, and your soul is condemned." I don't know that those were her *exact* words, but they were very much like those, and I use quotes to indicate they are not mine. Her phrasing was quite formal, straight from the Rule Book.

So it was suicide. But was the loss of my life less significant to her than the loss of my soul? It was not, because the undertones of fear and love in her voice were unmistakable: She was both

Mother and Catholic, and the losses were equivalent, the fear of one dominating the other depending only upon whether the emotions of motherhood or eternity presided over the moment. Although I'd thought about suicide a few times, I never figured they'd thought about me thinking about it, certainly not enough for them to want to do something about it.

Now Mom asked me point-blank if I had ever made the attempt, and I admired her courage. She was an old-world Catholic, and the idea that I didn't believe in God was bad enough; even I could imagine what she'd go through if I knocked myself off.

I told her I'd thought about it, and that this by itself had brought an interesting realization: Once you understand you can kill yourself whenever you want to, or imagine you'll find the guts for it when necessary, time ceases to exist and something strange happens. A lifetime seems both too long and too short at the same time. That's when you realize there'll be plenty of time to die in if it comes to that, and you learn to tough it out. It sounds like solid existential resolve now, but in fact it was cowardice. When I couldn't pull the trigger, I had to convince myself that living actually took more courage than quitting the game. This took place in Maine, where I'd gone to hide out after my relationships kept falling apart, in the years after my father died. It was on Father's Day, now that I think about it. I couldn't think of what I needed to do for myself, and struggled with the knowledge that I was always going to be alone because I couldn't figure out what it took to be with another person. The idea of spending the rest of my life without love was killing me.

Still, this wasn't a serious suicide attempt, it was just pushing myself in that direction to see if it made any more sense than the terminal isolation I was feeling. As I look back on it now, the hardest thing about that whole afternoon was the thought of the sadness I'd have to face before I pulled the trigger, when at the last second I'd finally admit to myself how much it all hurts. I feared that in the last second, between the dry metallic click of the hammer and the white light of annihilation, my pain would melt before some fabulous light of understanding, revealed to me perhaps by this God of my mother's. But by then it would be too late to avert my head, that last second being sufficient for regret but not for motor response.

But how could anybody tell his mother all that?

Instead, I tried to suggest my life was not her responsibility, that my lack of belief in her God was not her fault. I said we humans were not born as empty vessels waiting or needing to be topped off with the contents of our parents' minds. She didn't seem convinced of any of this, even though it would let her off the hook concerning my fate. What she was saying was that if I knocked myself off, both of us were headed for you-know-where. How could Christians even *have* kids if there was that much responsibility attached to it?

But the whereabouts of my soul did not concern me. What bothered me more were the anxiety and panic attacks; they'd followed me into my thirties, and fear of losing my mind sometimes drove me to extremes of despair. But I wasn't going to tell her about that, either. It seemed an impossibly difficult subject to bring up with her at the moment, and I said nothing. So she remained misinformed, because religion had little to do with my unhappiness, and what *was* tormenting me, I felt incapable of explaining. But in doubting her ability to understand, I failed to give her the opportunity to understand, or even to *not* understand, her son. I shortchanged her because I'd never had her to myself before and I didn't want to lose her on questions I figured didn't have answers. Now that I understand the questions better, I wish I'd tried harder back then to share them with her. She'd seen a lot in her day; it was not fair of me to second-guess either her intelligence or her courage.

She served a lunch of leftovers: her excellent meat loaf and the awful canned vegetables of my childhood. It was a minor miracle she'd kept sixteen people alive on that stuff for so many years. I reminded her of their failed attempt to convert us to powdered milk one year. It was the only group rebellion we kids ever pulled off.

Afterwards she asked me if I wanted to drive her to "Daddy's" grave. I said I wouldn't mind going for a drive and if that's where she wanted to go I'd take her, but I had no interest in going there myself and why didn't we go to the beach. Her tears were instantaneous, and I immediately regretted my bluntness. At the same time, I was glad it'd finally come out of me even though it hurt her to hear it. I fought my urge to take it back.

We played gin for a while (she killed me), and in the afternoon I drove her to the cardiologist's office to discuss the results of some pre-op tests. She was preparing for a bypass although she wasn't in such good shape for surgery. She could be very clipped when something was bothering her, speaking only in clearly delineated slices of pure information, without inflection of any kind. She was speaking like this in the car, and I couldn't help wondering how afraid she might be of what the doctor might have to tell her. There was plenty of heart disease in our family, especially on her side.

She was looking straight out the windshield when she said, "So why did you hate your father so much?" She said it just like that, using the "so" to make it sound casual. It wasn't an accusation, almost not even a question, just an observation that left no room for rebuttal. It was too big a question to answer. Instead, I thought about why mothers always call their husbands "your father" and not "my husband." The "your" and "my" imply that the man *belongs* to the son and the wife in distinct and separate ways; perhaps she was looking for insights on the man as he related to me. Knowing in advance what I might have to say, she could spare the memory of her husband by asking me about my father. I could denigrate one man while leaving the other man intact.

My feelings about my father were so familiar to me now, I didn't even have names for them anymore. Her word *hate* implied something active and participatory, something still ongoing between my father and me even though he was dead. I didn't have the courage to answer her. I just sat there wondering how long she'd been working up the courage to ask me that question, wondering whether she knew my father would have to be dead before she could even ask it. I knew then that my dislike of him had not escaped her notice, something I'd never considered. It had hurt her too, my dislike, probably more than it hurt him, although it wasn't intended to. I didn't know I couldn't punish him with hatred and not hurt her, that my parents were too close to each other for that. But hatred is like one of those underground fires burning in the peat bogs. You can never tell exactly where it's going or what it's going to do. Nor can you put it out even though you see how much destruction it's causing.

Being behind the wheel saved me, as if clinging to the responsibility of driving exempted me from feeling and responding. I didn't want to start talking about my father, mostly because I didn't have much good to say about him, and didn't want to get upset and start crying right there in the car. I just told her as simply as possible that I didn't feel he'd ever loved me, nor ever encouraged me to make something of myself, and that he'd made a large dent in my manhood and courage with the stick. At forty years of age, the most I could hope for was to figure out how not to spend the rest of my life resenting him.

"Do you have any idea," I asked her, "what happens to a child when you beat him with a stick?" I just wanted to get it over with; I just wanted to know if she'd ever thought about it in any other terms except discipline. But she had not. "Why did you have to steal?" she asked. I thought back to the time Catherine and I had gotten the stick for stealing those Cheerios, and wanted to ask Mom what she meant by stealing. Then I remembered a conversation Rita had overheard years earlier, while listening at our parents' bedroom door late one night in Nashua. "My kids are smart," Dad was saying. "They're strong. What I do makes them tough." But our mother clearly disagreed. "No, Marty, our kids are weak, our kids are insecure. What you do hurts them."

Why couldn't my mother remember that conversation now?

But I was already regretting that I'd brought up the beatings at all. I wasn't prepared for all the feelings they'd set off, and maybe neither was she. So I didn't say anything.

I didn't feel angry with her. She'd beaten me plenty of times, but somehow I don't think she beat me with anger like Dad did. Maybe with frustration, but not with hatred. At times she'd just dismiss me, too worn out to take disciplinary action, and I'd actually feel sorry that I'd done something wrong, because I'd caused her to become worked up about something she was too exhausted do anything about. But I didn't make peace with her even those times; I just dismissed them as miracles. I remember trying to hurt her with words, sinning in thought by wishing catastrophe upon her. I probably would have hurt her if I'd known how, if I'd been strong enough, but I was already too afraid of her. I'm not proud of this. That's just the way it was.

Mom's tests were positive in that they weren't negative, and she was cleared for surgery. The doctors' biggest concern was her circulatory system because they had to run her blood through a cooler and lower her temperature and metabolic rate while they operated. If her lung tissue had tightened up too much over the years, they'd be reluctant to do the work, and they'd certainly be more pessimistic concerning her prospects. I had no courage whatsoever to ask her how she felt about the operation. She was overweight and had smoked for thirty years and she was smart enough to calculate her chances.

She decided to drive on the way home. She talked with a cold, flat finality that suggested to me she knew she was going to have a difficult time. So many sentences sounded less like questions or responses, and more like statements. It made me sad to think she might be afraid to die, not because I'm not going to be afraid when it's my turn, but because it seemed to me God had cheated her if she had to spend her last years on earth alone and diseased and afraid. What good is faith if you have to die with fear?

"Then how come you came to your father's funeral?" Jesus, she was really asking for it. I realized once again how little we knew about each other, and it came as a shock to me to understand there was no need to fear her anymore, that she was just another woman trying to understand her son. I also realized she had a lot more courage than I did.

There wasn't really a simple answer to give her, and when one eventually evolved within me, it wasn't going to be something she'd want to hear. I knew, driving in that car, that I would never tell her what I really felt about him, mostly because she couldn't possibly live long enough, and also because inflicting hurt, no matter how satisfying, never fixes anything. And I wondered if either of us were in possession of the tools for taking and receiving those words I thought she'd like to have pass between us.

But I also knew she was trying to settle something, and it was obvious by the boldness of her inquiries that she wasn't interested in wasting time. Perhaps it was she who was striving within her limits for some aspect of understanding, while I with all my journals and reading and therapy clung to the despair of some dark and iron past. I smiled at her, perhaps the first real affection I'd ever felt for her.

That's as close as we ever got, driving in the car that next hour. She told me about the two stillborns she'd endured between Rita and Jane, how one of them dropped out when she was on the toilet. She fished it out of the bowl and wrapped it up in newspaper and had Father Kruzas baptize it. It was a boy, and his name would have been Thomas; she'd had a lot of girls and was disappointed she'd lost her chance for a boy. It happened again a year later, in the hospital this time, and she feared she would be unable to have any more children. Of course, Jane and Steffie eventually came along, but her admission shocked me. Would she have stopped at twenty? Or was the entire meaning of her life tied up in procreation? Was this what she wanted, or what she thought God wanted for her? I felt embarrassed because she'd never told me anything so graphic before, and sad because in her recounting it the pain of her loss was still evident after thirty years. But I was angry as well, angered by the ignorance that had caused her so much pain, and then sad again, because so much had gone wrong with her dreams for all those children. I tried to defuse my confused feelings with humor. I told her it was a good thing the last two girls were born, because I didn't know if I could have gotten by with just seven sisters. She was so lost in the reverie I don't even think she heard me.

That night we watched television, some British detective stuff. I felt uncomfortable sitting there and not enjoying it, trapped between her desire to watch and my inability to express that I didn't want to. I tried to observe her watching, but her lost and vacant gaze made me upset. It depressed me to think she might spend the rest of her days in front of a television because she and my father had alienated all their children. There was just enough distance between us all for détente, but not quite enough to grant forgiveness. It was sad to think she had nine daughters, any one of whom might have been a companion in her last years, but that she was doomed to be alone.

I lay on my bed in the spare room, staring at the ceiling. It struck me that our lives were painful and empty for the same reasons: We were furthest away from those we should have loved first, and it was too late to do anything about it. I'd spent my entire adult life up to that night afraid of having kids, fearful of all that could go wrong. But I'd only worried about disease and death and birth defects, I'd worried about the loss of my kids through fate, through the capricious acts of kindless gods. It never occurred to me there was a whole other category of loss, that you could have fourteen children and still end up alone in the end while they were all still walking the planet.

I no longer doubt that Johanna, as mother and a woman, did love her children on some plane, even if its surface remained unbroken by demonstrations of tenderness. In my hitchhiking days, she told me she'd rather not see me than have me take such a risk on her account. But her affection was not reciprocated; I was not taking those risks for her: I visited in the hope that she would finally come to love me. And maybe she did love me in her own way all along, but never understood what shape love had to come in for it to do a kid any good. Or maybe I was too selfish or dulled to understand that whatever shape her love came in, it was all I was going to get.

The next morning I raked her lawn: the compressed, weighted leaves of fall; the brown, layered volumes; the cold. I wanted to burn them in the open because of the smell, but there was a law. I did not know I would never see her again. There wasn't going to be any life-saving operation. The walls of her aorta had thinned away to nothing through the failure of a gene to issue instructions for the tissue to cease growing. There was no fixing her, no mechanical repairing of the damage, because all the surrounding material had rusted away. I talked to her once in the hospital at that time, and she was scared to death; it still bothered me that her faith could not allay her fear. But maybe we all fear death once we get so close to it that even God can't save us. The doctors cut her open, took one look at her aorta, closed her back up, and sent her home.

Three months later we put her in the ground a few feet from where we had put our father less than a year before.

I'm certain I cried at her funeral, but I can't remember why. My presence of mind was broken by the reading of the will. Dad's funeral had been uninterrupted by such details. But the will was nasty business, and reading it in the middle of visiting hours added an element to Mom's funeral that was almost political; a second batch of feelings got mixed up with those of loss and regret. Or maybe I'm just saying this because I didn't have strong feelings, at least not about loss and love regarding my mother, and it lets me off the hook for not having those feelings if I blame the reading of the will for interrupting their evolution.

It never occurred to me to wonder if she was going to be reunited with her husband in the afterlife, which I knew she believed was going to happen. If I think about that now, I shake my head. Not because I hated my father and couldn't imagine getting all the way to heaven just to meet up with him, even if you wanted to because you loved him as she did. The whole universe has just got to be more interesting than that. If you have to endure all the shit that happens to you here on earth just to get to a place where you meet up with other earthlings, picking up where you'd left off, following the happenings on earth like it was television, it's a pretty meager creation.

But I'll tell you something. Twice, walking up Sixth Avenue in lower Manhattan, I saw this old woman who looked just like her. Wavy white hair, very stout, same height, same type of cheap and indeterminate street shift my mother would wear. The first time completely stunned me; I followed her into the McDonald's at Twenty-Eighth Street before I remembered that my mother was dead. It took a few seconds for me to remember, and before those seconds were up, I knew I wanted to talk to her. I wanted to just meet her on the street, just the two of us walking along. The rest of my family didn't occur to me. Or maybe they did, in one of those seconds, because I realized that since our mother was dead, none of the others would be expecting her to be anywhere and so, through this miracle, I'd have her to myself, right there on Sixth Avenue. And the second time, even though I knew the woman was an impostor, I was disappointed. All I was going to be able to say to the others was, "I saw somebody who looked exactly like Mom."

Epilogue
1998

*I*t was still good sunlight when we emerged from the Penn Station tunnels and headed north up the Hudson. Louise gave me a lapel button with a line drawing of an old steam locomotive with a tiny red LED headlamp blinking on and off; she had a small bag of them. We settled in and talked about the river, all flat and pastel now because of the cooling daylight, but we didn't have much time together before Martha and Jimmy got on the train at Yonkers. Jimmy looked as thin, fragile, and wary as ever; even if you didn't know he'd had a hard time, he looked like a guy with a story to tell if you felt like taking a chance. He had a woman with him, a surprisingly bright, attractive, talkative blonde named Linda. Lou gave each of the newcomers a railroad pin. Jimmy's second marriage had been over for a few years, but none of us had met the wife, Stephanie, and there was some doubt as to her actual existence. Linda seemed attentive and curious about the rest of us. It's neither fair nor polite for me to refer to her as surprising, but the fact is she surprised us all; Jimmy had always clawed his way through life, always come up short. None of us were prepared for the possibility that the gods might grant him hope and happiness for the future. But there Linda was, with a fat ring on her finger, clinging to my brother like a love-wasted teen. It took me a while to accept the idea that, just possibly, Jimmy's luck had changed for the better.

They shared a seat behind me. I sat by myself, trying to eavesdrop on them, but they conversed in hushed tones. Martha and Louise sat side by side; they'd spent a lot of time since the funerals sweeping aside the differences that had separated them as kids, and hashing out Martha's handling of the will. I still tend to see my family through the dynamics of failed relationships, but the truth is, though our parents failed us and we've often failed with our spouses, we kids are learning how *not* to fail each other.

Our destination was Madison, Wisconsin. Elizabeth was already there, living in Madison, teaching at the university. She was the bride-to-be; the wedding, her second, was the excuse for our journey. The train idea belonged to Louise and me; I don't like to fly, and Lou's job gives her the summers off with no time constraints. It hadn't been that hard to rope the others into the adventure.

The train chugged lazily up the river and into the late dusk of the summer evening. The tracks run along the east bank, and I got to thinking of a winter a few years ago, when the river had frozen over. There'd been a rapid thaw, the Hudson had flooded, and the entire surface had shattered into innumerable ice floes, many as big as barn doors; the tracks we were on now had been underwater. Then the tide had turned and headed out, draining the river south into the sea. The ice chunks floated on the river, advancing like parade floats at three or four miles an hour, so crowded you could walk from bank to bank on them. It seemed as if the ice were being transported via conveyor belt to a huge melting machine, to be turned into drinking water for New York City.

We came to rest in Albany and met the train from Boston. Annie, Catherine, and Jane got on at Albany. Lou passed around more locomotive buttons. Annie still walked obliquely, like a three-legged dog; she greeted Jimmy with stiff and wary formality, and he reciprocated exactly in kind. I will never know the truth about them, but their behavior in one another's presence raises one's curiosity, to say the least. By now, all the kids knew something about Jimmy's time in Creedmore, but only I knew much about Annie's accusations against Jimmy, and nobody except me had ever asked either of them about their distant pasts. Letting sleeping dogs lie counts a lot if you're a Zanichkowsky, but it makes the truth hard to come by. Where do historical facts reside? Do the events in our lives leave a physical residue drifting untouchably through the ether like radiation? Or is history, as Milan Kundera says, merely the struggle of memory against forgetting?

Catherine and Annie sat together, still paired like twins as if nothing had changed in forty years. I remember them as skinny teens, braiding each other's hair as I spied upon them from that upper porch window, another world ago. Catherine had lined up the train tickets, brought Annie to the station (Annie doesn't drive), and would share a hotel room with her just as she had shared that attic dormer in Queens.

The train took a left at Albany and headed for Chicago. We reserved a few tables in the dining car. It was nicer than you'd expect, with cloth table covers, real flowers, candles, limited but decent menu. We were slightly conspicuous, taking up three tables and wearing our blinking railroad badges, not to mention the extremes of volume that result when six or eight of us get conversing. After supper, we stayed up reading and telling stories late into the night. Chocolate appeared from suitcases. I didn't do much interviewing, even though I'd started the process a year back and had brought along my recorder. I didn't want to commandeer the reunion for my own interests, unless quiet opportunities came along on the side.

We slept in various configurations in our seats, which were not at all designed for that purpose. Catherine opted for an open area on the floor where a wheelchair, had there been one on board, would have parked. Few of us had the money for the sleeper car, and those who did chose not to separate themselves from the rest of us.

In Chicago we picked up Kathy Willis, our cousin Tommy's widow; one of her daughters; and Catherine's son, Carl. Louise gave them all buttons. Carl works in the theater in New York, directing and acting. There was a layover while we switched trains in Chicago. We spent a few hours walking around town, admiring Union Station, having lunch. We took a boat ride in the canal off the Chicago River, then boarded a very luxurious double-decker train for Madison.

I sat with Martha and now learned I'd misinterpreted the tears she'd expressed while reading to us from the will eight years earlier. She *had* seen it before the funeral; she'd gone over the terms with Mom at the hospital. Martha had tried to soften the blow of our disinheritance, asking Mom to consider the needier kids, or to leave something for the five kids who'd not had children of their own. "I told her it seemed unfair to punish those of us who'd never gotten married," Martha says. "Because those of us with kids benefited indirectly through our kids' inheritance, I mean for college tuition and stuff." But our mother wouldn't listen to any talk of giving her children a leg up. She'd clenched her jaw and spoken through her teeth in a gesture we'd all seen a thousand times, and which Martha described as quite venomous. "We started out with *nothing*," Mom had said, "and made our own way." Which wasn't exactly the truth, because when her parents died that afternoon in 1946, they'd left their three kids the house, with Mom, Leon, and Helen getting equal shares. Why had she sounded so bitter? Had she spent those last weeks trying to sort out her family, her faith, and the paths she'd taken, only to come up short when cramming it all into her last few sentences?

Marty was flying in from California, as were Paul and Rita from Maine. That would make ten of us. Stephanie wasn't meeting us from California because, she says, she refuses to fly anymore. But skeptics among us wonder if her husband keeps her away from her family, because we hadn't seen her since the funerals. Our doubts were reinforced recently, when she booted her husband out. Tony, struggling to raise six kids from his second marriage, couldn't afford the time off even though some of us offered to chip in for his fare. Both his marriages were nightmares, at least from my perspective, but someday I'll ask him more about them. Grace drove out from Vermont on a road trip with her husband and two of her three kids.

It was just like Queens at the motel. Martha and Louise shared a room; Annie and Catherine shared a room; and I shared one with Paul and Marty. We three stayed up pretty late, knocking off some ouzo and bullshitting around. I found the idea of sharing a bed with Paul so difficult that I needed to sleep heads to feet. Marty and I were awakened in the middle of the night by the sound of Paul searching for his wallet with a flashlight. He'd stashed it under our mattress and had felt a sudden urge to verify its whereabouts. Marty, still in sleeper's fog, grasped the situation immediately. "Which one of us two did you think was going to steal it?" he asked.

The next morning, Marty told us about Jimmy's recent trip to California, the week they'd spent together camping and fishing. Both of them told me later how impossible it would have been to imagine such a trip even three years earlier, and that it was the best thing that had ever happened between them. Marty took Jimmy shooting and said Jimmy was the best shot with a pistol he'd ever seen. "I didn't *even* want to ask him who he was thinking about while he was shooting," Marty says.

The three girls were not sharing a room; Grace roomed with her husband and kids, while Rita stayed with her partner, Christine. As family groups go, only the three girls had endured beyond childhood, to become something special. Where we three boys, as kids, would cheat and lie and steal among one another, the three girls would lend and trade and borrow freely. They made up games to comfort themselves after their beatings; created hysterical routines about their teachers and their vaginas; they'd sung at each others' weddings. They were lucky; born all in a row and with nobody born after them for years, they were bound only to each other. Or maybe they were lucky simply because they were girls; I don't think boys bond like that. The three boys didn't, anyway.

Rita's commitment ceremony with Christine was difficult for Grace. She attended with what I saw as some courage and honesty, walking a fine line between not condoning the union and not turning her back on her sister. And it was difficult for Rita, who assumed that the bonds of three-girlhood would pave the way for Grace's acceptance without question. But there were questions, not just from Grace but from many of the kids, because Rita's gayness had appeared seemingly overnight. However, Rita tells me, she knew her earlier marriages were charades, that she'd swept her gayness under the carpet for twenty years. And while Grace had her doubts, Elizabeth did not; Liz had openly invited Rita to bring her mate out to Madison.

During the reception, a huge outdoor affair in one of the city parks, I thought about our five groups, our weddings and divorces and our spouses, and this train excursion to Wisconsin. My brothers and sisters are for the most part nonjudgemental; they do not expect you to go out of your way for them because they are your siblings; they do not evaluate each other's decisions about schooling, career choice, spouse. Because we grew up with so much judgment and criticism, and because our parents played no favorites, we kids are remarkably able to accept, or at least try to accept, each other as we are.

Such a train ride would have been unthinkable ten years earlier, before our parents died. They wouldn't have gone to the wedding anyway, since Elizabeth wasn't marrying in the Catholic Church. But neither would half of us kids. We'd become comfortable with celebrating our achievements in the absence of our siblings; we'd never developed a reliance on having our family as witnesses to our benchmarks. Not that we'd all been enemies, but we wouldn't go very far out of the way for one another. This seems to have turned around some since Mom and Dad died. When Jimmy turned fifty in 1996, he threw a party for himself at Tony's place in Merrimack, New Hampshire. Set the whole thing up himself. Most of the kids showed up with their spouses and kids, and even Tommy and Kathy were there. You could tell Jimmy was kind of embarrassed about it, shy about being the center of attention after being an outcast for all those decades.

Jimmy's party was not unlike Elizabeth's wedding, with people milling about outside, eating comfort foods, bouncing off each other in those same blind and pointless collisions I'd seen them in during my parents' funerals. Except now those collisions didn't seem so blind and pointless anymore.